BLUE RIBBON
CROCHET™

Exceptional Designs to Create Your Own Prizewinning Projects

EDITED BY CAROL ALEXANDER

HOUSE of
WHITE
BIRCHES

PUBLISHERS
SINCE 1947

BLUE RIBBON CROCHET

EDITOR	Carol Alexander
ASSOCIATE EDITOR	Cathy Reef, Brenda Stratton
TECHNICAL EDITOR	Agnes Russell
COPY EDITORS	Conor Allen, Michelle Beck, Marla Freeman, Nicki Lehman
PRODUCTION ASSISTANT	Marj Morgan
TECHNICAL ARTISTS	Chad Summers
PUBLISHING SERVICES MANAGER	Brenda Gallmeyer
GRAPHIC ARTS SUPERVISOR	Ronda Bechinski
PHOTOGRAPHY	Tammy Christian, Christena Green, Kelly Heydinger
PHOTOGRAPHY STYLIST	Tammy Nussbaum
GRAPHIC ARTIST	Pam Gregory
BOOK DESIGN	Brad Snow
COVER DESIGN	Erin Augsburger
CHIEF EXECUTIVE OFFICER	John Robinson
PUBLISHING DIRECTOR	David J. McKee
BOOK MARKETING DIRECTOR	Craig Scott
EDITORIAL DIRECTOR	Vivian Rothe

Printed in the United States of America
First Printing: 2004
Library of Congress Number: 2003108833
ISBN: 1-59217-035-8

Every effort has been made to ensure the accuracy and completeness of the instructions in this book. However, we cannot be responsible for human error or for the results when using materials other than those specified in the instructions, or for variations in individual work.

1 2 3 4 5 6 7 8 9

A NOTE FROM THE EDITOR

Many of us have experienced the special pleasure of receiving the beautiful crocheted handiwork of beloved family members passed to us through generations. These precious and prized pieces of needlework art inspire us to broaden our crochet horizons and develop our stitching skills to create our own crochet masterpieces worthy of prize-winning recognition.

The premier patterns in *Blue Ribbon Crochet* represent a glorious collection of prize-worthy projects for you to make and enjoy. The designs are as diverse as the talented artisans who created them and offer up a variety of styles in a wide color palette to satisfy the most discerning crochet tastes.

You'll find a stunning array of judges' choice afghans for your decorating pleasure or gift-giving needs and a stylish selection of first-place fashions and accessories to dress up your wardrobe. For the little folks, we've included a bevy of best-in-show designs for babies and toddlers and an enchanting assortment of top-notch toys and games for children. To showcase your home, you'll find everything from exquisite, heirloom-quality thread pieces to chic and contemporary decorating accents.

Whatever your skill level, whatever your crochet tastes, you'll love the variety and appreciate the quality of these first-class designs that are sure to make winning projects worthy of a blue-ribbon prize!

With warm regards,

Carol Alexander

6 40

68 96

124 148

CONTENTS

A crocheted afghan, lovingly made by hand one careful stitch at a time, is a unique creation that cannot be reproduced by machine. The timeless skills of hand and hook working together to create crochet magic are gloriously captured in these splendid examples of afghan artistry. Featuring

JUDGES' CHOICE AFGHANS

the handiwork of premier crochet designers, these original creations offer a tempting array of choices for all your afghan inspirations. Whether made to enhance a decorating scheme, give as a treasured gift to someone special or showcase your crochet skills in a judged exhibit, every afghan in this cream-of-the-crop collection is sure to be a winner!

DESIGN BY
DOT DRAKE

MAJESTIC BRAIDS

Elegant braid accents crocheted in sparkling, contrasting yarn adorn panels of deep blue to create an afghan treasure worthy of royalty. Gleaming wooden beads of rich garnet add the crowning touch.

GAUGE

7 sc = 2 inches; 7 sc rows = 2 inches
Check gauge to save time.

PATTERN NOTES

Weave in loose ends as work progresses.
Join rnds with a sl st unless otherwise stated.

PATTERN STITCH

Sc ch lp: Insert hook in st, yo, draw up a lp (2 lps on hook), [yo, draw through first lp on hook] 4 times, yo, draw through rem 2 lps on hook.

WIDE PANEL

Make 2

Row 1: With soft navy, ch 48, sc in 2nd ch from hook, sc in each of next 2 chs, [sc ch lp in next ch, sc in each of next 3 chs] 11 times, turn. (11 sc ch lps; 36 sc)

Row 2: Ch 1, sc in each st across, turn. (47 sc)

Row 3: Ch 1, sc in first sc, [sc ch lp in next st, sc in each of next 3 sts] 11 times, sc ch lp in next st, sc in next st, turn. (12 sc ch lps; 35 sc)

Row 4: Rep Row 2.

Row 5: Ch 1, sc in each of next 3 sts, [sc ch lp in next st, sc in each of next 3

INTERMEDIATE ●●●

SIZE 60 x 75 inches

MATERIALS

- Coats & Clark Red Heart Super Saver worsted weight yarn (8 oz per skein): 7 skeins soft navy #387
- Caron Victorian Gold Christmas worsted weight yarn: 24 oz lace #1952
- Size I/9 crochet hook or size needed to obtain gauge
- Several large safety pins
- Navy blue quilting thread
- 12 (15mm) red wooden beads
- Tracing or plain paper
- Pinning board
- Straight pins
- Yarn needle

Row 6: Rep Row 2.

Rows 7–10: Rep Rows 3–6.

Rows 11 & 12: Rep Rows 3 and 4.

Row 13: Ch 1, [sc in next 3 sts, sc ch lp in next st] 5 times, sc in each of next 7 sts, [sc ch lp in next st, sc in each of next 3 sts] 5 times, turn.

Row 14: Rep Row 2.

Row 15: Ch 1, sc in first st, [sc ch lp in next st, sc in each of next 3 sts] 5 times, sc in each of next 8 sts, [sc ch lp in next

st, sc in each of next 3 sts] 4 times, ch lp in next st, sc in last st, turn.

Row 16: Rep Row 2.

Row 17: Ch 1, [sc in each of next 3 sts, sc ch lp in next st] 4 times, sc in each of next 15 sts, [sc ch lp in next st, sc in each of next 3 sts] 4 times, turn.

Row 18: Rep Row 2.

Row 19: Ch 1, sc in first st, [sc ch lp in next st, sc in each of next 3 sts] 4 times, sc in each of next 13 sts, [sc in each of next 3 sts, sc ch lp in next st] 4 times, sc in next st, turn.

Row 20: Rep Row 2.

Row 21: Ch 1, [sc in each of next 3 sts, sc ch lp in next st] 3 times, sc in each of next 23 sts, [sc ch lp in next st, sc in each of next 3 sts] 3 times, turn.

Row 22: Rep Row 2.

Row 23: Ch 1, sc in first st, [sc ch lp in next st, sc in each of next 3 sts] 3 times, sc in each of next 21 sts, [sc in each of next 3 sts, sc ch lp in next st] 3 times, sc in last st, turn.

Row 24: Rep Row 2.

Rows 25–32: [Rep Rows 21–24] twice.

Rows 33 & 34: Rep Rows 21 and 22.

Row 35: Rep Row 19.

Row 36: Rep Row 2.

▶ CONTINUED ON PAGE 34

DESIGN BY
KATHLEEN GAREN

PERSIAN TILES

The intriguing tile design in this beautiful one-piece afghan is accomplished with an ingenious series of simple stitch patterns and creative color sequences. Surface chain stitch in a contrasting color gives the impression of individual blocks.

GAUGE

With size I hook, 10 sc = 3 inches; 10 sc rows = 3 inches
Check gauge to save time.

PATTERN NOTES

Weave in loose ends as work progresses. Row 1 establishes the RS of afghan. All rows are worked on RS only.

On all medium teal and royal rows, at beg and end of each row, leave a 6-inch length of yarn to be worked into fringe.

AFGHAN

Row 1 (RS): With soft white and I hook, ch 188, hdc in 2nd ch from hook, hdc in each rem ch across, fasten off. (187 sts)

Row 2: Attach medium teal with a sc in first st of previous row, ch 1, sk 1 st, [hdc in back bar of each of next 22 sts, ch 1, sk next st] rep across, ending with hdc in both lps of last st, fasten off.

Row 3: Attach royal with a sc in first st of previous row, ch 1, sk next st, [sc in back lp of each of next 22 sts, ch 1, sk next st] rep across, ending with a sc in both lps of last st, fasten off.

Note: *All sc sts will be worked in the back lp of the sts in previous row unless otherwise stated. All dc sts will*

BEGINNER ●●

SIZE 49 x 58 inches, excluding fringe

MATERIALS
- Coats & Clark Red Heart Super Saver worsted weight yarn: 24 oz medium teal #359, 20 oz royal #385, 6 oz soft white #316
- Sizes I/9 and K/10½ crochet hooks or sizes needed to obtain gauge
- Yarn needle

be worked in front lp of the 2nd row below in front of and skipping st directly behind the dc.

Row 4: Attach medium teal with a sc in both lps of first st of previous row, ch 1, sk next st, [dc in next st, sc in each of next 3 sts, dc in next st, sc in each of next 2 sts, dc in next st, sc in each of next 6 sts, dc in next st, sc in each of next 2 sts, dc in next st, sc in each of next 3 sts, dc in next st, ch 1, sk next st] rep across, ending with sc in both lps of last st, fasten off.

Row 5: Attach royal with a sc in both lps of first st of previous row, ch 1, sk next st, [sc in next st, dc in next st, {sc in each of next 3 sts, dc in each of next 2 sts} 3 times, sc in each of next 3 sts,

dc in next st, sc in next st, ch 1, sk next st] rep across, ending with sc in both lps of last st, fasten off.

Row 6: Attach medium teal with a sc in both lps of first st of previous row, ch 1, sk next st, [dc in next st, sc in next st, dc in next st, sc in each of next 6 sts, dc in each of next 2 sts, dc in next st, sc in each of next 6 sts, dc in next st, sc in next st, dc in next st, ch 1, sk next st] rep across, ending with sc in both lps of last st, fasten off.

Row 7: Attach royal with a sc in both lps of first st of previous row, ch 1, sk next st, [sc in each of next 3 sts, {dc in next st, sc in each of next 4 sts} 3 times, dc in next st, sc in each of next 3 sts, ch 1, sk next st] rep across, ending with sc in both lps of last st, fasten off.

Row 8: Rep Row 4.
Row 9: Rep Row 5.
Row 10: Rep Row 4.
Row 11: Rep Row 7.
Row 12: Rep Row 6.
Row 13: Rep Row 5.
Row 14: Rep Row 4.
Row 15: Rep Row 5.
Row 16: Rep Row 6.
Row 17: Rep Row 7.

► CONTINUED ON PAGE 35

DESIGN BY
ANGEL RHETT

CHARLESTON ROSE

Like the Southern city for which it is named, this exquisite pattern reflects the genteel beauty and gracious charm of bygone days. Sparkling filament thread worked into the design adds glittering elegance, and a delicate fan border completes the classic look.

GAUGE

3 sc = 1 inch; 3 sc rows = 1 inch
Check gauge to save time.

PATTERN NOTES

Weave in loose ends as work progresses.

Join rnds with a sl st unless otherwise stated.

Graph-reading knowledge is necessary. With color key as a guide, work with 1 strand each yarn and filament held tog. The only colors that do not use a filament are black, white and nickel.

AFGHAN

Row 1: With black, ch 127, sc in 2nd ch from hook, sc in each rem ch across, turn. (126 sc)

Rows 2–160: Foll graph (pages 14 and 15), ch 1, sc in each st across, changing colors as indicated, turn at the end of each row.

BORDER

Rnd 1: Attach black in top right corner, working across top edge of afghan, ch

INTERMEDIATE ●●●

SIZE 43 x 51 inches

MATERIALS
- Coats & Clark Red Heart TLC Essentials: 18 oz black #2112
- Coats & Clark Red Heart Classic worsted weight yarn: 3 oz each cardinal #917, cherry red #912 and jockey red #902, 2½ oz each claret #762 and paddy green #686, 2 oz each light lavender #579, forest green #689 and emerald green #676, 1½ oz each amethyst #588, lavender #584 and purple #596, 1 oz yellow #230, ½ oz white #1, ¼ oz each blue jewel #818 and olympic blue #849, small amount nickel #401
- Kreinik Blending Filament: 2¾ spools #003HL, 2½ spools each #032 and #031, 2 spools #061, 1½ spools each #008HL and #015HL, 1¼ spools #009, small amount of each #006 and #014HL
- Size J/10 crochet hook or size needed to obtain gauge
- Yarn needle

1, [3 sc in corner st, sc evenly sp across edge] rep around, join in beg sc.

Rnd 2: Ch 1, sc in first sc of corner 3-sc group, *ch 5, sk center corner sc, sc in each of next 7 sc, [ch 3, sk next sc, sc in each of next 7 sc] 14 times, ch 3, sk next sc, sc in each of next 6 sc, ch 5, sk next center corner sc, sc in each of next 7 sc, [ch 3, sk next sc, sc in each of next 7 sc] 18 times, ch 3, sk next sc, sc in each of next 8 sc, rep from * around, join in beg sc.

Rnd 3: Sl st into corner ch-5 sp, ch 5 (counts as first tr, ch 1), tr in corner ch-5 sp, [ch 1, tr] 7 times in same corner ch-5 sp, sk next 3 sc, sc in next sc, *[tr in next ch-3 sp, {ch 1, tr} 6 times in same ch-3 sp, sk next 3 sc, sc in next sc] rep across to next corner ch-5 sp **, tr in corner ch-5 sp, [ch 1, tr] 8 times in same corner ch-5 sp, rep from * around, ending last rep at **, join in 4th ch of beg ch-5.

Rnd 4: [Sk first tr of fan, sc in each ch-1 sp and each tr to last tr of same fan, sk last tr of fan, sc in sc between fan] rep around, join in beg sc, fasten off. ■

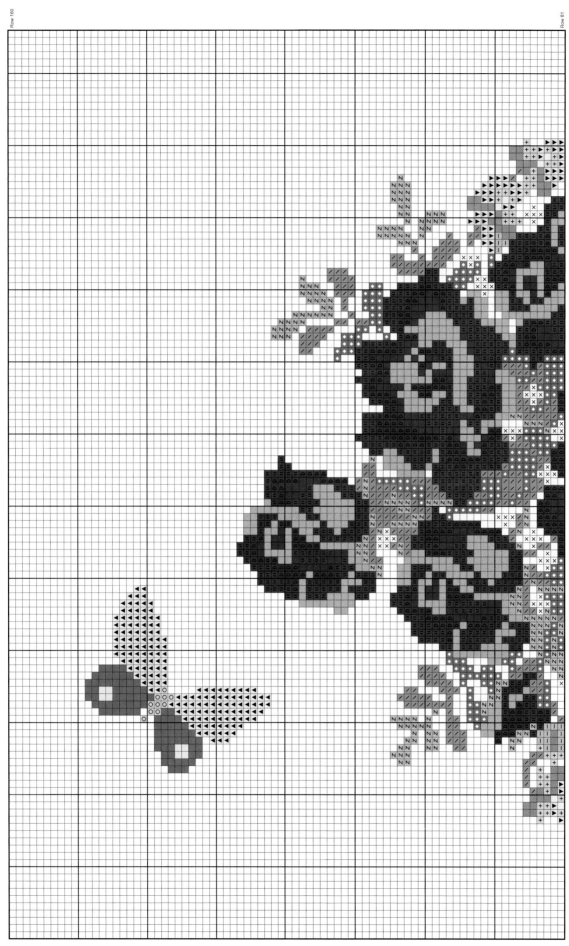

Charleston Rose
Upper Chart

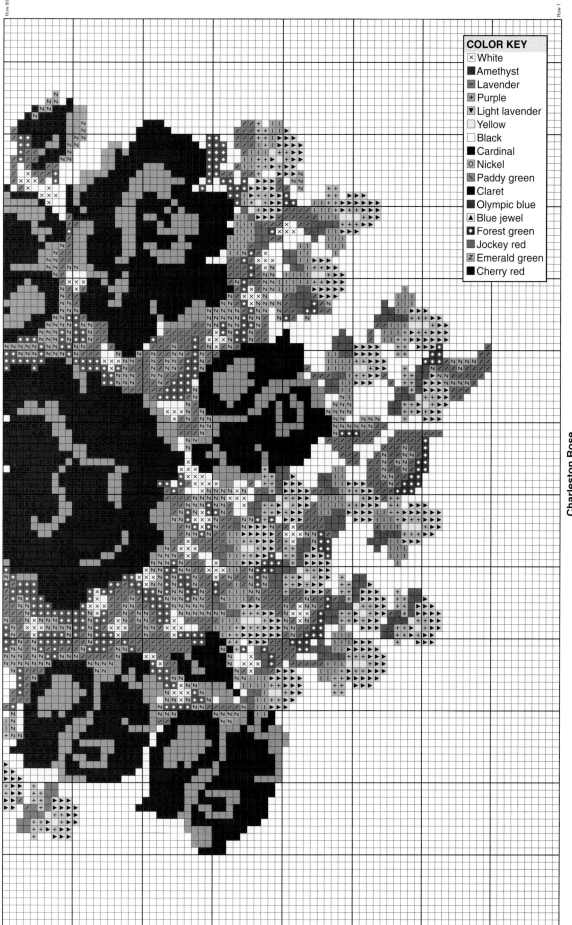

Charleston Rose
Lower Chart

COLOR KEY
- ⊠ White
- ■ Amethyst
- ▬ Lavender
- ＋ Purple
- ▼ Light lavender
- ☐ Yellow
- ☐ Black
- ■ Cardinal
- ⊙ Nickel
- ◩ Paddy green
- ■ Claret
- ■ Olympic blue
- ▲ Blue jewel
- ◈ Forest green
- ◼ Jockey red
- ☑ Emerald green
- ■ Cherry red

DESIGN BY
CAROL ALEXANDER

FRENCH PROVINCIAL

Rows of flowers captured in panels of delicate filet create the graceful elegance of this easy, join-as-you-go strip design that's as pretty as the blue skies of southern France.

GAUGE

4 dc = 1 inch; 2 rows = 1 inch; Rows 2–11 (pat rep) = 5¼ inches; completed strip 8½ x 66 inches
Check gauge to save time.

PATTERN NOTES

Weave in loose ends as work progresses.
Join rnds with a sl st unless otherwise stated.

PATTERN STITCHES

Tr cl: *Yo hook twice, insert hook in indicated st, yo, draw up a lp, [yo, draw through 2 lps on hook] twice, rep from * once, yo, draw through all 3 lps on hook.
Bobble: Yo hook, insert hook in indicated st, [draw up a ½-inch lp, yo] 5 times, draw through all 11 lps on hook, ch 1 tightly to lock.
Tr shell: [Tr, ch 1] 6 times in indicated st.
Beg tr shell: Ch 5, [tr, ch 1] 5 times in indicated st.
Dc shell: [Dc, ch 1] 4 times in indicated st.
Puff st: [Yo hook, insert hook in indicated st, yo, draw up a lp] 3 times, yo, draw through all 7 lps on hook.

FIRST STRIP

Row 1 (RS): Beg at bottom, ch 35,

INTERMEDIATE ● ● ●
SIZE 51 x 66 inches
MATERIALS
- Coats & Clark Red Heart Super Saver worsted weight yarn (8 oz per skein): 6 skeins light blue #381
- Size G/6 crochet hook or size needed to obtain gauge
- Yarn needle

dc in 9th ch from hook, [ch 2, sk next 2 chs, dc in next ch] 3 times, dc in each of next 5 chs, [ch 2, sk next 2 chs, dc in next ch] 4 times, turn.
Row 2: Ch 5 (counts as first dc, ch 2 throughout), dc in next dc (beg sp made), [ch 2, sk next 2 sts, dc in next dc] twice, dc in each of next 2 chs, dc in each of next 6 dc, dc in each of next 2 chs, dc in next dc, [ch 2, sk next 2 sts, dc in next dc] 3 times, placing last dc in top of turning ch, turn.
Row 3: Ch 5, dc in next dc, ch 2, sk next 2 sts, dc in next dc, dc in each of next 2 chs, dc in each of next 3 dc, ch 6, tr cl in 6th ch from hook, ch 7, tr cl in 6th ch from hook, ch 1, sk next 6 dc, dc in each of next 3 dc, dc in each of next 2 chs, dc in next dc, [ch 2, sk next 2 sts, dc in next dc] twice, turn.
Row 4: Ch 5, dc in next dc, dc in each of next 2 chs, dc in each of next 3 dc, ch 7,

tr cl in 6th ch from hook, ch 1, [sc, ch 2, sc] in ch-1 between next 2 tr cl, ch 6, tr in 6th ch from hook, ch 2, sk next tr cl and next 3 dc, dc in each of next 3 dc, dc in each of next 2 chs, dc in next dc, ch 2, sk next 2 sts, dc in next dc, turn.
Row 5: Ch 5, dc in each of next 6 dc, ch 7, tr cl in 6th ch from hook, ch 1, bobble in ch-2 sp between next 2 sc, ch 2, sc in top of same bobble, ch 6, tr cl in 6th ch from hook, ch 2, sk next tr cl, dc in each of next 6 dc, ch 2, dc in next dc, turn.
Row 6: Ch 5, dc in each of next 6 dc, ch 11, tr cl in 6th ch from hook, sl st in ch-2 sp in top of bobble, ch 6, tr cl in 6th ch from hook, ch 5, sk next tr cl, dc in each of next 6 dc, ch 2, sk 2 sts, dc in next dc, turn.
Row 7: Ch 5, dc in each of next 5 dc, sl st in 3rd ch of next ch-5 for 6th dc, fasten off. Attach yarn in 3rd ch of ch-5 after 2nd tr cl, sk next dc, dc in each of next 5 dc, ch 2, sk 2 sts, dc in next dc, turn.
Row 8: Ch 5, dc in next dc, ch 2, sk 2 sts, dc in each of next 3 dc, 3 dc in ch-2 sp before tr cl, ch 6, sk 2 tr cls, 3 dc in ch-2 sp after 2nd tr cl, dc in each of next 3 dc, [ch 2, sk 2 sts, dc in next dc] twice, turn.
Row 9: Ch 5, dc in next dc, ch 2, sk 2 sts, dc in next dc, ch 2, sk 2 sts, dc in

▶ CONTINUED ON PAGE 33

DESIGN BY
SANDY RIDEOUT

DESERT OASIS

A perfect blend of exotic inspiration and artistic imagination, this intriguing cultural creation effectively combines simple charted blocks with decorative borders and granny squares for a stunning tropical effect.

GAUGE

7 sc = 2 inches; 7 sc rows = 2 inches
Check gauge to save time.

PATTERN NOTES

Weave in loose ends as work progresses.
Join rnds with a sl st unless otherwise stated.

BLOCK

Make 9

Row 1: With linen, ch 38 loosely, sc in 2nd ch from hook, sc in each rem ch across, turn. (37 sc)

Rows 2–50: Foll graph (page 35), ch 1, sc in each st across, changing colors according to graph working over color not in use, turn at the end of each row. At the end of Row 50, fasten off.

BORDER

Rnd 1: With WS facing, attach warm brown in any st, ch 1, sc in same st as beg ch-1, hdc in next st, [sc in next st, hdc in next st] rep around, working 2 sts in each corner, join in beg sc, fasten off.

Rnd 2: With WS facing, attach medium brown in any hdc, ch 1, sc in same hdc as beg ch-1, hdc in next sc, [sc in next hdc, hdc in next sc] rep around, join in beg sc, fasten off.

INTERMEDIATE ○○●

SIZE 49 x 58 inches

MATERIALS
- Worsted weight yarn: 16 oz each linen and black, 9 oz medium brown, 8 oz warm brown, 6 oz artichoke, 3 oz rust
- Size H/8 crochet hook or size needed to obtain gauge
- Yarn needle

Rnd 3: With RS facing, attach black, ch 3 (counts as first dc throughout), dc in each st around, working 3 dc in each corner st, join in 3rd ch of beg ch-3, fasten off.

SIDE BORDER

Notes: *Side borders are worked in rows across each top, bottom and each side edge individually working from corner to corner and turning each row.*
On outer edges of blocks that will not be joined to another block, work 4 rows of side border and on inner edges that will be joined to an adjacent block work only 2 rows of side border. This will make the borders equal when joined to a previous block.

Row 1 (RS): Working from corner to corner on each side, with black, ch 3, [dc in next st, drawing through a lp of

warm brown in last 2 lps of dc, dc in next st, draw through lp of black in last 2 lps of dc, dc in next st] rep across edge until 13 warm brown dc across top and bottom edges of block and 17 warm brown dc across each side edge of block, turn.

Row 2: Ch 3, dc in each st with same color of previous row, turn or fasten off depending on the edge of the block.

ASSEMBLY

Place blocks on a flat surface 3 x 3, using care that edges that have 4 rows of side border are on the outer edge of afghan. Using matching yarns, sew side borders tog matching warm brown dc sts.

GRANNY SQUARE

Make 16

Rnd 1 (RS): With artichoke, ch 4, sl st to join to form a ring, ch 3, 2 dc in ring, ch 1, [3 dc in ring, ch 1] 3 times, join in 3rd ch of beg ch-3, fasten off.

Rnd 2 (RS): Attach linen in any corner ch-1 sp, [ch 3, 2 dc, ch 1, 3 dc] in same corner ch-1 sp, [{3 dc, ch 1, 3 dc} in next corner ch-1 sp] 3 times, join in 3rd ch of beg ch-3, fasten off.

Rnd 3 (RS): Attach warm brown in

► CONTINUED ON PAGE 35

DESIGN BY
BENDY CARTER

POST-STITCH REVIEW

Textured blocks featuring a variety of post-stitch patterns are creatively combined for a dramatic study in dimensional design in this afghan work of art. Lustrous pearl beads add shimmering highlights to alternating squares.

GAUGE

Square = 10 inches
Check gauge to save time.

PATTERN NOTES

Weave in loose ends as work progresses.
Join rnds with a sl st unless otherwise stated.

When working post sts, leave st directly behind post st unworked.

Ch 2 counts as first hdc throughout.
When pattern indicates to "mark last st," tie a scrap piece of yarn around post of indicated st.

PATTERN STITCHES

Fptrtr: Yo hook 4 times, insert hook around vertical post of indicated st, yo, draw up a lp, [yo, draw through 2 lps on hook] 5 times.

Fptr: Yo hook twice, insert hook front to back to front again around vertical post of indicated st, yo, draw up a lp, [yo, draw through 2 lps on hook] 3 times.

Bptr: Yo hook twice, insert hook back to front to back again around vertical post of indicated st, yo, draw up a lp, [yo, draw through 2 lps on hook] 3 times.

Fpdtr split: Yo hook 3 times, insert hook around front vertical post of indi-

ADVANCED ●●●
SIZE 53 x 73 inches
MATERIALS
• Patons Decor worsted weight yarn (3½ oz per skein): 19 skeins pale aqua #1610
• Size I/9 crochet hook or size needed to obtain gauge
• 108 (8mm) white pearl beads
• Beading needle
• Yarn needle

cated st 2 rows below or around same st as last fpdtr split or fpdtr, yo, draw up a lp, [yo, draw through 2 lps on hook] 3 times, yo hook 3 times, sk next 3 sts on same row, insert hook around front vertical post of next st or fpdtr split or fpdtr, yo hook, draw up a lp, [yo, draw through 2 lps on hook] 3 times, yo, draw through rem 3 lps on hook.

Fp bobble: Yo hook, insert hook around vertical post of st, yo, draw up a lp, yo, insert hook around post of same st, yo, draw up a lp, yo, draw through 4 lps on hook, yo, draw through rem 2 lps on hook.

Fpdtr bobble: Yo hook 3 times, insert hook around vertical post of indicated st, yo, draw up a lp, yo, insert hook around post of same st, yo, draw up a

lp, yo, draw through 4 lps on hook, [yo, draw through 2 lps on hook] 3 times.

Fptr bead split: Yo hook twice, insert hook around vertical post of marked st on last row, yo, draw up a lp, [yo, draw through 2 lps on hook] twice, yo hook 5 times, insert hook around post of marked st 4 rows below, yo, draw up a lp, push bead up next to hook, yo, [draw through 2 lps on hook] 5 times, yo hook twice, insert hook around post of next post st, yo, draw up a lp, [yo, draw through 2 lps on hook] twice, yo, draw through rem 4 lps on hook.

SQUARE ONE

Make 3

Row 1: Ch 26, hdc in 3rd ch from hook, hdc in each of next 3 sts (mark last st), [hdc in each of next 8 sts (mark last st)] twice, hdc in each of next 4 sts, turn. (25 sts)

Row 2: Ch 2, hdc in each st across, turn.

Row 3: Ch 2, hdc in next st, fpdtr around first marked st, hdc in each of next 3 sts, fpdtr around same st as last fpdtr, [hdc in each of next 3 sts, fpdtr around next marked st, hdc in each of next 3 sts, fpdtr around same st as last fpdtr] twice, hdc in each of next 2 sts, turn.

Row 4: Rep Row 2.

Row 5: Ch 2, hdc in each of next 3 sts (mark last st), [fptrtr 3 rows below, hdc in next st (make last st), hdc in each of next 6 sts (mark last st)] twice, fptrtr 3 rows below, hdc in next st (mark last st), hdc in each of next 3 sts, turn

Row 6: Rep Row 2.

Row 7: Ch 2, hdc in next st, [fpdtr bobble around marked st, hdc in next st, fpdtr bobble around fptrtr, hdc in next st, fpdtr bobble around next marked st, hdc in each of next 3 sts] twice, fpdtr bobble around marked st, hdc in next st, fpdtr bobble around fptrtr, hdc in next st, fpdtr bobble around next marked st, hdc in each of next 2 sts, turn.

Rows 8 & 9: Rep Row 2.

Row 10: Ch 2, hdc in each of next 4 sts (mark last st), [hdc in each of next 8 sts (mark last st)] twice, hdc in each of next 4 sts, turn. (25 sts)

Rows 11–17: Rep Rows 2–8, *at the same time*, make all FP sts BP sts. At the end of Row 17, fasten off.

SQUARE TWO
Make 2

Row 1: Ch 26, hdc in 3rd ch from hook, hdc in each rem ch across, turn. (25 sts)

Row 2: Ch 2, hdc in each of next 3 sts, bpdc around each of next 6 sts, hdc in each of next 5 sts, bpdc around each of next 6 sts, hdc in each of next 4 sts, turn.

Row 3: Ch 2, hdc in each of next 3 sts, *sk next 3 post sts, fpdtr around each of next 3 sts, with hook in front of sts just made, fpdtr around first sk post st, [fpdtr around next sk post st] twice *, hdc in each of next 5 sts, rep from * to *, hdc in each of next 4 sts, turn.

Row 4: Rep Row 2.

Row 5: Ch 2, hdc in each of next 3 sts, fpdc around each of next 6 sts, hdc in each of next 5 sts, fpdc around each of next 6 sts, hdc in each of next 4 sts, turn.

Rows 6–17: [Rep Rows 2–5] 3 times. At the end of Row 17, fasten off.

SQUARE THREE
Make 2

Row 1: Ch 27, hdc in 3rd ch from hook, hdc in each rem ch across, turn. (26 sts)

Row 2: Ch 2, hdc in next 3 sts, *sk next

3 sts, [fpdtr around next st] 3 times, with hook in front of sts just made, fpdtr around first sk st, [fpdtr around next sk st] twice *, hdc in each of next 6 sts, rep from * to *, hdc in each of next 4 sts, turn.

Note: *All post sts are worked around post of post st on row below now and throughout.*

Row 3: Ch 2, hdc in next 3 sts, bpdc around each of next 6 sts, hdc in each of next 6 sts, bpdc around each of next 6 sts, hdc in each of next 4 sts, turn.

Row 4: Ch 2, hdc in each of next 3 sts, *sk each of next 3 post sts, fpdtr around each of next 3 sts, with hook in front of sts just made, fpdtr around first sk post st, [fpdtr around next sk post st] twice *, hdc in each of next 6 sts, rep from * to *, hdc in each of next 4 sts, turn.

Row 5: Ch 2, [hdc in each of next 2 sts, bptr around next 3 sts] twice, hdc in each of next 4 sts, bptr around each of next 3 sts, hdc in each of next 2 sts, bptr around each of next 3 sts, hdc in each of next 3 sts, turn.

Row 6: Ch 2, hdc in next st, [fptr around each of next 3 sts, hdc in each of next 4 sts, fptr in each of next 3 sts, hdc in each of next 2 sts] twice, turn.

Row 7: Ch 2, bptr around each of next 3 sts, hdc in each of next 6 sts, bptr around each of next 6 sts, hdc in each of next 6 sts, bptr around each of next 3 sts, hdc in next st, turn.

Row 8: Ch 2, fpdc around each of next 3 sts, hdc in each of next 6 sts, sk next 3 post sts, fpdtr around next 3 sts, with hook in front of sts just made, fpdtr around first sk st, [fpdtr around next sk st] twice, hdc in each of next 6 sts, fpdc around each of next 3 sts, hdc in next st, turn.

Row 9: Ch 2, bpdc around each of next 3 sts, hdc in each of next 6 sts, bpdc around each of next 6 sts, hdc in each of next 6 sts, bpdc around each of next 3 sts, hdc in next st, turn.

Row 10: Rep Row 8.

Row 11: Rep Row 6 making all fp sts, bp sts.

Row 12: Rep Row 5 making all bp sts, fp sts.

Row 13: Ch 2, hdc in each of next 3 sts, bptr around each of next 6 sts, hdc in each of next 6 sts, bptr around each of next 6 sts, hdc in each of next 4 sts, turn.

Row 14: Rep Row 4.

Rows 15–17: Rep Rows 3–5. At the end of Row 17, fasten off.

SQUARE FOUR
Make 2

Row 1: Ch 26, hdc in 3rd ch from hook, hdc in each rem ch across, turn. (25 sts)

Row 2: ch 2, hdc in each st across, turn.

Note: *On the following rows, work all post sts around post of post sts 2 rows below now and throughout.*

Row 3: Ch 2, [sk next 4 sts, fptrtr around each of next 3 sts, hdc in next st, with hook in front of sts just made, fptrtr around first sk st, {fptrtr around next sk st} twice, hdc in next st] 3 times, turn.

Row 4: Rep Row 2.

Row 5: Ch 2, fpdtr around each of next 3 sts, hdc in next st, [sk next 3 post sts, fptrtr around each of next 3 sts, hdc in next st, with hook behind sts just made, fptrtr around first sk st, {fptrtr around next sk st} twice, hdc in next st] twice, fpdtr around each of next 3 sts, hdc in next st, turn.

Row 6: Rep Row 2.

Row 7: Ch 2, [sk next 3 post sts, fptrtr around each of next 3 sts, hdc in next st, with hook in front of sts just made, fptrtr around first sk st, {fptrtr around next sk st} twice, hdc in next st] 3 times, turn.

Rows 8–15: [Rep Rows 4–7] twice.

Rows 16 & 17: Rep Rows 2 and 5. At the end of Row 17, fasten off.

SQUARE FIVE
Make 2

Row 1: Ch 26, hdc in 3rd ch from hook, hdc in each rem ch across, turn. (25 sts)

Row 2: Ch 2, hdc in each st across, turn.

Note: *On the following rows, work all post sts around post sts 2 rows below now and throughout.*

Row 3: Ch 2, hdc in next st, [fpdtr around next st, hdc in next st, fpdtr around next st, hdc in each of next 3 sts] 3 times, fpdtr around next st, hdc in next st, fpdtr around next st, hdc in each of next 2 sts, turn.

Row 4: Rep Row 2.

Row 5: Ch 2, hdc in next st, [sk next post st, fpdtr around next st, hdc in next st, with hook in front of sts just made, fpdtr around sk st, hdc in each of next 3 sts] 3 times, sk next post st, fpdtr around next st, hdc in next st, with hook in front of sts just made, fpdtr around sk st, hdc in each of next 2 sts, turn.

Row 6: Rep Row 2.

Row 7: Ch 2, hdc in next st, [fpdtr around next st, hdc in next st, fpdtr around next st, hdc in each of next 3 sts] 3 times, fpdtr around next st, hdc in next st, fpdtr around next st, hdc in each of next 2 sts, turn.

Rows 8–15: [Rep Rows 4–7] twice.

Rows 16 & 17: Rep Rows 4 and 5. At the end of Row 17, fasten off.

SQUARE SIX
Make 2

Row 1: Ch 26, hdc in 3rd ch from hook, hdc in each of next 3 sts (mark last st), [hdc in each of next 8 sts (mark last st)] twice, hdc in each of next 4 sts, turn. (25 sts)

Row 2: Ch 2, hdc in each st across, turn.

Row 3: Ch 2, hdc in next st, fpdtr around first marked st 2 rows below, hdc in each of next 2 sts (mark last st), hdc in next st, fpdtr around same st as last fpdtr, [hdc in each of next 3 sts, fpdtr around next marked st 2 rows below, hdc in each of next 2 sts (mark last st), hdc in next st, fpdtr around same st as last fpdtr] twice, hdc in each of next 2 sts, turn.

Rows 4–17: [Rep Rows 2 and 3] 7 times. At the end of Row 17, fasten off.

SQUARE SEVEN
Make 2

Row 1: Ch 26, hdc in 3rd ch from hook, hdc in next st (mark last st), hdc in each rem st across, turn. (25 sts)

Row 2: Ch 2, hdc in each st across, turn.

Row 3: Ch 2, hdc in next st, fp bobble in next st, hdc in next st, fpdtr split (work first part around marked st of Row 1), [hdc in next st, fp bobble, hdc in next st, fpdtr split (work first part around same st as last part of last fpdtr split)] 4 times, hdc in next st, fp bobble, hdc in each of next 2 sts, turn.

Row 4: Rep Row 2.

Row 5: Ch 2, hdc in next st, fpdtr (around first fpdtr split 2 rows below),

[hdc in next st, fp bobble, hdc in next st, fpdtr split] 4 times, hdc in next st, fp bobble, hdc in next st, fpdtr (around post of last fpdtr split 2 rows below), hdc in next 2 sts, turn.

Row 6: Rep Row 2.

Row 7: Ch 2, hdc in next st, fp bobble, hdc in next st, fpdtr split (work first part around fpdtr 2 rows below), [hdc in next st, fp bobble, hdc in next st, fpdtr split] 4 times, hdc in next st, fp bobble, hdc in next 2 sts, turn.

Rows 8–15: [Rep Rows 4–7] twice.

Rows 16 & 17: Rep Rows 4 and 5. At the end of Row 17, fasten off.

SQUARE EIGHT
Make 2

Row 1: Ch 27, hdc in 3rd ch from hook, hdc in each rem ch across, turn. (26 sts)

Row 2: Ch 2, hdc in each st across, turn.

Row 3: Ch 2, *sk next 2 sts, fpdtr around next 2 sts of Row 1, with hook in front of sts just made fpdtr around first sk st of Row 1, fpdtr around next sk st of Row 1 *, hdc in each of next 7 sts (mark last st), [hdc in next st and mark st] twice, hdc in each of next 2 sts, fpdtr around each of next 2 sts of Row 1, hdc in each of next 3 sts, rep from * to *, hdc in next st, turn.

Row 4: Rep Row 2.

Row 5: Ch 2, fpdtr around each of next 4 fpdtr sts, hdc in each of next 3 sts, fpdtr around first marked st, fpdtr around 2nd marked st (leave st marked), hdc in each of next 3 sts, fpdtr around each of next 2 fpdtr, with hook in front of sts just made, fpdtr around 2nd marked st, fpdtr around 3rd marked st, hdc in each of next 4 sts, fpdtr around each of next 4 fpdtr sts, hdc in next st, turn.

Row 6: Rep Row 2.

Note: *Work all post sts around post of post sts 2 rows below throughout.*

Row 7: Ch 2, *sk next 2 post sts, fpdtr around next 2 sts, with hook in front of sts just made, fpdtr around first sk st, fpdtr around next sk st *, hdc in each of next 3 sts, fpdtr around each of next 4 sts, hdc in each of next 5 sts, fpdtr around next 2 sts, hdc in each of next 2 sts, rep from * to *, hdc in next st, turn.

Row 8: Rep Row 2.

Row 9: Ch 2, fpdtr around each of next 4 sts, hdc in each of next 2 sts, sk next 2 post sts, fpdtr around each of next 2 sts, hdc in next 2 sts, with hook behind post sts just made, fpdtr around first sk st, fpdtr around next sk st, hdc in next st, fpdtr around next 2 sts, hdc in next 5 sts, fpdtr around each of next 4 sts, hdc in next st, turn.

Row 10: Rep Row 2.

Row 11: Ch 2, *sk next 2 post sts, fpdtr around next 2 sts, with hook in front of sts just made, fpdtr around first sk st, fpdtr around next sk st *, hdc in each of next 2 sts, fpdtr around next 2 sts, hdc in each of next 2 sts, sk next 2 post sts, fpdtr around each of next 2 sts, hdc in next st, with hook in front of post sts just made, fpdtr around first sk st, fpdtr around next sk st, hdc in each of next 5 sts, rep from * to *, hdc in next st, turn.

Row 12: Rep Row 2.

Row 13: Ch 2, fpdtr around next 4 sts, hdc in each of next 3 sts, sk next 2 post sts, fpdtr around next 2 sts, with hook behind sts just made, fpdtr around first sk st, fpdtr around next sk st, hdc in each of next 5 sts, fpdtr around next 2 sts, hdc in each of next 2 sts, fpdtr around next 4 sts, hdc in next st, turn.

Row 14: Rep Row 2.

Row 15: Ch 2, *sk next 2 sts, fpdtr around next 2 sts, with hook in front of sts just made, fpdc around first sk st *, hdc in each of next 2 sts, fpdtr around next 2 sts, hdc in each of next 4 sts, fpdtr around next st, [yo hook 3 times, insert hook around post of next st, yo, draw up a lp, {yo, draw through 2 lps on hook} 3 times] twice, yo, draw through rem 3 lps on hook, fpdtr around next st, hdc in each of next 5 sts, rep from * to *, hdc in next st, turn.

Row 16: Rep Row 2.

Row 17: Ch 2, fpdtr around each of next 4 sts, hdc in each of next 2 sts, fpdtr around each of next 2 sts, hdc in each of next 12 sts, fpdtr around each of next 4 sts, hdc in next st, fasten off.

▶ CONTINUED ON PAGE 36

UNDERWATER ADVENTURES

Colorful sea life and underwater creatures come alive in this enchanting, multipattern afghan that is sure to capture the imagination of any child who has dreamed of daring exploits under the sea!

GAUGE

13 sc = 4 inches; 13 sc rows = 4 inches; 13 sh sc = 4 inches; 16 rows sh sc = 4 inches
Check gauge to save time.

PATTERN NOTES

Weave in loose ends as work progresses.

Join rnds with a sl st unless otherwise stated.

When working with 2 yarn colors, work over yarn color not in use.

Use afghan order and direction of construction as a guide for section being worked and the arrows indicated for the direction of the rows.

Most of the afghan is worked with 2 colors in each row, which may cause your tension to be slightly tighter. Use care to maintain a proper tension.

PATTERN STITCHES

Shallow sc (sh sc): Insert hook under the 2 horizontal threads and bet the 2 vertical threads, yo, draw up a lp, yo, draw through 2 lps on hook.

5-tr cl: *Yo hook twice, insert hook in

SIZE 48 x 54 inches
MATERIALS
- Coats & Clark Red Heart Kids worsted weight yarn (5 oz per skein): 3 skeins turquoise #2850, 2 skeins each orange #2252, yellow #2230 and red #2390, 1 skein lime #2652
- Phentex Merit worsted weight yarn (50 gram balls): 3 balls each black #106 and white #101
- Oddments of worsted weight yarn in small amounts of shades of turquoise and jade
- Size H/8 crochet hook or size needed to obtain gauge
- 2 yarn bobbins
- Yarn needle

indicated st, yo, draw up a lp, [yo, draw through 2 lps on hook] twice, rep from * 4 times, yo, draw through all 6 lps on hook, ch 1 to lock.

Lp st: Insert hook in indicated st, wrap yarn around finger of left hand, insert hook under lps on finger and draw sts through, yo, draw through all lps on hook, remove lps from finger.

CENTER SECTION

Row 1 (RS): With turquoise, ch 65, sc in 2nd ch from hook, sc in each rem ch across, turn. (64 sc)

Row 2: Ch 1, sh sc in first st, sh sc in each rem st across, turn.

Rows 3–96: Rep Row 2.

Note: *If you choose, randomly work in oddments of yarn in shades of turquoise and jade to simulate wave movement in the water.*

INNER TRIM

Row 1 (RS): Attach white, ch 1, work sh sc in each of next 4 sts, join black, sh sc in each of next 4 sts, [with white, sh sc in each of next 4 sts, with black sh sc in each of next 4 sts] 7 times, turn. (64 sts)

Rows 2–8: Ch 1, continue in established color, working 4 sh sc across each color section. At the end of last rep, fasten off.

SIDE EDGE INNER TRIM

Note: *Prepare 2 bobbins with lime yarn.*

Row 1 (RS): Attach black in side edge of Row 8 of inner trim, ch 1, work 8 sc across inner trim, join turquoise, work 80 sc across center section, change to black, work 8 sc across inner trim, fasten off, turn. (96 sc)

Row 2: Attach lime, ch 1, sh sc in each of next 8 sts, [with black, 4 sh sc, with white, 4 sh sc] 10 times, with lime, sh sc in each of next 8 sts, turn. (96 sts)

Rows 3–7: Rep as for Row 2, working sh sc in each st across in established color sequence.

Row 8: Rep as for Row 2, inc 1 sh sc in middle of row, fasten off. (97 sts)

Rep Rows 1–8 of side edge inner trim on opposite side of afghan.

ARGYLE SECTIONS

With WS facing, attach orange along edge of top at the corner of a lime sec-tion, working in sc, foll chart and work until all 32 rows are completed. There will be 81 sts in argyle pattern across top and bottom, and 97 sts in argyle pattern on each side.

LARGE DIAMOND CORNER SQUARE

Note: *2 squares are worked in red with yellow diamonds and 2 are worked in yellow with red diamonds.*

With RS facing, working across right edge of top argyle section, with yellow, sc in each of next 15 sts, with red, work 1 sc, with yellow, sc in each of next 15 sts, turn. Foll large diamond corner diagram to complete. After corner square is com-pleted, sew open edge to the argyle sec-tion along side.

Rep rem 3 corners remembering to alter-nate colors and work the squares from the top or bottom sides out to the edges.

OUTER TRIM

Row 1: With RS facing, working across top (bottom) edge, attach black, ch 1, work 16 sh sc, [with white, sh sc in each of next 16 sts, with black, sh sc in each of next 16 sts] 4 times, *at the same time*, work 1 sh sc dec near center of row, turn. (144 sts)

Rows 2–4: With black, ch 1, sh sc in each of next 16 sts, [with white, sh sc in each of next 16 sts, with black, sh sc in each of next 16 sts] rep across, turn.

Note: *Row 5 is worked in reverse color order of previous rows.*

Row 5: With white working, ch 1, sh sc in each of next 16 sts, [with black, sh sc in each of next 16 sts, with white, sh sc in each of next 16 sts] rep across, turn.

Rows 6–8: Rep same color sequence as previ-ous row, turn. At the end of Row 8, fasten off.

SECTION KEY	
1	Center Section
2 & 3	Inner Trim
4 & 5	Side Edges of Inner Trim
6–9	Argyle Sections
10–13	Large Diamond Corner Squares
14 & 15	Outer Trim
16 & 17	Side Edges of Outer Trim

Afghan
Order and Direction of Construction

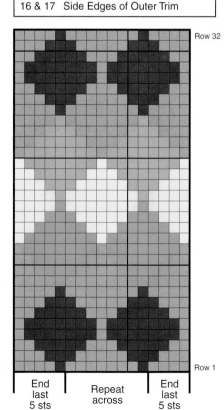

Argyle Section

SIDE EDGE OUTER TRIM

Row 1: Attach black in side edge of Row 8 of outer trim, ch 1, work 8 sh sc across outer trim, [with white, sh sc in each of next 16 sts, with black, sh sc in each of next 16 sts] 5 times, *at the same time*, work 1 sh sc dec near center of row, with black, sh sc in each of next 8 sts across outer trim, turn. (176 sts)

Rows 2–4: With black, ch 1, sh sc in each of next 8 sts, matching color of previous row, sh sc in each st across, turn.

Row 5: With black, ch 1, sh sc in each of next 8 sts, sh sc in each st across, reversing color order of previous row to last 8 sts, with black, sh sc in each of next 8 sts, turn.

Rows 6–8: With black, ch 1, sh sc in each of next 8 sts, working same color sequence as previous row, sh sc in each st across, turn. At the end of Row 8, fasten off. Rep side edge of outer trim on opposite edge of afghan, do not fasten off.

BORDER

Rnd 1: Ch 1, reverse sc in same st as beg ch-1, ch 1, sk 1 st, [reverse sc in next st, ch 1, sk next st] rep around, join in beg sc, fasten off.

APPLIQUÉS

Note: Appliqués are sewn with turquoise on center section of afghan. Use photo as a guide for placement.

LARGE PLANT

Row 1: With lime ch 2, sc in 2nd ch from hook, *insert hook into the single vertical thread that forms the left side of previous sc and work another sc *, rep * to * until 35 sc completed, do not turn, working in the left vertical thread, sl st in each st to beg, 1 sc in beg st, rep from * to * until 40 sc completed, do not turn, working in the left vertical thread, sl st in each st to beg, 1 sc in beg st, rep from * to * until 30 sc completed, do not turn, working in the left vertical thread, sl st in each st to beg, 1 sc in beg st, work 3 sc across base of leaves, turn.

Row 2: Ch 1, sc in each of the 3 base sc, turn.

Row 3: Ch 1, 2 sc in first sc, sc in next sc, 2 sc in last sc, fasten off.

SMALL PLANT

Row 1: Work as for large plant making leaves 25, 30 and 20 sts long.

Rows 2 & 3: Rep Rows 2 and 3 of small plant.

ROCK

With lime, ch 18, sc in 2nd ch from hook, [ch 2, sk 1 ch, 5-tr cl in next ch, ch 2, sk 1 ch, sc in next ch] 4 times, fasten off.

With red, ch 14, sc in 2nd ch from hook, [ch 2, sk 1 ch, 5-tr cl in next ch, ch 2, sk 1 ch, sc in next ch] 3 times, fasten off.

With orange, ch 10, sc in 2nd ch from hook, [ch 2, sk 1 ch, 5-tr cl in next ch, ch 2, sk 1 ch, sc in next ch] twice, fasten off.

LARGE ANEMONE

Rnd 1: With orange, ch 4, join to form a ring, ch 1, 8 sc in ring, do not join. (8 sc)

Rnd 2: Holding a length of red with the orange and working with both strands held tog, [lp st in next st, 2 lp sts in next st] rep until 30 lp sts are completed, turn.

Row 3: Ch 1, sc in each of next 3 sts, turn.

Rows 4–8: Rep Row 3.

Row 9: Ch 3, sl st in 2nd ch from hook, sl st in next ch, sl st in each of next 3 sc, ch 3, sl st in 2nd ch from hook, sl st in next ch, sl st in next st, fasten off.

SMALL ANEMONE

Rnd 1: With yellow, rep Rnd 1 of large anemone.

Rnd 2: With yellow and lime, rep Rnd 2 of large anemone.

Rows 3–6: Rep Row 3 of large anemone.

Row 9: Rep Row 9 of large anemone.

STARFISH

Rnd 1: With orange, ch 5, join to form a ring, ch 1, 10 sc in ring, join in beg sc. (10 sc)

Rnd 2: Ch 1, sc in same sc as beg ch-1, 2 sc in next sc, [sc in next sc, 2 sc in next sc] 4 times, join in beg sc. (15 sc)

Rnd 3: [Ch 9, sl st in 2nd ch from hook, sl st in next ch, sc in each of next 2 chs, hdc in each of next 2 chs, dc in each of next 2 chs, sk next 2 sc of Rnd 2, sl st in next sc] 5 times, fasten off.

YELLOW FISH

Row 1: With yellow, ch 4, sc in 2nd ch from hook, sc in each of next 2 chs, turn. (3 sc)

Row 2: Ch 1, 2 sc in first sc, sc in next sc, 2 sc in next sc, turn. (5 sc)

Row 3: Ch 1, 2 sc in first sc, sc in each sc across to last sc, 2 sc in last sc, turn. (7 sc)

Row 4: Rep Row 3. (9 sc)

Row 5: Ch 1, sc in each sc across, attach red, fasten off yellow, turn.

Row 32

Row 1

Large Diamond Corner Square

▶ CONTINUED ON PAGE 37

DESIGN BY
GLENDA WINKLEMAN

TAPESTRY FLORAL

In the old-fashioned elegance of bygone days, delicate bouquets cross-stitched on a Tunisian crochet background create the look of fine embroidery. A lacy border of dainty shells adds a pretty petaled edging.

GAUGE

12 afghan sts = 3 inches; 10 rows = 3 inches
Check gauge to save time.

PATTERN NOTES

Weave in loose ends as work progresses.
Join rnds with a sl st unless otherwise stated.

BLOCK

Make 12

Row 1: With afghan hook and winter white, ch 40, insert hook in 2nd ch from hook, yo, draw up a lp, [insert hook in next ch, yo, draw up a lp] rep across retaining all lps on hook (40 lps on hook), yo, draw through 1 lp on hook, [yo, draw through 2 lps on hook] rep across until 1 lp rem on hook.

Row 2: First rem lp from previous row counts as regular afghan st, [with yarn to the front of work on right hand side of next vertical st, insert hook in next vertical st, yarn underneath and to the back of hook, yo, draw through st, with yarn to back of work, insert hook in next vertical st, yo, draw yarn through st] rep across to last st, yarn to back

ADVANCED ● ● ●

SIZE 45 x 61 inches
MATERIALS
- Coats & Clark Red Heart TLC Essentials worsted weight yarn (6 oz per skein): 8 skeins winter white #2316, 2 skeins light country rose #2772, 1 skein light plum #2531, 1 oz each butter #2220, baby yellow #2222, medium thyme #2673
- Size J/10 afghan crochet hook or size needed to obtain gauge
- Size J/10 crochet hook
- Yarn needle

of work, insert hook in last st, yo, draw yarn through st (40 lps on hook), yo, draw through first lp on hook, [yo, draw through 2 lps on hook] rep across until 1 lp rem on hook.

Row 3: First lp counts as regular afghan st, [with yarn to back of work, insert hook in next vertical st, yo, draw up a lp, with yarn to the front of work right hand side of next vertical st, insert hook in next vertical st, yarn underneath and to the back of hook, yo, draw yarn through st] rep across to last st, with yarn to back of work, insert hook in last st, yo, draw yarn through st (40 lps on

hook), yo, draw through first lp on hook, [yo draw through 2 lps on hook] rep across until 1 lp rem on hook.

Rows 4 & 5: Rep Rows 2 and 3.

Row 6: First lp on hook counts as regular afghan st, *with yarn to the front of work on right hand side of next vertical st, insert hook in next vertical st, yarn underneath and to the back of hook, yo, draw yarn through st, with yarn to the back of work, insert hook in next vertical st, yo, draw yarn through st *, rep from * to * twice, [with yarn to the back, insert hook in next vertical st, yo draw up a lp] 28 times, rep from * to * twice, yarn to back of work, insert hook in last st, yo, draw yarn through st (40 lps on hook), yo, draw through first st on hook, [yo, draw through 2 lps on hook] rep across until 1 lp rem on hook.

Row 7: First lp counts as regular afghan st, *with yarn to back of work, insert hook in next vertical st, yo, draw up a lp, with yarn to the front of work on right hand side of vertical st, insert hook in next vertical st, yarn underneath and to the back of hook, yo, draw yarn through st *, rep from * to *, [with yarn to the back, insert hook in next vertical

► CONTINUED ON PAGE 38

DESIGN BY
MARGRET WILLSON

AMERICAN MOSAIC

Like the colorful blend of America's diverse cultures, the patriotic montage in this beautiful afghan presents an artful design cleverly created with different types of motifs of various shapes and sizes.

GAUGE

Rnds 1–3 of square = 4 inches
Check gauge to save time.

PATTERN NOTES

Weave in loose ends as work progresses.

Join rnds with a sl st unless otherwise stated.

Make and join triangles first. Centers and squares are joined to the circles formed by joining the triangles.

For assistance in joining a circle of triangles to a previous circle of triangles, tag each with the number of the triangle. Once you have a clear understanding of the joining process, it will no longer be necessary to mark the triangles.

The 192 triangles will make a total of 24 circles consisting of 8 triangles each when joined.

PATTERN STITCHES

Beg 3-dc cl: Ch 2 (counts as first dc), [yo hook, insert hook in indicated st, yo, draw up a lp, yo, draw through 2 lps on hook] twice, yo, draw through all 3 lps on hook.

3-dc cl: [Yo hook, insert hook in indicated st, yo, draw up a lp, yo, draw through 2 lps on hook] 3 times, yo, draw

INTERMEDIATE ◒◒●

SIZE 44½ x 67 inches
MATERIALS
- Coats & Clark Red Heart Super Saver worsted weight yarn (8 oz per skein): 32 oz soft white #316, 15 oz cherry red #319, 3 oz soft navy #387
- Size H/8 crochet hook or size needed to obtain gauge
- Yarn needle

through all 4 lps on hook.

Beg pc: Ch 3, 2 dc in ring, draw up a lp, remove hook, insert hook in 3rd ch of beg ch-3, pick up dropped lp and draw through st on hook.

Pc: Work 3 dc in ring, draw up a lp, remove hook, insert hook in first dc of 3-dc group, pick up dropped lp, draw through st on hook.

TRIANGLE

Make 192

Rnd 1 (RS): With soft white, ch 4, sl st to join in beg ch to form a ring, beg 3-dc cl in ring, ch 3, [3-dc cl in ring, ch 3] 5 times, join in top of beg cl, fasten off. (6 cl sts; 6 ch-3 sps)

Rnd 2: Attach cherry red in any ch-3

sp, ch 3 (counts as first dc throughout), [2 dc, ch 3, 3 dc] in same sp, 3 dc in next ch-3 sp, [{3 dc, ch 3, 3 dc} in next ch-3 sp, 3 dc in next ch-3 sp] twice, join in 3rd ch of beg ch-3, fasten off.

Notes: *Explanation of joining of the triangles: The point of each triangle on inside of the circle is not joined but is left free for attaching center. Using afghan diagram (page 33) as a guide, beg by making Circle A pattern for upper left corner, then work Circle B pattern 3 times to finish the row. On each of the rem rows, first work Circle C pattern on the left edge, then work Circle D pattern 3 times to finish the row. Triangles are numbered for joining clockwise and are marked with a • at the point of attaching yarn to each triangle to beg joining.*

CIRCLE A

Triangle 1

Attach soft white as indicated on diagram in corner ch-3 sp, ch 1, [{sc, ch 3, sc} in corner ch-3 sp, {ch 3, sc in sp bet dc groups} twice] 3 times, join in beg sc, fasten off.

Triangles 2–7

Attach soft white as indicated on diagram in corner ch-3 sp, ch 1, [sc, ch 3, sc] in

corner ch-3 sp, [ch 3, sc in next sp bet dc groups] twice, ch 3, sc in next corner ch-3 sp, ch 1, sc in corner ch-3 sp of previous triangle, ch 1, sc in same corner ch-3 sp of working triangle, [ch 1, sc in next ch-3 sp of previous triangle, ch 1, sc in next sp bet dc groups of working triangle] twice, ch 1, sc in next ch-3 sp on previous triangle, ch 1, sc in next sp bet dc groups on working triangle, ch 1, [sc, ch 3, sc] in next ch-3 corner sp (center inner circle point), [ch 3, sc in next sp bet dc groups] twice, ch 3, join in beg sc, fasten off.

Triangle 8

Attach soft white as indicated on diagram in corner ch-3 sp, ch 1, sc in same corner ch-3 sp of working triangle, ch 1, sc in ch-3 sp of first triangle, ch 1, sc in same corner ch-3 sp of working triangle, [ch 3, sc in next sp bet 3-dc groups] twice, ch 3, sc in next ch-3 sp, ch 1, sc in next corner ch-3 sp of 7th triangle, ch 1, sc in same ch-3 corner sp on working triangle, [ch 1, sc in next ch-3 sp of 7th triangle, ch 1, sc in next sp bet 3-dc groups on working triangle] twice, ch 1, sc in next ch-3 sp on 7th triangle, ch 1, [sc, ch 3, sc] in corner ch-3 sp, [ch 1, sc in next ch-3 sp on first triangle, ch 1, sc in next sp bet 3-dc groups] twice, ch 1, sc in next ch-3 sp of first triangle, ch 1, join in beg sc, fasten off.

CIRCLE B
Triangle 1
Rep Circle A, triangle 1.
Triangles 2–5
Attach soft white in corner ch-3 sp, ch 1, [sc, ch 3, sc] in corner ch-3 sp, [ch 3, sc in next sp bet 3-dc groups] twice, ch 3, sc in next corner ch-3 sp, ch 1, sc in ch-3 sp of previous triangle, ch 1, sc in ch-3 sp on working triangle, [ch 1, sc in adjacent ch-3 sp of previous triangle, ch 1, sc in next sp bet 3-dc groups] twice, ch 1, sc in adjacent ch-3 sp on previous triangle, ch 1, [sc, ch 3, sc] in next corner ch-3 sp, [ch 3, sc in next sp bet 3-dc groups] twice, ch 3, join in beg sc, fasten off.
Triangle 6
Attach soft white in indicated corner ch-3 sp, ch 1, sc in corner ch-3 sp, ch 1, sc in joining of triangle 2 and 3 of previous

circle, ch 1, sc in same ch-3 sp on working triangle, [ch 1, sc in next ch-3 sp of triangle 3 of previous circle, ch 1, sc in next sp bet 3-dc groups on working triangle] twice, ch 3, sc in corner ch-3 sp, ch 1, sc in corner ch sp of triangle 5, ch 1, sc in same ch-3 sp of working triangle, [ch 1, sc in next ch-3 sp of triangle 5, ch 1, sc in next sp bet 3-dc groups] twice, ch 1, sc in next ch-3 sp of triangle 5, ch 1, [sc, ch 3, sc] in corner ch-3 sp, [ch 3, sc in next sp bet 3-dc groups] twice, ch 3, join in beg sc, fasten off.

Triangle 7
Attach soft white in indicated corner ch-3 sp, ch 1, [sc, ch 3, sc] in corner ch-3 sp, ch 3, [sc in next sp bet dc groups, ch 1, sc in adjacent ch-3 sp of triangle 2 of previous circle, ch 1] twice, sc in next ch-3 sp, ch 1, sc in joining, ch 1, sc in same ch-3 sp of working triangle, [ch 1, sc in adjacent ch-3 sp of triangle 6, ch 1, sc in next sp bet 3-dc groups] twice, ch 1, sc in adjacent ch-3 sp of triangle 6, ch 1, [sc, ch 3, sc] in next corner ch-3 sp, [ch 3, sc in next sp bet 3-dc groups] twice, ch 3, join in beg sc, fasten off.

Triangle 8
Rep Circle A, triangle 8.

CIRCLE C
Triangle 1
Attach soft white in indicated corner ch-3 sp, ch 1, [sc, ch 3, sc] in corner sp, ch 3, [sc in next sp bet 3-dc groups, ch 1, sc in adjacent ch-3 sp of triangle 4 in circle above, ch 1] twice, sc in corner ch-3 sp of working triangle, ch 1, sc in joining of adjacent triangle, ch 1, sc in same ch-3 sp of working triangle, [ch 3, sc in next sp bet 3-dc groups] twice, ch 3, [sc, ch 3, sc] in next corner ch-3 sp, [ch 3, sc in next sp bet 3-dc groups] twice, ch 3, join in beg sc, fasten off.

Triangles 2–7
Rep Circle A, triangles 2–7.

Triangle 8
Attach soft white in indicated ch-3 sp, ch 1, sc in same ch-3 sp, ch 1, sc in joining of triangle 4 and 5 above, ch 1, sc in same ch-3 sp on working triangle, [ch 1, sc in adjacent ch-3 sp of triangle 5 above, ch 1, sc in next sp bet 3-dc groups on working triangle] twice, ch 3, sc in next corner ch-3 sp, ch 1, sc in adjacent ch-3 sp of triangle 7, ch 1, sc in same ch-3 sp on working triangle, [ch 1, sc in adjacent ch-3 sp of triangle 7, ch 1, sc in next sp bet 3-dc groups on working

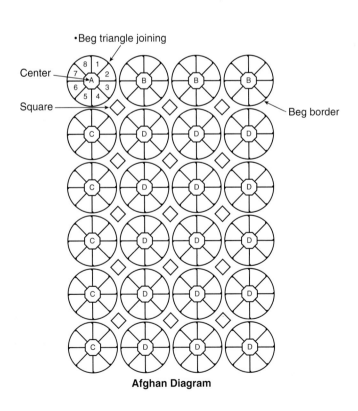

Afghan Diagram

triangle] twice, ch 1, sc in adjacent ch-3 sp on triangle 7, ch 1, [sc, ch 3, sc] in next corner ch-3 sp, [ch 1, sc in adjacent ch-3 sp on triangle 1 of working circle, ch 1, sc in next sp bet 3-dc groups] twice, ch 1, sc in adjacent ch-3 sp of triangle 1, ch 1, join in beg sc, fasten off.

CIRCLE D
Triangle 1
Rep Circle C, triangle 1.
Triangles 2–5
Rep Circle A, triangles 2–5.
Triangle 6
Rep Circle B, triangle 6.
Triangle 7
Rep Circle B, triangle 7.
Triangle 8
Rep Circle C, triangle 8.

CIRCLE CENTERS
Make 24
Rnd 1: With soft white, ch 5, sl st to join to form a ring, beg pc in ring, ch 3, [pc in ring, ch 3] 7 times, join in top of beg pc, fasten off. (8 pc; 8 ch-3 sps)
Rnd 2: Attach soft navy in any ch-3 sp,

ch 3, [dc, ch 1, sc in ch-3 tip of any triangle, ch 1, 2 dc] in same sp, *[2 dc, ch 1, sc in tip of next triangle, ch 1, 2 dc] in next ch-3 sp, rep from * 6 times, join in 3rd ch of beg ch-3, fasten off.

SQUARE
Make 15
Rnd 1: With soft white, ch 5, sl st to join to form a ring, beg pc in ring, ch 3, [pc in ring, ch 3] 7 times, join in top of beg pc.
Rnd 2: Sl st into ch-3 sp, ch 3, [2 dc, ch 3, 3 dc] in same ch sp, 3 dc in next sp bet 3-dc groups, *[3 dc, ch 3, 3 dc] in next ch-3 sp, 3 dc in next sp bet 3-dc groups, rep from * twice, join in 3rd ch of beg ch-3.
Rnd 3: Sl st across into corner ch-3 sp, [ch 3, 2 dc, ch 3, 3 dc] in same corner ch-3 sp, 3 dc in each of next 2 sps bet 3-dc groups, *[3 dc, ch 3, 3 dc] in corner ch-3 sp, 3 dc in each of next 2 sps bet 3-dc groups, rep from * twice, join in 3rd ch of beg ch-3.
Rnd 4: Ch 1, sc in sp to the right created by the joining, ch 1, sc in adjacent free sp of triangle, ch 1, *[sc in corner ch-3 sp, ch 1, sc in joining, ch 1, sc in corner ch-3

sp] corner joining, ch 1, sc in next free sp of triangle, ch 1, sc in next sp bet 3-dc groups on square, [ch 1, sc in next ch-3 sp of triangle, ch 1, sc in next sp bet 3-dc groups on square] twice, ch 1, sc in next adjacent free sp, ch 1, rep from * 3 times, ending with join in beg sc, fasten off.

BORDER
Working across short edge, attach soft white with sc in first in ch-3 sp at beg of upper right corner scallop as indicated on afghan diagram, ch 3, 3 dc in sc just made, *[sc in next ch-3 sp or ch-3 corner, ch 3, 3 dc in sc just made] 24 times, sc in next sp, [{sc in next ch-3 lp or ch-3 sp, ch 3, 3 dc in sc just made} 15 times, sc in next sp] twice, [sc in next ch-3 lp or ch-3 sp, ch 3, 3 dc in sc just made] 25 times, sc in next sp, working across long edge, [{sc in next ch-3 lp or ch-3 sp, ch 3, 3 dc in sc just made} 15 times, sc in next sp] 4 times, sc in next sp, sc in next sp, ch 3, 3 dc in sc just made, rep from * around, join in beg sc, fasten off. ■

FRENCH PROVINCIAL ▶ CONTINUED FROM PAGE 16

each of next 3 dc, 6 dc in ch-6 sp, dc in each of next 3 dc, [ch 2, sk 2 sts, dc in next dc] 3 times, turn.
Row 10: Ch 5, dc in next dc, [ch 2, sk 2 sts, dc in next dc] 3 times, dc in each of next 5 dc, [ch 2, sk 2 sts, dc in next dc] 4 times, turn.
Row 11: Rep Row 10.
[Rep Rows 2–11] 10 times for pattern, then rep Rows 2–10, at the end of last rep, fasten off.

EDGING
Note: *Loosen tension as needed to keep edges flat.*
Rnd 1: With RS of strip facing, attach yarn in bottom right corner sp, ch 3, [2 dc, ch 2, 3 dc] in same sp, *[dc in next dc, dc in next turning sp] rep across long side, dc in last

dc before corner sp, [3 dc, ch 2, 3 dc] in corner sp, working across short side, [dc in next dc, 2 dc in next ch sp] 3 times, dc in each of next 6 dc, [2 dc in next ch sp, dc in next dc] 3 times, [3 dc, ch 2, 3 dc] in corner sp **, rep from * around, ending last rep at **, join in 3rd ch of beg ch-3.
Rnd 2: Sl st in each of next 2 dc, sl st in corner ch-2 sp, beg tr shell in same sp, *sk next 3 sts of corner group, [puff st around FP of next st, ch 1, sk 2 sts, dc shell in next dc, sk 2 sts] rep across, ending with puff st around FP of st just before next corner group, ch 1, sk next 3 sts of corner group **, tr shell in corner ch-2 sp, rep from * 3 times, ending last rep at **, join in 4th ch of beg ch-5, fasten off. (4 corner tr shells; 4 dc shells and 5 puff sts each short side; 39 dc

shells and 40 puff sts each long side)

SECOND STRIP
Rep instructions for first strip through Rnd 1 of edging.
Rnd 2 (joining rnd): Work joining side as follows, work the 4th and 5th ch-1's of beg corner tr shell as a sl st in the corresponding ch-1 sps of corner tr shell on previous strip, work the 2nd ch-1 of each dc shell as a sl st in the corresponding ch-1 sp of dc shell on previous strip, work the first and 2nd ch-1's of the 2nd corner tr shell as a sl st in corresponding ch-1 sps of corner tr shell on previous strip. Work rem of rnd same as Rnd 2 of edging of first strip.
Make and join 4 more strips the same as 2nd strip. ■

Row 37: Rep Row 17.
Row 38: Rep Row 2.
Row 39: Rep Row 15.
Row 40: Rep Row 2.
Row 41: Rep Row 13.
Row 42: Rep Row 2.
Rows 43–242: [Rep Rows 3–42] 5 times.
Rows 243–254: [Rep Rows 3–6] 3 times. At the end of last rep, fasten off.

NARROW PANEL

Make 3

Row 1: With soft navy, ch 25, sc in 2nd ch from hook, sc in each rem ch across, turn. (24 sc)
Rows 2–254: Ch 1, sc in each sc across, turn. At the end of Row 254, fasten off.

QUATREFOIL

Make 12

Note: *If you have never worked braid before, it is recommended that you practice first with scrap yarn.*

Step 1: To make the braid, with lace, ch 2, sc in 2nd ch from hook, turn to the right, sc in 1 vertical lp, turn to the right, sc in 2 verticals lps, [turn to the left and keeping your thumb on the yarn just below the last sc made, sc in 2 vertical lps, turn to the right, sc in 2 vertical lps] rep until piece measures approx 27 inches, leaving a 15 inch length of yarn, fasten off.

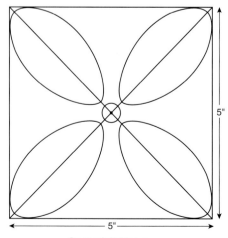

Quatrefoil Diagram

Note: *One side of the braid will look like braiding and one side will have horizontal bars.*

Step 2: The following will guide you when shaping the braid. Trace pattern of square of quatrefoil onto tracing paper. Or on a sheet of paper make a 5-inch square. Draw lines from corner to corner, crossing at center. Place a red bead at center and trace around the bead.
Step 3: Draw lps around each diagonal line from center bead to outer corner.
Step 4: Place sheet of paper over pinning board and pin in place.
Step 5: Using the lp lines as a guide, shape the braid from 1 lp to the next pinning in place as work progresses around bead in center, hiding ends underneath. With care, sew braid tog, remove pins.
Step 6: Mark the center of each flat diamond shape on each panel and with a double length of navy thread, sew a bead to the center of each diamond.
Step 7: Place 1 quatrefoil on diamond with bead coming through center square, pin in place. With a length of navy thread, sew around outer edges of quatrefoil.

SCROLL

Make 3

Step 1: To make the braid, follow directions as for quatrefoil, but make the braid 8 yds long.
Step 2: Using photo as a guide, arrange the braid on narrow panel beg at one end with a lp in the center, pin in place. Now beg to work lps going side to side, keeping each lp the same size and distance from the edge. Work all the way down the panel, pinning each lp as work progresses and end with a single lp at bottom center. Place the panel on a flat surface where you can make sure they are evenly placed and make needed adjustments. Recommended to have 27–29 lps on each panel. If you have excess braid, simply cut it off.

Step 3: With navy thread, sew braid in place onto panel.

INSIDE BORDER

Note: *Inside border is worked on each long edge of each wide panel, each long edge of 1 narrow panel, left side on long edge of 1 narrow panel and right side on long edge of 1 narrow panel. Inside border is not worked on outer edges of the 2 narrow panels.*

Row 1 (RS): With lace, beg at top edge and working down side edge of long edge, sl st in end of each row across, turn.
Row 2 (WS): Ch 11, sk first sl st, sc in 2nd sl st, [ch 10, sc in each of next 2 sl sts] rep across, fasten off. (126 lps)

Joining panels

Lay out panels on a flat surface. Beg at one side to join lps, pass right lp through left lp, then pass left lp through right lp, alternating from side to side. Work all the way to the top and with a safety pin, secure last lp in place. To join next panel, beg with the opposite side with pass left lp through right lp. Alternate in this manner until all panels are joined.

OUTER BORDER

Rnd 1 (RS): Working around outer edge of afghan, attach lace, sc in each sc, ch and end of each row around, working 3 sc in each corner and 4 sc across the inside border of joining of panels, join in beg sc.
Note: *On the following rnd, work with lace and soft navy simultaneously as indicated.*
Rnd 2 (RS): With lace, ch 4, sk 1 sc, sc in next sc, ch 4, drop lp from hook, pick up soft navy, sc in skipped sc, [ch 4, fold lace to front, sc in next sc, ch 4, drop soft navy, pick up lp of lace, fold soft navy to front, sc in next sc, ch 4, drop lp from hook, pick up soft navy] rep around, ending with join each color in beg sc of same color, fasten off. ■

PERSIAN TILES ▶ CONTINUED FROM PAGE 10

Row 25: Attach soft white with hdc in both lps of first st of previous row, ch 1, sk next st, [hdc in back lp of each of next 22 sts, ch 1, sk next st] rep across, ending with last hdc in both lps of last st, fasten off.
Rep Rows 2–25 until 6 patterns are completed.
Final Row 25: Attach soft white with a hdc in both lps of first st, hdc in back lp of each st across to last st, hdc in both lps of last st, fasten off. (187 sts)
Row 26: Attach soft white with a sc in both lps of first st, sc in back bar of each st across to last st, sc in both lps of last st, turn, do not fasten off.
Row 27: Ch 1, sl st in each sc across, fasten off.
Row 28: With opposite side of foundation ch of Row 1 facing, attach soft white, sl st in each ch across, fasten off.

Row 18: Rep Row 4.
Row 19: Rep Row 5.
Row 20: Rep Row 4.
Row 21: Rep Row 7.
Row 22: Rep Row 6.
Row 23: Rep Row 5.
Row 24: Rep Row 4.

VERTICAL LINE

Working with hook size K and 2 strands of soft white, ch 1, beg at bottom of afghan, holding strands of yarn at back and hook at front, insert hook in next ch-1 sp, yo, draw up a lp of soft white and draw through st on hook (sl st completed), continue to sl st in each ch sp to top of afghan, fasten off, secure ends.
Rep vertical line from bottom to top in each section of ch-1 sps.

FRINGE

Cut 12-inch lengths of royal and medium teal. Matching royal and medium teal color to beg and ending of each row, fold 2 strands of matching color in half, insert hook in side edge of row, draw strands through at fold to form a lp on hook, draw cut ends including rem beg or ending length through lp on hook, pull ends to secure. Attach 2 strands of royal or medium teal in each row of soft white row. Trim ends even. ■

DESERT OASIS ▶ CONTINUED FROM PAGE 18

any corner ch-1 sp, [ch 3, 2 dc, ch 1, 3 dc] in same corner ch-1 sp, 3 dc in sp between 3-dc groups on side of square, [{3 dc, ch 1, 3 dc} in next corner ch-1 sp, 3 dc in sp between 3-dc groups on side of square] 3 times, join in 3rd ch of beg ch-3, fasten off. With matching yarn, sew a granny square in each open corner created by the side borders.

AFGHAN BORDER

Rnd 1 (RS): Attach black in first black dc of black 2-dc group of side border, ch 3, dc in next black dc, [dc in next st, ch 3, sl st in top of dc just made, dc in each of next 2 dc] rep evenly sp around entire outer edge of afghan, ending with ch 3, sl st in top of last dc made, join in 3rd ch of beg ch-3, fasten off. ■

Row 50

COLOR KEY
■ Artichoke
■ Rust
□ Linen

Row 1

Chart A

twice, fptr bead split, hdc in each of next 4 sts, turn.

Row 9: Ch 2, hdc in each of next 3 sts, [bptr, hdc in each of next 7 sts] twice, bptr, hdc in each of next 4 sts, turn.

Row 10: Ch 2, hdc in each of next 2 sts, [fptr in next st, hdc in next st, fptr around same st as last fptr, hdc in each of next 5 sts] twice, fptr around next st, hdc in next st, fptr around same st as last fptr, hdc in each of next 3 sts, turn.

Rows 11–17: Rep Rows 3–9. At the end of Row 17, fasten off.

SQUARE BORDER

Note: *Work border on each square.*

Rnd 1: With RS facing, attach yarn in corner, ch 1, work 22 sc evenly sp on each side and 3 sc in each corner, join in beg sc. (100 sc)

Rnds 2 & 3: Ch 1, sc in each sc around, working 3 sc in each center corner sc, join in beg sc.

At the end of Rnd 3, leaving a length of yarn, fasten off.

ASSEMBLY

Using diagram as a guide, sew squares tog as indicated.

9	1	9	8	9
7	9	6	9	3
9	4	9	5	9
2	9	1	9	8
9	7	9	6	9
3	9	4	9	5
9	2	9	1	9

Assembly Diagram

AFGHAN BORDER

Rnd 1: With RS facing, attach yarn in any corner, ch 1, work 148 sc evenly sp across each short side and 208 sc across each long side and 3 sc in each corner st, join in beg sc. (724 sc)

Rnd 2: Ch 1, sc in each sc around, working 3 sc in each center corner sc, join in beg sc.

Rnd 3: Rep Rnd 2, fasten off. ∎

SQUARE NINE

Make 18

Note: *String 6 beads onto yarn before beg each square.*

Row 1: Ch 26, hdc in 3rd ch from hook, hdc in each of next 33 sts (mark last st), [hdc in each of next 8 sts (mark last st)] twice, hdc in each of next 4 sts, turn. (25 sts)

Row 2: Ch 2, hdc in each of next 2 sts, [fptr around marked st, hdc in next st, fptr around same st as last fptr, hdc in each of next 5 sts] twice, fptr around marked st, hdc in next st, fptr around same st as last fptr, hdc in each of next 3 sts, turn.

Note: *Work all post sts around post of post sts on row below throughout unless otherwise stated.*

Row 3: Ch 2, hdc in next st, bptr around next st, [hdc in each of next 3 sts, bptr around next st] 5 times, hdc in each of next 2 sts, turn.

Row 4: Ch 2, [fptr around next st, hdc in each of next 3 sts (mark last st), hdc in each of next 2 sts, fptr around next st, hdc in next st] 3 times, turn.

Row 5: Ch 2, [bptr around next st, hdc in each of next 5 sts, bptr around next st, hdc in next st] 3 times, turn.

Row 6: Ch 2, hdc in next st, fptr around next st, [hdc in each of next 3 sts, fptr around next st] 5 times, hdc in each of next 2 sts, turn.

Row 7: Ch 2, hdc in each of next 2 sts, [bptr around next st, hdc in next st, bptr around next st (mark last st), hdc in each of next 5 sts] twice, bptr around next st, hdc in next st, bptr around next st (mark last st), hdc in each of next 3 sts, turn.

Row 8: Ch 2, hdc in each of next 3 sts, [fptr bead split, hdc in each of next 7 sts]

Row 6: Ch 1, sc in first st, [tr in next st, sc in next st] rep across, turn.

Row 7: Ch 1, sc in each st across, attach lime, fasten off red, turn.

Rows 8 & 9: Rep Rows 6 and 7. At the end of Row 9, attach red, fasten off lime, turn.

Row 10: Rep Row 6

Row 11: Ch 1, sc dec over next 2 sts, sc in each st across to last 2 sts, sc dec over next 2 sts, join lime, fasten off red, turn. (7 sc)

Row 12: Rep Row 6.

Row 13: Rep Row 11, attach red, fasten off lime, turn. (5 sc)

Row 14: Ch 1, sc in each sc across, turn.

Row 15: Ch 1, sc dec over next 2 sts, sc in next st, sc dec over next 2 sts, turn. (3 sc)

Tail fin

Row 16: Ch 9, sl st in 2nd ch from hook, sl st in next ch, sc in each of next 2 chs, hdc in each of next 2 chs, dc in each of next 2 chs, sl st to join in side edge of Row 13.

Attach red in opposite end of Row 15, rep Row 16.

Top fin

Row 1: Attach yellow on top edge in Row 8 (lime row), ch 6, sl st in 2nd ch from hook, sc in next ch, hdc in next ch, dc in each of next 2 chs, sl st in side edge of Row 6, fasten off.

Trim

Rnd 1: Attach yellow in center foundation ch of Row 1 of fish, ch 1, work 3 sc in center ch, sc evenly sp around entire outer edge of fish, working sl sts around each fin, join in beg sc, fasten off.

Mouth

Attach red in center sc of 3-sc at center front of fish, ch 1, 3 sc in same sc, fasten off.

Eye

With turquoise, embroider straight sts for eye over Row 1.

RED FISH

Make a red fish, working the scales with lime and yellow, tail fins with yellow and top fin with red. Work trim with red and make a yellow mouth.

SNAIL

Rnd 1: With turquoise, ch 4, join to form a ring, ch 1, 8 sc in ring, join in beg sc, drop turquoise, do not fasten off. (8 sc)

Rnd 2: Draw up a lp of lime, ch 1, sc in same sc as beg ch-1, 2 sc in next sc, [sc in next sc, 2 sc in next sc] rep around, join, drop lime, draw up a lp of turquoise. (12 sc)

Rnd 3: Ch 1, sc in first sc, 2 sc in next sc, [sc in next sc, 2 sc in next sc] rep around, draw up a lp of lime, fasten off turquoise. (18 sc)

Rnd 4: Ch 1, sc in same sc as beg ch-1, sc in next sc, 2 sc in next sc, [sc in each of next 2 sc, 2 sc in next sc] rep around, join in beg sc, fasten off. (24 sc)

Row 5: Draw up a lp of yellow in first sc of Rnd 4, ch 5, sc in 2nd ch from hook, hdc in next ch, dc in each of next 2 chs (tail), sk next 2 sc of Rnd 4, sc in next sc, sc in each of next 3 sc, [sc, hdc] in next sc, [hdc, dc] in next sc, [2 dc in next sc] twice, tr in next sc, ch 2, sc in 2nd ch from hook, [hdc, dc] over side edge of tr st (head), fasten off.

Row 6: Attach yellow in same st as beg st of Row 5, sl st in each st around tail, body and head, fasten off.

With a length of turquoise, embroider eye with straight sts over head.

ANTENNA

Make 2

Attach red to top of head, ch 2, sl st in 2nd ch from hook, fasten off. ■

[ch 1, sk next st, sc in next st] rep across to next corner, ch 2, working across side edge of rows, sc in end of row, [ch 1, sk next st, sc in next st] rep across, ending with ch 2, join in beg sc, fasten off.

Rnd 2: Attach winter white in joining sc, ch 3 (counts as first dc), dc in each ch-1 sp and each sc around, working [dc, ch 2, dc] in each corner ch-2 sp, join in 3rd ch of beg ch-3.

Rnd 3: Ch 1, *sc in each of next 7 dc, sk next dc *, rep from * to * across to within 8 dc of corner, sc in each of next 8 dc, [sc, ch 2, sc] in corner ch-2 sp, sc in each dc down length to next corner ch-2 sp, [sc, ch 2, sc] in corner ch-2 sp, sc in each of next 8 dc, rep from * to * across to within 8 dc of corner, sc in each of next 8 dc, [sc, ch 2, sc] in corner ch-2 sp, sc in each dc across length to next corner, [sc, ch 2, sc] in corner ch-2 sp, sc in next dc, join in beg sc, fasten off.

EMBROIDERY

Foll graph, cross-stitch floral design on the center front of each block in the regular afghan st section.

ASSEMBLY

With hook size J and winter white, working in back lps only, sl st block tog 3 x 4. When joining blocks tog, make sure that each junction of 4 blocks and all other corners are evenly sp so that design will not be distorted.

AFGHAN BORDER

Rnd 1 (RS): With hook size J, attach winter white in top right corner sc, ch 1, sc in each sc and each ch sp on each side of each joining seam around, working [sc, ch 2, sc] in each corner ch-2 sp, join in beg sc.

Rnd 2: Ch 3 (counts as first dc throughout), working backwards, dc in sc to the right of beg ch-3, *[sk next sc, dc in next sc, dc in sk sc] rep across to within 1 sc from corner, dc in next sc, [2 dc, ch 2, 2 dc] in corner ch-2 sp, working down length, [sk next sc, dc in next sc, dc in sk

st, yo, draw up a lp] 28 times, rep from 8 to * 3 times, with yarn to the back of work, insert hook in last st, yo, draw yarn through st (40 lps on hook), yo, draw through first lp on hook, [yo, draw through 2 lps on hook] rep across until 1 lp rem on hook.

Rows 8–33: [Rep Rows 6 and 7] 13 times.

Row 34: Rep Row 2.

Row 35: Rep Row 3.

Row 36: Rep Row 2.

Row 37: [With yarn to back, sl st in next vertical st, with yarn to front, sl st in next vertical st] rep across, fasten off.

BLOCK BORDER

Rnd 1 (RS): With hook size J, attach light country rose in top right corner st of block, ch 1, sc in corner st, [ch 1, sk next st, sc in next st] rep across to next corner, ch 2, working across side edge of rows, sc in end of row, [ch 1, sk next st, sc in next st] rep across to 1 st from corner, sc in next st, ch 2, working across width, sc in first st, sc] rep across to corner, [2 dc, ch 2, 2 dc] in corner ch-2 sp, rep from * around, join in 3rd ch of beg ch-3.

Rnd 3: Ch 1, sc in each dc around, work-

ing [sc, ch 2, sc] in each corner ch-2 sp, join in beg sc.

Rnd 4: Ch 3, working backwards, dc in sc to the right of beg ch-3, *[sk next

sc, dc in next sc, dc in sk sc] rep across to within 1 sc of corner, dc in next sc, [dc, ch 2, dc] in corner ch-2 sp, working down length, [sk next sc, dc in next sc, dc in sk sc] rep across to corner, [dc, ch 2, dc] in corner ch-2 sp, rep from * around, ending with sk next sc, dc in next sc, dc in sk sc, join in 3rd ch of beg ch-3, fasten off.

Rnd 5: Attach light country rose in right hand corner dc, ch 1, sc in each dc around, working 4 sc in each corner ch-2 sp, join in beg sc, fasten off.

Rnd 6: Attach light plum in joining sc, ch 1, [hdc, dc, ch 1, tr, ch 1, dc, hdc] in same st as beg ch-1, [sk next sc, sc in next sc, sk next sc, {hdc, dc, ch 1, tr, ch 1, dc, hdc} in next sc] rep around to within last 9 sc, sk next 2 sc, sc in next sc, sk next sc, [hdc, dc, ch 1, tr, ch 1, dc, hdc] in next sc, sk next 2 sc, sc in next sc, sk next sc, join in top of beg hdc, fasten off. ■

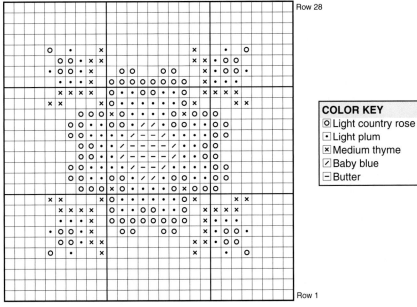

Row 28

Row 1

Tapestry Floral Chart

COLOR KEY
- ○ Light country rose
- • Light plum
- ✕ Medium thyme
- ⁄ Baby blue
- — Butter

CHAPTER 2

With styles ranging from retro to contemporary, this classy

collection of fashions and accessories is sure to give a

winning look to any wardrobe, whether flirty and

fun, cool and casual, or sleek and

sophisticated. Tempting textures and rich

details abound in every pattern, from jazzy

FIRST PLACE FASHIONS

jackets to sophisticated sweaters, and

purses with panache to

just-right jewelry. You'll find it easy to

achieve designer looks with the fabulous

mix of trendy yarns and fashionable

colors featured in these fresh and flattering designs that are

sure to complement anyone's sense of style.

DESIGN BY
MARGRET WILLSON

WOODLAND JACKET

Wide stripes of rich, earthy colors accented with feathery fringe throughout the design create the bold, rustic look of this sensational sporty jacket that's worked in a combination of two trendy yarns. It's sure to be a head-turning addition to any casual-chic wardrobe!

GAUGE

2-dc tog 10 times = 4 inches; 9 pat rows = 4 inches
Check gauge to save time.

PATTERN NOTES

Weave in loose ends as work progresses.

Join rnds with a sl st unless otherwise stated.

Work with 1 strand each Celebrity and Frolic held tog throughout unless otherwise stated.

Color sequence of Frolic yarn is

INTERMEDIATE ●●●

SIZE Extra-small (small, medium, large, extra-large and extra-extra-large)

Finished bust: 36 (40, 44, 48, 52, 56) inches

Back length: 22½ (23, 24, 24¾, 26¼, 27½) inches

MATERIALS

- CGOA Presents Celebrity (200 yds per skein) or wool/ray on blend sport weight yarn: 9 (9, 10, 11, 12, 14) skeins thicket
- CGOA Presents Frolic (200 yds per skein) or wool sport weight yarn: 2 (2, 3, 3, 4, 4) skein(s) each chocolate, terra-cotta, mustard and taupe, 1 (2, 2, 2, 3, 3) skein basil
- Size I/9 crochet hook or size needed to obtain gauge
- 6 (⅞-inch) leather buttons
- Tapestry needle

chocolate, mustard, terra-cotta, basil and taupe.

PATTERN STITCHES

2-dc tog: Yo, insert hook in same st

as last st, yo, draw up a lp, yo, draw through 2 lps on hook, sk next ch, yo, insert hook in next st, yo, draw up a lp, yo, draw through 2 lps on hook, yo, draw through rem 3 lps on hook.

2-sc tog: [Insert hook in next st, yo, draw up a lp] twice, yo, draw through all 3 lps on hook.

BACK

Foundation row (RS): With 1 strand each thicket and chocolate held tog, ch 90 (100, 110, 120, 130, 140), yo, insert hook in 3rd ch from hook, yo, draw up a lp, yo, draw through 2 lps on hook, ch 1, sk next ch, yo, insert hook in next ch, yo, draw up a lp, yo, draw through 2 lps on hook, yo, draw through all 3 lps on hook, ch 1, sk next ch, [2-dc tog, ch 1, sk next ch] rep across, ending with dc in last ch, turn. (43, 48, 53, 58, 63, 68 2-dc tog sts)

Row 1: Ch 1, sc in next sp, [ch 1, sc in next sp] rep across, turn.

Row 2: Ch 3, yo, insert hook in first sc, yo, draw up a lp, yo, draw through 2 lps on hook, yo, insert hook in next sc, yo, draw up a lp, yo, draw through 2 lps on

▶ CONTINUED ON PAGE 65

DESIGN BY
DEBORAH DAVIDSON

SCARLET RIBBONS SHAWL

The accent is on simplicity in this flirtatious and feminine evening shawl worked in a light and lacy pattern of easy double crochet and chain stitches. Trendy ribbon yarn gives it glitz, glamour and style!

GAUGE

7 rows = 3 inches
Check gauge to save time.

PATTERN NOTES

Weave in loose ends as work progresses.

Join rnds with a sl st unless otherwise stated.

Work loosely throughout. Stitches will vary in size due to the way the thread is designed.

PATTERN STITCHES

Beg dec: Ch 3, dc in next dc.

Ending dec: Work across row to last 2 dc, yo, insert hook in next dc, yo, draw up a lp, yo, draw through 2 lps on hook, yo, insert hook in next dc, yo, draw up a lp, yo, draw through 2 lps on hook, yo, draw through rem 3 lps on hook.

Dtrtr: Yo hook 5 times, insert hook in

BEGINNER ●●
SIZE Adult
MATERIALS
- Binario Trendsetter yarns: 12 balls red #103
- Size G/6 crochet hook or size needed to obtain gauge
- Yarn needle

indicated st, yo, draw up a lp, [yo, draw through 2 lps on hook] 6 times.

SHAWL

Row 1: Ch 269 loosely, sc in 2nd ch from hook, sc in each rem ch across, turn. (268 sc)

Row 2: Ch 4 (counts as first dc, ch 1), sk 1 sc, dc in next sc, [ch 1, sk next sc, dc in next sc] rep across, turn.

Row 3: Beg dec, ch 1, [dc in next dc, ch 1] rep across to last 2 dc, ending dec over last 2 dc, turn.

Rep Row 3 until 16 dc sts rem, fasten off.

BORDER

Row 1: Attach thread in side edge of Row 1, ch 1, sc in side edge of Row 1, *ch 6, sk next row, dtrtr in end of next row, ch 6, sk next row **, 3 sc in end of next row] rep evenly sp across edge, last row of shawl and up opposite edge of shawl, ending last rep at **, sc in side edge of Row 1, turn.

Row 2: Ch 1, sc in first sc, [7 sc over next ch-6 sp, {sc, ch 4, sc} in dtrtr, 7 sc over next ch-6 sp, sc in each of next 3 sc] rep across Row 1 of border, ending with 1 sc in last sc, fasten off.

FRINGE

For each fringe, cut 12 strand each 16 inches long. Knot 12 strands in each ch-4 sp of shawl. ∎

DESIGN BY
MARGRET WILLSON

JAZZY JEWELS VEST

Chic metallic-blend yarn adds a touch of dazzle to a sleek, sporty vest that's the perfect go-with-anything wardrobe accessory. Striking and simple, it defines a style that is both casual and romantic, and always contemporary.

GAUGE

4 shells = 3 inches; 7 pat rows = 3 inches
Check gauge to save time.

PATTERN NOTES

Weave in loose ends as work progresses.

Join rnds with a sl st unless otherwise stated.

Body of vest is worked with 1 strand each Blithe and Jewel FX held tog.

Edging is worked with 2 strands of Blithe held tog.

PATTERN STITCHES

Shell: 3 dc in indicated st.

2-dc dec: Yo hook, insert hook in same sc as last dc, yo, draw up a lp, yo, draw through 2 lps on hook, yo, insert hook in next sc, yo, draw up a lp, yo, draw through 2 lps on hook, yo, draw through all 3 lps on hook.

BACK

Foundation row: With 1 strand each color held tog, ch 69 (75, 81, 93, 99, 105), sc in 2nd ch from hook, ch 1, sk next ch, sc in next ch, [ch 2, sk next 2 chs, sc in next ch] rep across to last 2 chs, ch 1, sk 1 ch, sc in last ch, turn.

INTERMEDIATE ●●●

SIZE Extra-small (small, medium, large, extra-large and extra-extra-large)
Finished bust: 34 (37, 40, 46, 49, 52) inches

MATERIALS

- Berroco Jewel FX (57 yds per ball) or rayon/metallic blend sport weight yarn: 9 (9, 10, 12, 13, 15) balls #6913
- CGOA Presents Blithe (200 yds per skein) or cotton/rayon blend fingering weight yarn: 4 (4, 5, 5, 6, 6) skeins natural #13
- Size I/9 crochet hook or size needed to obtain gauge
- 6 (⁵⁄₈-inch) buttons
- Tapestry needle

across to last sc, dc in last sc, turn. (22, 24, 26, 30, 32, 34 shells)

Row 2: Ch 1, sc in first dc, ch 1, sc in center dc of next shell, [ch 2, sc in center dc of next shell] rep across, ending with ch-1, sc in last dc, turn.

Rep Rows 1 and 2 of pat 11 (10, 10, 10, 9, 9) times, rep Row 1 of pat, fasten off, turn.

Armhole shaping

Sk 5 (8, 8, 11, 11, 11) sts, attach yarn with sc in next st, [ch 2, sc in center dc

of next shell] rep across leaving last 5 (8, 8, 11, 11, 11) sts unworked, turn. (18, 18, 20, 22, 24, 26 shells)

Rep Rows 1 and 2 of pat 7 (8, 9, 10, 11, 12) times, rep Row 1 of pat, turn.

First neck shaping

Row 1: Ch 1, sc in first dc, ch 1, sc in center dc of next shell, [ch 2, sc in center dc of next shell] 4 (4, 5, 5, 6, 7) times, turn.

Row 2: Ch 3, shell in each sc across to last sc, dc in last sc, turn.

Row 3: Ch 1, sc in first dc, ch 1, sc in center dc of next shell, [ch 2, sc in center dc of next shell] rep across, ending with ch 1, sc in last dc, turn.

Row 4: Ch 3, shell in each sc across to last sc, dc in last sc, fasten off.

Second neck shaping

Row 1: With WS facing, sk center 26 (26, 26, 32, 32, 32) sts, attach yarn with sc in next st, [ch 2, sc in center dc of next shell] 4 (4, 5, 5, 6, 7) times, ch 1, sc in last dc, turn.

Row 2: Rep Row 1 of pat across 4 (4, 5, 5, 6, 7) shells, turn.

Row 3: Rep Row 2 of pat across, turn.

Row 4: Rep Row 1 of pat across, fasten off.

▶ CONTINUED ON PAGE 66

PURSE PANACHE!

A variety of styles and an assortment of beautiful yarns and threads create this stunning collection of ultra-chic purses that are the perfect complement for a fashionable wardrobe.

SILVER MOON

DESIGN BY

AMY BREWER

It's your night to shine when you accent your evening ensemble with this glamorous little purse stitched in sumptuous, metallic-mix yarn. Rich, luxurious texture and glimmering highlights add drama and elegance.

GAUGE

4 hdc = ½ inch; 4 hdc rnds = 1 inch
Check gauge to save time.

PATTERN NOTES

Weave in loose ends as work progresses.
Join rnds with a sl st unless otherwise stated.
Do not turn at the end of each rnd.

PATTERN STITCHES

Popcorn (pc): 4 dc in next st, draw up a lp, remove hook, insert hook in first dc of 4-dc group, pick up dropped lp and draw lp through st on hook.

Beg popcorn: Ch 3, 3 dc in same st as beg ch-3, draw up a lp, remove hook, insert hook in 3rd ch of beg ch-3, pick up dropped lp and draw through st on hook.

PURSE

Rnd 1: With MC, ch 46, 2 hdc in 3rd

INTERMEDIATE ●●●

SIZE 5½ x 6½ inches; strap 36 inches

MATERIALS
- South Maid crochet cotton size 10: 100 yds black #12 (CC)
- Charming Trendsetter Yarn: 20-gram ball black magic/silver #310S (MC)
- Size 2 steel crochet hook or size needed to obtain gauge
- 7 x 12 inches black satin lining material
- 7-inch black zipper
- Black sewing thread
- Sewing needle
- Tapestry needle

chs, 3 hdc in last ch, working on opposite side of foundation ch, hdc in each of next 42 chs, join. (90 hdc)

Rnd 2: Ch 2 (counts as first hdc throughout), hdc in each st around, join in 2nd ch of beg ch-2.
Rep Rnd 2 until purse measures 4 inches, fasten off.

Trim

Rnd 1: Attach CC with a sl st on side of purse 13 sts to the left of joining, ch 1, sc in each st around, join in beg sc. (90 sc)

Rnd 2: Ch 1, sc in each st around, join in beg sc.

Rnds 3 & 4: Rep Rnd 2.

Rnd 5: Ch 3 (counts as first dc), pc in next st, [dc in each of next 2 sts, pc in next st] rep around, ending with dc in last st, join in 3rd ch of beg ch-3.

Rnd 6: Rep Rnd 2.

Rnd 7: Beg pc in first st, dc in each of next 2 sts, [pc in next st, dc in each of next 2 sts] rep around, join in top of beg pc.

Rnds 8–10: Rep Rnd 2.

Rnd 11: Ch 1, reverse sc in each st around, join in beg sc, fasten off.

STRAP

With CC, leaving a 6-inch length at beg, ch 4, [dc in 4th ch from hook] 4 times, draw up a lp, remove hook, insert hook in top of ch-4, pick up dropped lp and draw through st on hook, [ch 6, [4 dc in 4th ch from hook, draw up a lp, remove hook, insert hook in top of ch-6, pick up dropped lp and draw through st on hook] rep until strap measures 36 inches, leaving a 6-inch length, fasten off.

With tapestry needle, sew strap to each side of purse trim, weaving the 6-inch length through last pc and last 3 rnds of trim.

FINISHING

Fold lining material in half and press. Sew sides of lining closed and zipper into top opening. Place lining in purse and sew top edge to Rnd 10 of trim.

BLACK ICE

DESIGN BY
DONNA COLLINSWORTH

For the "little black dress" that is a fashion essential in any feminine wardrobe, this dazzling little drawstring purse, crocheted with glittering sequin accents, is the perfect finishing touch!

GAUGE

16 sts = 1 inch; 10 rnds = 1 inch
Check gauge to save time.

PATTERN NOTES

Weave in loose ends as work progresses. Join rnds with a sl st unless otherwise stated.

Beg ch-3 does not count as a dc unless otherwise stated.

BAG

Note: Thread sequins onto crochet cotton. Push sequins along cotton until pattern calls for sequins.

Rnd 1: With black, ch 30, dc in 3rd ch from hook, dc in each ch across, working on opposite side of foundation ch, dc in each ch across, join in top of first dc, turn. (56 dc)

Rnd 2: Ch 3, 2 dc in each of next 2 sts, dc in each of next 24 sts, 2 dc in each of

next 4 sts, dc in each of next 24 sts, 2 dc in each of next 2 sts, join in top of first dc, turn. (64 dc)

Rnd 3: Ch 3, 2 dc in each of next 4 sts, dc in each of next 26 sts, 2 dc in each of next 6 sts, dc in each of next 26 sts, 2 dc in each of next 2 sts, join in top of first dc, turn. (76 dc)

Rnd 4: Ch 3, 2 dc in each of next 4 sts, dc in each of next 30 sts, 2 dc in each of next 8 sts, dc in each of next 30 sts, 2 dc in each of next 4 sts, join in top of beg dc, turn. (92 dc)

Rnd 5: Ch 3, dc in each st around, join in top of first dc, turn.

Rnd 6: Ch 3, 2 dc in each of next 5 sts, dc in each of next 36 sts, 2 dc in each of next 10 sts, dc in each of next 36 sts, 2 dc in each of next 5 sts, join in first dc, turn. (112 dc)

Rnd 7: Rep Rnd 5.

Rnd 8: Ch 1, [push a sequin up next to hook, sc in next st, dc in next st] rep around, join in beg sc, turn.

Rnd 9: Ch 1, [sc in next st, dc in next st] rep around, join in beg sc, turn.

Rnds 10–41: Rep Rnds 8 and 9.

Rnds 42 & 43: Rep Rnd 9.

Rnd 44: Ch 7 (counts as first tr, ch 3), sk next 3 sts, [tr in next st, ch 3, sk next 3 sts] rep around, join in 4th ch of beg ch-7, turn.

Rnd 45: Ch 1, sc in first st, dc in next st, [sc in next st, dc in next st] rep around, join in beg sc, turn.

Rnds 46 & 47: Rep Rnd 9.

Rnd 48: Ch 3 (counts as first dc), sk next 3 sts, 8 tr in next st, sk next 3 sts, [dc in next st, sk next 3 sts, 8 tr in next st, sk next 3 sts] rep around, join in 3rd

ch of beg ch-3.

Rnd 49: Sl st in next tr, ch 7, sl st in 4th ch of ch-7, [dc in next tr, ch 4, sl st in top of last dc] rep in each tr around, join in 3rd ch of beg ch-7, fasten off.

FINISHING

Starting at side edge, weave ribbon through sps of Rnd 44, holding ends even, knot ends tog.

LIMPET SHELLS

DESIGN BY
MAGGIE PETSCH

If good things come in small packages, this charming little purse is truly a treasure! Stitched in glimmering metallic nylon thread in a beautiful, textured shell pattern that dates back to Victorian days, this dainty accessory will add sparkling elegance to any evening ensemble.

GAUGE

29 sc = 4 inches
Check gauge to save time.

Weave in loose ends as work progresses. Join rnds with a sl st unless otherwise stated.

PATTERN STITCH

Limpet shell: *Insert hook into indicated st, yo, draw up a lp, wrap working thread around index finger of left hand from back of finger to front to form lp, pass hook in front of lp; twist hook with point up behind lp, insert tip of hook into lp from right to left, slide finger out of lp and pull working thread to form loose lp on hook, rep from * 7 times in same st (9 lps on hook), yo, draw through 8 lps, yo, draw through 2 lps to form eye; twisting limpet shell downward, insert hook through eye and into next st, yo, draw up a lp through st and eye on hook, yo, draw through 2 lps on hook.

PURSE

Rnd 1: Ch 20, 2 sc in 2nd ch from hook, sc in each of next 17 chs, 3 sc in last ch, working on opposite side of foundation ch, sc in each of next 17 chs, sc in last ch, join in back lp only of beg sc. (40 sc)

Rnd 2 (RS): Ch 1, working in back lps for this rnd only, sc in same st as joining, sc in each rem st around, join in beg sc, turn. (40 sc)

Rnd 3: Ch 1, sc in same st as joining, sc in each rem sc around, join in beg sc, turn. (40 sc)

Rnd 4: Ch 1, sc in same sc as joining, sc in next st, [limpet shell, sc in each of next 2 sc] 9 times, limpet shell, join in beg sc, turn. (10 limpet shells)

Rnds 5–7: Ch 1, sc in same st as joining, sc in each rem st around, join in beg sc. (40 sc)

Rnd 8: Beg in same st as joining, [limpet shell, sc in each of next 2 sts] rep around, join in beg limpet shell, turn.

Rnds 9–11: Rep Rnds 5–7.

Rnds 12–16: Rep Rnds 4–8.

Rnd 17: Ch 1, sc in same st as joining, *sc dec over next 2 sts, sc in each of next 15 sts, sc dec over next 2 sts *, sc in next st, rep from * to *, join in beg sc, turn. (36 sts)

FRONT

Row 1: Sk joining sl st, ch 1, sc in each of next 17 sts, turn.

Row 2: Ch 1, sc in each st across, turn.

Row 3: Ch 1, sc in each of next 2 sts, [limpet shell, sc in each of next 2 sts] 3 times, limpet shell, sc in last st, turn. (4 limpet shells)

Row 4: Ch 1, sc dec over next 2 sts, sc in each st across to last 2 sts, sc dec over next 2 sts, turn. (15 sts)

Row 5: Rep Row 4. (13 sts)

Row 6: Rep Row 2.

Row 7: Ch 1, sc in each of next 3 sts, limpet shell, sc in each of next 2 sts, limpet shell, sc in each of next 4 sts, turn.

Row 8: Rep Row 4. (11 sts)

Row 9: Rep Row 2, fasten off.

BACK

Row 1: With RS facing, sk next st on Rnd 17, attach thread with a sl st in next st, ch 1, sc in same st as joining, sc in each of next 16 sts, turn. (17 sc)

Rows 2–9: Rep Rows 2–9 of front.

FINISHING

With sewing needle and ecru thread, sew 1 metallic rainbow bead at center of each limpet shell.

Sew top of purse to purse clasp. Attach gold chain to purse clasp.

ZEBRA STRIPES

DESIGN BY

ANN E. SMITH

A striking black and white chevron pattern adds exotic flair to this simple yet sophisticated drawstring purse stitched in easy-care mercerized cotton yarn and worked in easy single crochet stitches.

GAUGE

24 sc = 4 inches; 36 rnds = 5 inches
Check gauge to save time.

PATTERN NOTES

Weave in loose ends as work progresses. Do not join rnds, use a stitch marker to mark rnds.

PURSE

Rnd 1: Beg at bottom, with MC, ch 2, 6 sc in each of next 3 sc, 2 sc in next sc] 6 times. (30 sc)

SIZE 7½ x 8½ inches
MATERIALS
- Patons Grace (136 yds per ball) or cotton sport weight yarn: 2 balls night #60040 (MC), 1 ball snow #60005 (CC)
- Size C/2 crochet hook or size needed to obtain gauge
- Stitch marker
- Tapestry needle

next sc] 6 times. (36 sc)

Rnd 7: [Sc in each of next 5 sc, 2 sc in next sc] 6 times. (42 sc)

Rnd 8: [Sc in each of next 6 sc, 2 sc in next sc] 6 times. (48 sc)

Rnd 9: [Sc in each of next 7 sc, 2 sc in next sc] 6 times. (54 sc)

Rnd 10: [Sc in each of next 8 sc, 2 sc in next sc] 6 times. (60 sc)

Rnd 11: [Sc in each of next 9 sc, 2 sc in next sc] 6 times. (66 sc)

Rnd 12: [Sc in each of next 10 sc, 2 sc in next sc] 6 times. (72 sc)

Rnd 13: [Sc in each of next 11 sc, 2 sc

in next sc] 6 times. (78 sc)

Rnd 14: [Sc in each of next 12 sc, 2 sc in next sc] 6 times. (84 sc)

Rnd 15: [Sc in each of next 13 sc, 2 sc in next sc] 6 times. (90 sts)

Rnds 16–52: Working in sc with MC and CC, beg each rnd at A and work to B, rep A–B for 9 times, then go to the next rnd. Read each rnd from right to left.
When working Rnds 16–24, carry color not in use loosely along top of last rnd, working over the strand as you go to create the look of dotted Swiss. For Rnds 25–52, carry color not in use loosely along WS of fabric, do not work over the strands as this will make the dots again. At the end of Rnd 52, leaving a 3-inch length of CC, fasten off.

Rnd 53: With MC, sc in first 2 sc, ch 2, sk next 2 sc (buttonhole), [sc in each of next 3 sc, ch 2, sk next 2 sc (buttonhole)] rep around, ending with sc in last sc.

Rnd 54: [3 sc in next sc, sc in next sc, 2 sc in next ch-2 sp, sc in next sc] rep around.

Rnds 55–59: Sc in each sc around.

Rnd 60: [Sl st in next sc, ch 1] rep around,

ending with join in beg sl st, fasten off.

STRAP
With a strands of MC, ch 275, sl st, ch 1 in 2nd ch from hook, [sl st in next ch, ch 1] rep across, working on opposite side of foundation ch, [sl st in next ch, ch 1] rep across, ending with sl st in beg st, fasten off.
Take one end of strap from WS to RS through buttonhole, tie end into an overhand knot on the RS of bag. Sk next 2 buttonholes, using care not to twist strap, pass opposite end from WS to RS through the next buttonhole and tie into an overhand knot on the RS of bag.

TIE
With double strand of MC, ch 125, sl st in 2nd ch from hook, sl st in each rem ch across, fasten off. Take first end from RS to WS through the first sk buttonhole between the strap ends. Take the 2nd end from RS to WS through the 2nd buttonhole between the strap ends. Weave each end through the rem buttonholes until they meet. Pull ends out so that the ends match. Tie into an overhand knot.

VICTORIAN PRINCESS

DESIGN BY
BRENDA STRATTON
As regal and refined as the royal reticule of a Victorian princess, this dainty thread purse, embellished with lustrous bead and button trims, is a stunning accent for today's high-fashion formal wear.

GAUGE
4 rows = 1 inch; 6 sts = 1 inch
Check gauge to save time.

PATTERN NOTES
Weave in loose ends as work progresses.
Join rnds with a sl st unless otherwise stated.
Beg ch-2 counts as a hdc except when working hdc dec.

PATTERN STITCHES
Hdc dec: Yo, [insert hook in next st, yo, draw up a lp] twice, yo, draw through all

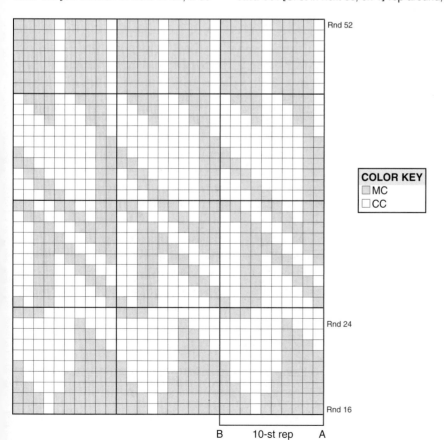

COLOR KEY
☐ MC
☐ CC

Rnd 52

Rnd 24

Rnd 16

B   10-st rep   A

Zebra Stripes Chart

4 lps on hook.
Shell: 7 dc in indicated st.

FRONT

Row 1: Beg at bottom with 2 strands of wood violet held tog and size D hook, ch 22, sc in 2nd ch from hook, [dc in next ch, sc in next ch] rep across, turn. (21 sts)

Row 2: Ch 2 (counts as first hdc), sc in next st, [dc in next st, sc in next st] rep across, ending with hdc in last st, turn.

Row 3: Ch 1, sc in first st, [dc in next st, sc in next st] rep across, turn.

Rep Rows 2 and 3 until piece measures 5 inches.

Row 4 (RS): Ch 1, sc in each st across, fasten off.

BACK

Row 1: Rep Row 1 of front. (21 sts)

Rep Rows 2 and 3 of front until piece measures 6 inches. Do not work Row 4.

Flap

Row 1: Ch 2, hdc dec over next 2 sts, sc in each dc, dc in each sc across to last 2 sts, hdc dec over last 2 sts, turn. (19 sts)

Rep Row 1 until 3 sts rem.

Row 2: Ch 2, yo, draw up a lp in each

SIZE 4 x 5 inches

MATERIALS

- Aunt Lydia's Classic crochet cotton size 10: 2 balls wood violet #495
- Size D/3 crochet hook or size needed to obtain gauge
- Size 5 steel crochet hook
- ¼ yd ¼-inch-wide lavender ribbon
- ½ yd lavender bead trim
- Size 3/0 snap fastener
- Straight pins
- Craft glue
- Matching sewing thread
- Sewing needle
- ⅝-inch lavender shank button
- 1¼-inch silver filigree craft backing
- Tapestry needle

of next 2 sts, yo, draw through all lps on hook, fasten off.

EDGING

Note: *Pin both pieces tog with RS of front facing.*

Rnd 1: With hook size 5, attach 1 strand of wood violet in lower right corner and working through both thicknesses, ch 1, sc evenly to top of front, continue working through back piece only around flap, sc evenly sp to point of flap, 3 sc in point, sc evenly down opposite side of flap and to top edge of opposite side of front, working through both thicknesses, sc evenly down side of front to bottom edge, do not fasten off.

Rnd 2: Sl st to front lp of foundation ch, working in front lps of front only, ch 1, sc in first st, [sk 1 st, shell in next st, sk 1 st, sc in next st] rep across front, turn and work across opposite side of foundation ch of back to beg st of front, sl st to join in beg sc, leaving a length of cotton, fasten off. Cut a piece of bead trim 5 inches long and place inside bottom opening of purse. Thread rem strand onto tapestry needle and sew opening closed with strand through BL of foundation ch.

Lightly tack the bottom centers of the shell sts tog.

FLAP TRIM

With size 5 steel hook, attach 1 strand of crochet cotton with a sl st at top left edge of purse in next st above where front piece ends, sc in each of next 4 sc, sk 1 sc, *shell in next sc, sk next sc, sc in next sc, shell in next sc, sk next sc, rep from * until 11 shells are completed, adjusting as necessary to allow 6th shell to fall at center point of flap, ending with sc in each of next 4 sc, sl st in last sc, fasten off. (11 shells)

Cut bead trim to fit underside of flap, sew in place, mitering at point.

HANDLE

With hook size D and 2 strands of wood violet held tog, ch 3, dc in 3rd ch from hook, ch 2, dc between last ch-3 and dc worked, [ch 2, dc bet last ch-2 and dc worked] rep until handle measures 20 inches long, fasten off.

Taking care not to twist handle, tack each end of handle at side seam on inside of purse.

Cut rem of beaded trim apart as needed to obtain 10 matching beads. Sew 9 beads evenly sp across handle.

JEWELED FRONT TRIM

Remove shank from lavender button and glue to silver backing and let dry. Glue rem bead left from those removed for handle to center of button and let dry.

FINISHING

Sew snap to flap and corresponding position on front of bag.

Tie ribbon into a bow and tack to front of flap slightly above snap.

Sew jeweled front trim in place over bow. ■

DESIGN BY
NORMA GALE

EARRING ELEGANCE

Crocheted in sparkling metallic embroidery floss on purchased hoops and adorned with bright bead accents, these glittering earrings add dazzle to evening wear or dress up a stylish daytime wardrobe.

GAUGE

Rnd 1 = 5/16 inch in diameter
Check gauge to save time.

PATTERN NOTES

Weave in loose ends as work progresses.

Join rnds with a sl st unless otherwise stated.

Remove 1 single strand from gold embroidery floss 6-strand skein.

EARRING

Make 2

Rnd 1: With 1 strand of gold, ch 6, sl st to join to form a ring, ch 1, 12 sc in ring, join in beg sc. (12 sc)

Rnd 2: Working in fl only, ch 1, sc in first st, ch 3, [sc in next st, ch 3] rep around, join in beg sc. (12 ch-3 sps; 12 sc)

Rnd 3: Ch 1, working in rem bl only of Rnd 1, sl st in first sc, ch 1, 2 sc in same st as beg ch-1, 2 sc in each rem st around, join in beg sc, fasten off. (24 sc)

Rnd 4: Attach aquamarine with a sl st in first sc, holding hoop behind crocheted piece and working over hoop as indicated, ch 4, tr in st as ch-4, sc over

INTERMEDIATE ●●●

SIZE 1¼-inch earring hoops

MATERIALS

- DMC Metallic embroidery floss: 1 skein gold #5282
- Kreinik Metallic Balger Fine #8 Braid: 6 yds aquamarine
- Size 11 steel crochet hook or size needed to obtain gauge
- Pair 1¼-inch gold earring hoops
- 2 (4mm) gold beads
- Pair 4mm gold ball and drop earrings
- Pair gold ear post nuts
- 2 (4mm) gold jump rings
- Fabric stiffener
- Glue
- Needle-nose pliers

hoop, ch 4, sl st in same st as last tr, sk next st, [sl st in next st, ch 4, tr in same st as sl st, sc over hoop, ch 4, sl st in same st as first sl st] rep around, fasten off. (12 spokes)

FINISHING

Spray crocheted piece with fabric stiffener, let dry. Glue a gold bead to the

center of each hoop, let dry.

Using needle-nose pliers, open jump ring. Insert jump ring through hole at top of hoop and through lp below ball of earring, making sure ball faces front of hoop, close jump ring. ■

FUCHSIA FANTASY RIPPLE PULLOVER

An eye-catching ripple pattern accented with a handkerchief-style hem in front and back makes this fashion-friendly pullover easy to wear and hard to resist! Trendy sport yarn in luscious, coordinated colors creates a feminine and flirtatious look that's perfect for any wardrobe.

GAUGE

With size 1 steel hook, 30 dc = 4 inches; 16 dc rows = 4 inches
Check gauge to save time.

PATTERN NOTES

Weave in loose ends as work progresses.

Join rnds with a sl st unless otherwise stated.

To change colors, work to last st of WS row, with 2 lps rem on hook, yo with next color, draw through rem 2 lps on hook. Do not fasten off old color, carry unused color along side of work.

Ch-3 counts as first dc throughout.

PATTERN STITCHES

2-dc inc: Work 2 dc in indicated st.

2-dc dec: [Yo, insert hook in next st, yo, draw up a lp, yo, draw through 2 lps on hook] twice, yo, draw through all 3 lps on hook.

3-dc dec: [Yo, insert hook in next st, yo,

INTERMEDIATE ○○●

SIZE Extra-small (small, medium, large, extra-large and extra extra-large)
Finished bust: 32 (36, 40, 44, 48, 52) inches

MATERIALS

- CGOA Presents Celebrity (200 yds per skein) or wool/rayon blend sport weight yarn: 9 (10, 10, 11, 11, 12) skeins fuchsia, 4 (4, 4, 5, 5, 6) skeins pink licorice
- Sizes 1, 2 and 3 steel crochet hooks or sizes needed to obtain gauge
- Tapestry needle

hook] 3 times, yo, draw through all 4 lps on hook.

4-dc dec: [Yo, insert hook in next st, yo, draw up a lp, yo, draw through 2 lps on hook] 4 times, yo, draw through all 5 lps on hook.

Back

Row 1 (RS): With size 2 hook and fuchsia, ch 131 (147, 163, 179, 195, 211), dc in 3rd ch from hook, dc in each

of next 62 (70, 78, 86, 94, 102) chs, 3-dc dec over next 3 chs, dc in each of next 62 (70, 78, 86, 94, 102) chs, 2 dc in last ch, turn. (129, 145, 161, 177, 193, 209 dc)

Row 2: Ch 3, dc in same dc as beg ch-3, dc in each of next 62 (70, 78, 86, 94, 102) sts, 3-dc dec over next 3 sts, dc in each of next 62 (70, 78, 86, 94, 102) sts, 2 dc in last st, changing to pink licorice with last yo, turn.

Rep Row 2 for pattern working 2 rows each pink licorice and fuchsia for a total of 66 (66, 68, 70, 72, 72) rows from beg. (33, 33, 34, 35, 36, 36 stripes)

Shoulder shaping

Row 1: Ch 3, 3-dc dec, work in established pat to last 4 sts, 4-dc dec, turn. Maintaining striped pat and carrying unused color loosely across shoulder, rep Row 1 in established pat 8 (9, 11, 12, 14, 15) times. At the end of last rep, fasten off.

▶ CONTINUED ON PAGE 67

DESIGN BY
BENDY CARTER

COTTON CANDY CAPELET SET

The name says it all in the luscious look and feel of this glamorous, classic-style capelet and matching gauntlet gloves. Lightweight mohair yarn gives ultra soft texture, and shiny metallic thread and glittering glass beads add sparkling highlights!

GAUGE

19 sc = 5 inches; 20 sc rows = 5 inches
Check gauge to save time.

PATTERN NOTES

Weave in loose ends as work progresses.

Join rnds with a sl st unless otherwise stated.

Gauntlets and cape are made holding 2 strands each mohair yarn and holographic thread tog throughout.

Mark indicated sts by wrapping a piece of yarn around the post of indicated st. Sk st directly behind any post st.

For cape, place a yarn marker at center st on each shoulder edge. When working a 4 st dec, dec 2 sts each shoulder. When working an 8 st dec, dec 4 sts at each shoulder.

For a 4 st dec, keeping with established pat as much as possible, work sc dec before and after marker on each side.

For an 8 st dec, keeping with estab-

ADVANCED ● ● ●

SIZE Adults: Extra-small (small, medium and large)

MATERIALS

- Berroco Mohair Classic yarn (1.5 oz per ball): 9 (10, 11, 12) balls #B1212
- Sulky Holoshimmer Holographic thread (250 yds per ball): 4 (4, 4, 5) balls light pink #145-6033
- Size G/6 crochet hook or size needed to obtain gauge
- Yarn needle

evenly sp dec across shoulder, work [sc dec] twice before marker and [sc dec] twice after marker on each side.

PATTERN STITCHES

Front lp sc (flsc): Work in front lp of indicated st.

Back lp sc (blsc): Work in back lp of indicated st.

Front post tr (fptr): Yo hook twice, insert hook, front to back to front again around the vertical post of indicated st, yo, draw up a lp, [yo, draw through 2 lps on hook] 3 times.

Front post dtr (fpdtr): Yo hook 3 times, insert hook front to back to front again around vertical post of indicated st, yo, draw up a lp, [yo, draw through 2 lps on hook] 4 times.

CAPE PATTERN RNDS

Pat rnd 1: Ch 1, [flsc in next st, blsc in next st] rep across to last st, flsc in last st, join in beg st, turn.

Note: *All post sts are worked around post of post st 2 rows below now and throughout.*

Pat rnd 2: Ch 1, [blsc in next st, flsc in next st] rep until 1 st before marked st, blsc in next st, fptr around next st, [blsc in next st, flsc in next st] 3 times, fptr around next st, flsc in next st, blsc in next st, flsc in next st, fptr around next st, flsc in next st, blsc in next st, flsc in next st, fptr around next st, [flsc in next st, blsc in next st] 3 times, fptr around next st, [blsc in next st, flsc in next st] rep to last st, blsc in last st, join in beg st, turn.

Pat rnd 3: Rep Pat rnd 1.

Pat rnd 4: Ch 1, [blsc in next st, flsc in next st] rep until 1 st before marked st, blsc in next st, fptr around next st, [blsc in next st, flsc in next st] twice, fptr around next st, [flsc in next st, blsc in next st] twice, flsc in next st, fptr around next st, [flsc in next st, blsc in next st] twice, flsc in next st, fptr in around next st, [flsc in next st, blsc in next st] twice, fptr around next st, [blsc in next st, flsc in next st] rep to last st, blsc in last st, join in beg st, turn.

Pat rnd 5: Rep Pat rnd 1.

Pat rnd 6: Ch 1, [blsc in next st, flsc in next st] rep until 1 st before marked st, blsc in next st, fptr around next st, blsc in next st, flsc in next st, fptr around next st, [flsc in next st, blsc in next st] 3 times, flsc in next st, fptr around next st, [flsc in next st, blsc in next st] 3 times, flsc in next st, fptr around next st, flsc in next st, blsc in next st, fptr around next st, [blsc in next st, flsc in next st] rep to last st, blsc in last st, join in beg st, turn.

Pat rnd 7: Rep Pat rnd 1.

Pat rnd 8: Ch 1, [blsc in next st, flsc in next st] rep until 1 st before marked st, blsc in next st, fptr around next st, fpdtr around next st, [flsc in next st, blsc in next st] 4 times, flsc in next st, fptr around next st, [flsc in next st, blsc in next st] 4 times, flsc in next st, fpdtr around next st, fptr around next st, [blsc in next st, flsc in next st] rep to last st, blsc in last st, join in beg st, turn.

Pat rnd 9: Rep Pat rnd 1.

Pat rnd 10: Ch 1, [blsc in next st, flsc in next st] rep until 1 st before marked st, blsc in next st, fptr around next st, [blsc in next st, flsc in next st] 4 times, sk next post st 2 rnds below, fpdtr around next post st, flsc in next st, fptr around post of same st as last post st, flsc in next st, fpdtr around post of same st as last post st, [flsc in next st, blsc in next st] 4 times, sk next post st 2 rnds below, fptr around next st, [blsc in next st, flsc in next st] rep to last st, blsc in last st, join in beg st, turn.

CAPE

Ribbing

Row 1: Ch 4, sc in 2nd ch from hook, sc in each rem ch across, turn. (3 sc)

▶ CONTINUED ON PAGE 67

DESIGN BY
ANN SMITH

LEMON DROPS SWEATER

Stitched in sunny yellow, cloud-soft sport weight cotton yarn, this bright, cheery cardigan features a sweetly feminine design accented with a dainty scalloped border. It's the perfect fashion accent to top off a spring or summer outfit.

GAUGE

17 sts = 4 inches; 22 rows = 4 inches
Check gauge to save time.

PATTERN NOTES

Weave in loose ends as work progresses.

Body of cardigan is crocheted from the lower edge in one piece.

When working body pat Row 1, remember to work in established pat so that fpdc sts are even.

PATTERN STITCHES

Puff st: [Yo, insert hook in next st, yo, draw up a lp] 4 times, yo, draw through 8 lps on hook, yo, draw through rem 2 lps on hook.

Fpdc: Yo, insert hook front to back to front again around the vertical of next dc of post st, yo, draw up a lp, [yo, draw through 2 lps on hook] twice.

Fpsc: Insert hook front to back to front again around post of indicated st, yo, draw up a lp, yo, draw through 2 lps on hook.

Sc 3 tog: Draw up a lp in each of next 3

INTERMEDIATE ●●●

SIZE Small (medium, large and extra-large)

Finished buttoned bust: 35 (38, 40¾, 43½) inches

Length: 22¾ (23¼, 23¾, 24¼) inches

MATERIALS

- Tahki Cotton Classic sport weight yarn (50 grams per ball): 18 (19, 21, 23) balls yellow #3533
- Size E/4 crochet hook or size needed to obtain gauge
- 7 (⅝-inch) buttons
- Yarn needle

---

sts, yo, draw through all 4 lps on hook.

Sc 2 tog: Draw up a lp in each of next 2 sts, yo, draw through all 3 lps on hook.

BODY PATTERN

Row 1 (RS): Ch 1, sc in each of next 5 sts, [fpdc over next fpdc, sk sc directly behind post st, sc in each of next 5 sts] rep across, turn.

Row 2 (WS): Ch 1, sc in each st across, turn.

CARDIGAN BODY

Row 1 (WS): Beg at lower edge and above the border, ch 144 (156, 168, 180), sc in 2nd ch from hook, sc in next ch, puff st in next ch, sc in each of next 2 chs, [dc in next ch, sc in each of next 2 chs, puff st in next ch, sc in each of next 2 chs] rep across, turn. (143, 155, 167, 179 sts)

Row 2 (RS): Ch 1, sc in each of next 2 sc, sc in next puff st, sc in each of next 2 sc, [fpdc over dc, sc in each of next 2 sc, sc in next puff st, sc in each of next 2 sc] rep across, turn.

Row 3 (WS): Ch 1, sc in each st across, turn.

Work body pat Rows 1 and 2 until from beg piece measures approx 13¾ inches, ending with a WS row.

RIGHT FRONT
Armhole shaping

Row 1: With RS facing, work in established pat across 31 (34, 37, 40) sts, turn.

Row 2: Rep Row 2 of body pat.

Row 3: With RS facing, rep Row 1 of body pat, ending with sc 3 tog, turn.

Row 4: Rep Row 2 of body pat.
[Rep Rows 3 and 4] twice. (25, 28, 31, 34 sts)
Work even in body pat until from beg piece measures approx 20¼ (20¾, 21¼, 21¾) inches, ending with a WS row, fasten off.

Neck shaping
Row 1: With RS facing, sk first 10 sts, attach yarn in next st, ch 1, sc in same st, work in body pat to end of row, turn.
Row 2: Rep Row 2 of body pat.
Row 3: Ch 1, sc 2 tog, work body pat across rem of sts, turn.
Rows 4 & 5: Rep Rows 2 and 3. (13, 16, 19, 22 sts)
Work even in body pat until from beg piece measures approx 21¼ (21¾, 22¼, 22¾) inches, ending with a RS row, fasten off.

BACK
Row 1: With RS facing, sk 9 sts from right front, attach yarn with a sl st in next st, ch 1, sc in same st, work in body pat across next 62 (68, 74, 80) sts, turn. (63, 69, 75, 81 sts)

Armhole shaping
Row 2: Rep Row 2 of body pat.
Row 3: Ch 1, sc 3 tog, work in body pat across to last 3 sts, sc 3 tog, turn.
[Rep Rows 2 and 3] twice. (51, 57, 63, 69 sts)
Work even in pat until back is the same length as right front, ending with a RS row, fasten off.

LEFT FRONT
Armhole shaping
Row 1: With RS facing, sk next 9 sts from back, attach yarn with sl st in next

st, ch 1, sc in same st, work in body pat across row, turn.
Row 2: Rep Row 2 of body pat.
Row 3: Ch 1, sc 3 tog, work in pat across row, turn.
[Rep Rows 2 and 3] twice. (25, 28, 31, 34 sts)
Work even in body pat until from beg piece measures approx 20¼ (20¾, 21¼, 21¾) inches, ending with a WS row.

Neck shaping
Row 1: Work in pat across, leaving last 10 sts unworked, turn.
Row 2: Rep Row 2 of body pat.
Row 3: Work even in pat across to last 2 sts, sc 2 tog, turn.
Rows 4 & 5: Rep Rows 2 and 3. (13, 16, 19, 22 sts)
Work even in body pat until from beg piece measures the same as right front. Matching sts, sew shoulder seams.

SLEEVE
Make 2
Row 1 (WS): Beg at lower edge above the border, ch 42 (42, 48, 48), sc in 2nd ch from hook, sc in next ch, puff st in next ch, sc in each of next 2 chs, [dc in next ch, sc in each of next 2 chs, puff st in next ch, sc in each of next 2 chs] rep across, turn. (41, 41, 47, 47 sts)
Row 2 (RS): Ch 1, sc in each of next 2 sts, sc in next puff st, sc in each of next 2 sts, [fpdc over dc, sc in each of next 2 sts, sc in next puff st, sc in each of next 2 sts] rep across, turn.
Row 3 (WS): Ch 1, sc in each st across, turn.

Work body pat until sleeve measures approx 4½ inches, ending with a WS row. Including new sts into body pat as they accumulate, inc 1 st each edge now and then every 6th row 10 (8, 9, 7) more times, then every 4th row 0 (4, 2, 6) times. (63, 67, 71, 75 sts)
Work even in pat to approx 18½ inches, ending with a WS row.

Sleeve cap shaping
Row 1 (RS): Sl st in first 6 sts, ch 1, sc in same st as beg ch-1, pat across leaving last 5 sts unworked, turn. (53, 57, 61, 65 sts)
Row 2: Rep Row 2 of body pat.
Row 3: Ch 1, sc 2 tog, work body pat Row 1 across to last 2 sts, sc 2 tog, turn.
[Rep Rows 2 and 3] 15 times. (21, 25, 29, 33 sts)
Row 4: Rep Row 2 of body pat.
Row 5: Ch 1, sc 3 tog, work body pat Row 1 across to last 3 sts, sc 3 tog, turn.
[Rep Rows 4 and 5] twice, fasten off. (9, 13, 17, 21 sts)

LEFT FRONT BORDER
Row 1 (RS): Working from neck to lower edge, [sl st over each of next 10 rows, sk 1 row] rep for a total of 100 (102, 104, 106) sts, turn.
Row 2: Ch 1, working in fl only, sc in each st across, turn.
Rows 3–6: Ch 1, sc in each st across, turn.
Row 7 (RS): Ch 1, sc in each sc across, sl st across lower edge of border to rem free lps of Row 1, [sl st, ch 1] in each rem st of Row 1 to neckline edge for rickrack trim, sl st across top edge of border to

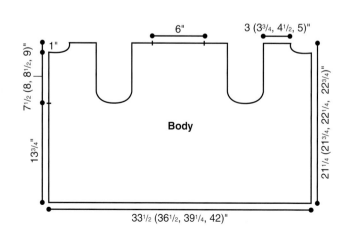

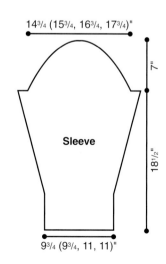

edge of beg of Row 7.

Row 8 (RS): Ch 1, sc in each sc to lower edge, fasten off.

RIGHT FRONT BORDER

Row 1 (RS): Working from lower edge to neck, [sl st over each of next 10 rows, sk 1 row] rep for a total of 100 (102, 104, 106) sts, turn.

Row 2: Ch 1, working in fl only, sc in each st across, turn.

Rows 3–5: Ch 1, sc in each st across, turn.

Row 6: Ch 1, sc in each of next 2 sc, [ch 2, sk next 2 sc, sc in each of next 10 sc] 7 times, sc in each rem sc across row, turn. (7 buttonholes)

Row 7 (RS): Ch 1, sc in each sc across, working 2 sc in each ch-2 sp, sl st across top edge of border to rem free lps of Row 1, [sl st, ch 1] in each rem st of Row 1 to lower edge, sl st across lower edge of border to edge of beg of Row 7.

Row 8 (RS): Ch 1, sc in each sc to neckline edge, fasten off.

LOWER BORDER

Row 1: With RS facing, attach yarn with sl st at lower edge of left front border, ch 1, sc in same st as beg ch-1, sc in each sl

st to rickrack, fpsc over rickrack, working along opposite side of foundation ch, *ch 1, sk next 2 chs, 5 dc in next ch directly beneath puff st, ch 1, fpsc over dc st, rep from * across bottom edge, ending last rep with fpsc over rickrack, sc in each sl st across right front border, fasten off.

REVERSE SC BORDER

Row 1: With RS facing, attach yarn with sl st in corner of right front border at neckline edge, ch 1, reverse sc in each sc to bottom corner of right front, reverse sc in each st across bottom edge of cardigan, do not work up left front, fasten off.

SLEEVE BORDER

Make 2

Row 1: With RS facing, working in opposite side of foundation ch, attach yarn with sl st in first ch at right edge, ch 1, sc in same ch as beg ch-1, [ch 1, 5 dc in ch directly below puff st, ch 1, fpsc over dc post] rep across, ending with sc in last ch.

Row 2: Ch 1, reverse sc in each st across, fasten off.

Sew sleeve seam and sew sleeve into armhole opening.

COLLAR

Row 1: With RS facing, attach yarn with sl st 1 inch from right front edge at neckline edge, ch 1, work 4 sc over rem of right front border, 17 sc evenly sp to shoulder, 27 sc across back neck, 17 sc from shoulder to left front border, 4 sc across border, leaving last 1 inch free, turn. (69 sts)

Note: *Row 2 is the RS of collar when completed.*

Row 2: Ch 1, [sc in each of next 2 sc, dc in next sc] 7 times, 2 sc in next sc, dc in next sc, [sc in each of next 2 sc, dc in next sc] 8 times, 2 sc in next sc, [dc in next sc, sc in each of next 2 sc] 7 times, turn. (71 sts)

Row 3: Ch 1, sc in each st across, turn.

Row 4: Ch 1, sc in each of next 2 sc, [fpdc over next dc, sc in each of next 2 sc] rep across, turn.

Row 5: Ch 1, sc in first sc, 2 sc in next st, [sc in each of next 2 sts, 2 sc in next st] rep across, turn. (95 sts)

Row 6: Ch 1, sc in each of next 3 sts, [fpdc over fpdc, sc in each of next 3 sts] rep across, turn.

Row 7: Ch 1, sc in each of next 2 sc, [2 sc in next st, sc in each of next 3 sts] rep across, ending with 2 sc in last sc, turn. (119 sts)

Row 8: Ch 1, sc in each of next 4 sc, [fpdc over fpdc, sc in each of next 4 sc] rep across, turn.

Row 9: Ch 1, sc in each of next 3 sc, [2 sc in next st, sc in each of next 4 sts] rep across, ending with 2 sc in last sc, turn. (143 sts)

Row 10: Ch 1, sc in each of next 5 sc, [fpdc over fpdc, sc in each of next 5 sc] rep across, turn.

Row 11: Ch 1, sc in each of next 2 sc, puff st in next st, [sc in each of next 5 sts, puff st in next st] rep across, ending with sc in each of last 2 sc, turn.

Row 12: Ch 1, sc in first sc, *ch 1, sk next 2 sc, 5 dc in next puff st, ch 1, sk next 2 sc **, fpdc over fpdc, rep from * across, ending last rep at **, sc in last sc, do not turn.

Row 13: Ch 1, reverse sc in each st across, fasten off.

Sew buttons opposite buttonholes. ∎

DESIGN BY
MARGRET WILLSON

DIAMOND RIO JACKET

Simple styling and basic stitches create the easy design of this classic-style jacket, but it's the decorative pattern of filet diamond outlines in a brilliant mix of metallic yarns and accented with rich gold buttons that defines the dazzle!

GAUGE

With size I hook, 14 dc = 4 inches; 8 rows = 4 inches
Check gauge to save time.

PATTERN NOTES

Weave in loose ends as work progresses.

Join rnds with a sl st unless otherwise stated.

Jacket is crocheted with black yarn. Embellishments are added after completion.

BACK

Row 1: With black yarn and hook size I, ch 61 (69, 77, 85, 93), dc in 4th ch from hook, dc in each rem ch across, turn. (59, 67, 75, 83, 91 dc)

Rows 2–40 (41, 42, 44, 47): Ch 3 to beg each row (counts as first dc throughout), follow graph, turn at the end of each row. At the end of last rep, fasten off.

RIGHT FRONT

Row 1: With black yarn and hook size I, ch 31 (35, 39, 43, 47), dc in 4th ch from hook, dc in each rem ch across, turn. (29, 33, 37, 41, 45 dc)

Rows 2–40 (41, 42, 44, 47): Ch 3 to

INTERMEDIATE ●●●

SIZE Extra-small (small, medium, large and extra-large)
Finished bust: 34 (38, 42, 46, 50) inches

MATERIALS

- Plymouth Encore worsted weight yarn (3½ oz per ball): 5 (5, 6, 7, 8) balls black #217
- Plymouth Firenze (55 yds each ball): 3 balls #440
- Plymouth Gold Rush (109 yds per cone): 2 cones gold # 2
- Sizes H/8, I/9 and J/10 crochet hooks or sizes needed to obtain gauge
- 4 (⅞-inch) gold shank buttons
- 10 (⅝-inch) gold shank buttons
- Yarn needle

end of each row. At the end of last rep, fasten off.

LEFT FRONT

Row 1: With black yarn and hook size I, ch 31 (35, 39, 43, 47), dc in 4th ch from hook, dc in each rem ch across, turn. (29, 33, 37, 41, 45 dc)

Rows 2–40 (41, 42, 44, 47): Ch 3 to beg each row, follow graph, turn at the end of each row. At the end of last rep, fasten off.

SLEEVE

Make 2

Row 1: With black yarn and hook size I, ch 33 (35, 37, 39, 43), dc in 4th ch from hook, dc in each rem ch across, turn. (31, 33, 35, 37, 41 dc)

Row 2: Ch 4 (counts as first dc, ch 1 throughout), sk next dc, dc in next dc, [ch 1, sk next dc, dc in next dc] rep across, turn.

Row 3: Ch 4, dc in next dc, [ch 1, dc in next dc] rep across, turn.

Row 4: Ch 3, dc in same st as beg ch-3, dc in each dc and each ch-1 sp across, ending with 2 dc in last dc, turn.

Rows 5–44 (44, 45, 44, 43): Ch 3, work dc in each st across, inc by working 2 dc in first and last st of every row 0 (0, 0, 0, 4) times, inc in every 2nd row 8 (7, 13, 17, 14) times, then inc every 4 rows 5 (5, 2, 0, 0) times, work even on 59 (59, 67, 73, 81) sts until all rows are completed, fasten off.

ASSEMBLY

Sew shoulder seams, matching center of sleeve to shoulder seam, set in sleeves, sew sleeve and side seams.

EDGING

Rnd 1: With black and hook size H, attach

in right side seam on lower edge, ch 1, sc
in each st to right front corner, 3 sc in corner st, sc up right front edge placing 2 sc
around end of each dc row to beg of neck
shaping (64, 62, 64, 68, 72 sc between
corner and beg neck shaping), working
across neck edge, sc in dc at beg of neck
shaping, [ch 3, sc in end dc of next row] 6
(7, 7, 7, 8) times, 4 sc around ends of next
2 rows, sc in shoulder seam, sc around end
of first back row, ch 3, sc in end of next row,
ch 3, sk 1 dc, sc in next dc, work 18 (22,
22, 26, 26) sc across back edge, [ch 3, sc
in end of next row] twice, sc in left shoulder
seam, 4 sc around ends of next 2 rows, [ch
3, sc in end of next row] 6 (7, 7, 7, 8) times,
work 2 sc around end of row to left front
bottom corner, 3 sc in corner, sc in each
rem st of bottom edge, join in beg sc.

Rnd 2: Ch 1, sc in each sc to corner, 3 sc
in center corner sc, sc in each st up right
front to beg of neckline shaping, 2 sc in
corner at beg of neck, [2 sc in next ch-3
sp, sc in next sc] 6 (7, 7, 7, 8) times, sc in
each of next 6 sc, [2 sc in next ch-3 sp,
sc in next sc] twice, sc in each sc across
back, [2 sc in next ch-3 sp, sc in next
sc] twice, sc in each of next 5 sc, [sc in
next sc, 2 sc in next ch-3 sp] 6 (7, 7, 7, 8)
times, 2 sc in corner at beg of neck shaping, sc in each sc down left front corner, 3
sc in center corner sc, sc in each rem sc
across bottom, join in beg sc.

Rnd 3: Ch 1, sc in each sc across to
center corner, 3 sc in center corner sc, sc
in each of next 4 (4, 4, 8, 10) sc, ch 2, sk
next 2 sc, [sc in each of next 18 sc, ch 2,
sk next 2 sc] 3 times, matching buttonholes to dc rows between diamonds, sc in
each st to neck edge, 2 sc in next corner,
sc in each st around neckline, 2 sc in left
neck corner, sc in each sc down left front,
3 sc in left front corner, sc in each rem sc
across bottom, join in beg sc.

Rnds 4 & 5: Ch 1, sc in each st around,
placing 3 sc in each lower front corner
and 2 sc at each neckline corner, join in
beg sc. At the end of Rnd 5, fasten off.

EMBELLISHMENT

Note: *Embellishments are worked in
filet sps according to each graph on*

back and fronts and on lower portion of each sleeve.

With hook size J, holding 1 strand of firenze and 2 strands of gold rush tog, work full surface sc in filet sps according to each graph. Work 1 sc in each ch-1 sp and 2 sc around each dc, sl st to join in beg sc, fasten off.

BUTTONS

Sew 4 (⁷/₈-inch) buttons on left front opposite buttonholes. Sew ⁵/₈-inch buttons to center st of each diamond. ■

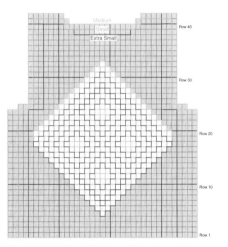

**Diamond Rio
Jacket Back Chart**

Note: This chart shows diamond placement for the M,S & XS sizes only.

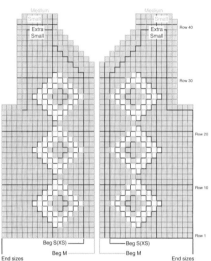

**Diamond Rio
Jacket Front Chart**

Note: This chart shows diamond placement for the M,S & XS sizes only.

STITCH KEY	
	3 dc
	3 dc, ch 1, 3 dc
	5 dc
	dc (ch 1, sk 1, dc) 3 times

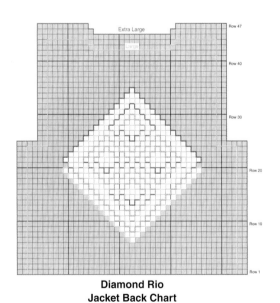

**Diamond Rio
Jacket Back Chart**

Note: This chart shows diamond placement for the M,S & XS sizes only.

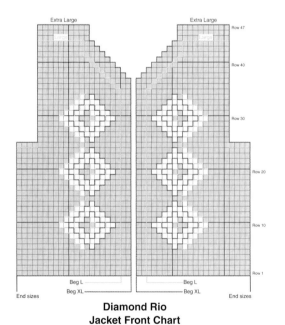

**Diamond Rio
Jacket Front Chart**

Note: This chart shows diamond placement for the M,S & XS sizes only.

hook, yo, draw through all 3 lps on hook, ch 1, [2-dc tog, ch 1] rep across, ending with dc in beg ch-1, turn.

[Rep Rows 1 and 2] twice with chocolate, [rep Rows 1 and 2] 4 times with each color in sequence until there are 20 (20, 20, 20, 20, 22) 2-dc tog RS rows, fasten off.

Armhole shaping

Turn, sk 4 (4, 4, 4, 5, 5) 2-dc tog, attach yarn with sc in next sp, [ch 1, sc in next sp] rep across until 4 (4, 4, 4, 5, 5) 2-dc tog rem, turn.

Work pat Row 2 across rem 35 (40, 45, 50, 53, 58) 2-dc tog, turn.

Rep Rows 1 and 2, maintaining color sequence, 9 (10, 11, 12, 13, 14) times.

First shoulder shaping

Row 1: Work Row 1 of pat across 8 (10, 12, 14, 15, 17) 2-dc tog, turn.

Row 2: Ch 3, sk first sc, dc in next sc, work Row 2 of pat to end, fasten off.

Second shoulder shaping

Row 1: Sk center 19 (20, 21, 22, 23, 24) 2-dc tog, attach yarn with sc in next sp, rep Row 1 of pat across rem of row, turn.

Row 2: Work Row 2 of pat across rem of row, fasten off.

RIGHT FRONT

Foundation row: With 1 strand of each thicket and chocolate, ch 44 (50, 54, 60, 64, 70), work as for back on 20 (23, 25, 28, 30, 33) 2-dc tog to armhole shaping. At the end of last rep, fasten off, turn.

Armhole shaping

Sk 4 (4, 4, 4, 5, 5) 2-dc tog, attach yarn with sc in next sp, rep Row 1 of pat across, turn.

Work Row 2 of pat across 16 (19, 21, 24, 25, 28) 2-dc tog.

Neck shaping

Work Rows 1 and 2 of pat 1 (1, 2, 2, 3, 3) times.

Row 1 (dec): Sc in next sp, [ch 1, sc in next sp] rep across, turn.

Row 2 (dec): Ch 2, sk first sc, dc in next sc, ch 1, [2-dc tog, ch 1] rep across, ending with ch 1, dc in ch-1 ch, turn.

Rep dec Rows 1 and 2 for neck shaping 7 (8, 8, 9, 9, 10) times. At the end of last dec row 9 (10, 12, 14, 15, 17) 2-dc tog rem, turn.

Work Row 1 of pat across, turn.
Work Row 2 of pat across, fasten off.

LEFT FRONT

Work as for right front to armhole shaping.

Armhole shaping

Work Row 1 of pat across leaving last 4 (4, 4, 4, 5, 5) 2-dc tog unworked.

Work Row 2 of pat across 16 (19, 21, 24, 25, 28) 2-dc tog.

Neck shaping

Work Rows 1 and 2 of pat 1 (1, 2, 2, 3, 3) times.

Row 1 (dec): Ch 1, sc in next sp, [ch 1, sc in next sp] rep across, turn.

Row 2 (dec): Ch 3, [2-dc tog, ch 1] rep across omitting last ch 1 and dc, turn.

Rep dec Rows 1 and 2 for neck shaping 7 (8, 8, 9, 9, 10) times.

At the end of last dec row 9 (10, 12, 14, 15, 17) 2-dc tog rem, turn.

Work Row 1 of pat across, turn.
Work Row 2 of pat across, fasten off.

SLEEVE

Make 2

Foundation row: With 1 strand each thicket and chocolate, ch 46 (48, 48, 50, 54, 56), sk 2 chs, [2-dc tog, ch 1, sk 1 ch] rep across, ending with dc in last ch, turn. (21, 22, 22, 23, 25, 26 2-dc tog)

Row 1: Ch 1, sc in sp, [ch 1, sc in next sp] rep across, turn.

Row 2 (inc): Ch 3, dc in first sc, ch 1, [2-dc tog, ch 1] rep across, ending with dc in last sc, dc in ch-1, turn.

Row 3: Ch 1, sc bet first and 2nd dc, [ch 1, sc in next sp] rep across, ending with ch 1, sc bet last 2 dc, turn.

Row 4: Ch 3, [2-dc tog, ch 1] rep across, ending with ch 1, dc in last st, turn.

Inc every 4th row 0 (3, 9, 13, 14, 15) times, then every 6th row 9 (7, 3, 0, 0, 0) times for a total of 39 (42, 46, 49, 53, 56) 2-dc tog. Work even until 29 (29, 29, 29, 30, 30) RS row are completed, ending with a RS row, fasten off.

FRINGE

On first row of each new color using same color for fringe, cut 3 strands each 6 inches long, fold strand in half, insert hook from front to back in sp bet 2-dc tog and from back to front in sc above, hold fringe tails and draw fold through forming a lp on hook, draw tails through lp on hook and tighten. Trim fringe even.

To secure fringe, thread tapestry needle with same color as fringe and work a row of back st across top of fringe.

ASSEMBLY

Sew shoulder seams, set in sleeves and sew side and sleeve seams.

EDGING

Rnd 1: With 1 strand each of thicket and taupe, attach with sc in right side seam, sc in each st or sp to corner, 3 sc in corner st, sc up right front working 2 sc around end of each 2-dc tog row and 1 sc around edge of each sc row to beg of neck shaping, 2 sc at corner, sc around neck edge, place 2 sc at beg of left neck shaping, sc down left front, 3 sc in left lower corner, sc in each st and sp across bottom, join in beg sc, do not turn.

Rnd 2: Ch 1, sc in same st as joining, sc in each st around, working 3 sc in each lower front corner and 2 sc in each front neckline corners, join in beg sc, do not turn.

Rnd 3: Ch 1, sc in same st as joining, sc in each st around, working 3 sc in each lower front corner, 2 sc in each front neckline corner and 2-sc tog at each back neck corner, join in beg sc, do not turn.

Rnd 4: Ch 1, sc in same st as joining, sc in each st to corner, 3 sc in corner st, sc in each of next 6 sc, ch 3, sk next 3 sc, [sc in each of next 9 sc, ch 3, sk next 3 sc] 5 times, work 2 sc in front neckline corner, sc in each st to beg of back neck, 2-sc tog, sc in each st across back neckline to last 2 sts, 2-sc tog, sc in each st to left front, 2 sc in front corner neckline, sc in each st down front, 3 sc in corner, sc in each rem sc across bottom, join in beg sc, do not turn.

Rnd 5: Ch 1, sc in same st as joining, sc in each st and each ch around maintaining inc and dec sts at corners, join in beg sc, do not turn.

Rnds 6 & 7: Rep Rnd 3. At the end of Rnd 7, fasten off.

Sew buttons opposite buttonholes. ∎

LEFT FRONT

With 1 strand each color held tog, ch 33 (36, 39, 45, 48, 51), sc in 2nd ch from hook, ch 1, sk next ch, sc in next ch, [ch 2, sk next 2 chs, sc in next ch] rep across to last 2 chs, ch 1, sc in last ch, turn. Work as for back on 10 (11, 12, 14, 15, 16) shells to armhole shaping, ending with a RS row, turn.

Armhole shaping

Ch 1, sc in first dc, ch 1, [sc in center dc of next shell, ch 2] 8 (8, 9, 10, 11, 12) times, sc in center dc of next shell, turn. Rep Rows 1 and 2 of pat 3 (4, 5, 6, 7, 8) times, rep Row 1 of pat, fasten off, turn.

Neck shaping

Row 1: Sk 6 (6, 6, 6, 9, 9) sts, attach yarn with sc in next st, ch 1, sc in center dc of next shell, [ch 2, sc in center dc of next shell] 5 (5, 6, 6, 7, 8) times, ch 1, sc in last dc, turn.

Row 2: ch 3, [shell in next sc] 5 (5, 6, 6, 7, 8) times, dc in next sc, work 2-dc dec, turn.

Row 3: Ch 1, sc in top of dec, ch 1, sc in center dc of next shell, [ch 2, sc in center dc of next shell] 4 (4, 5, 5, 6, 7) times, ch 1, sc in last dc, turn.

Row 4: Ch 3, [shell in next sc] 4 (4, 5, 5, 6, 7) times, dc in next sc, work 2-dc dec, turn.

Row 5: Ch 1, sc in top of dec, ch 1, sc in center dc of next shell, [ch 2, sc in center dc of next shell] 3 (3, 4, 4, 5, 6) times, ch 1, sc in last dc, turn.

[Rep Rows 1 and 2 of pat] 3 times. Rep Row 1 of pat, fasten off.

RIGHT FRONT

Work as for left front to armhole shaping, fasten off, turn.

Armhole shaping

Sk 5 (8, 8, 11, 11, 11) sts, attach yarn with sc in next st, [ch 2, sc in center dc of next shell] 8 (8, 9, 10, 11, 12) times, ch 1, sc in last dc, turn. Rep Rows 1 and 2 of pat 3 (4, 5, 6, 7, 8) times, rep Row 1 of pat.

Neck shaping

Row 1: Ch 1, sc in first dc, ch 1, sc in center dc of next shell, [ch 2, sc in center dc of next shell] 5 (5, 6, 6, 7, 8) times, ch 1, sk next dc, sc in next dc, turn.

Row 2: Ch 2, 2 dc in next sc, [shell in next sc] 5 (5, 6, 6, 7, 8) times, dc in next sc, turn.

Row 3: Work Row 2 of pat across, ending with sc in last dc (sk beg ch-2 ch), turn.

Row 4: Ch 2, 2 dc in next sc, [shell in next sc] 4 (4, 5, 5, 6, 7) times, dc in next sc, turn.

Row 5: Work Row 2 of pat across, ending with sc in last dc (sk beg ch-2 ch), turn.

[Rep Rows 1 and 2 of pat] 3 times. Rep Row 1 of pat, fasten off.

ASSEMBLY

With 1 strand of natural, sew shoulder and side seams.

EDGING

Rnd 1: With 2 strands natural held tog, attach with sc in right side seam at bottom edge, work sc evenly across bottom, up right front, around back neck, down left front and across rem of bottom edge, working 3 sc in corners at bottom front and at beg of neck shaping, join in beg sc, do not turn.

Rnd 2: Ch 1, sc in each sc around, working 3 sc at each front bottom corner and 2 sc in corner at beg of neck shaping, join in beg sc, do not turn.

Rnd 3: Ch 1, sc in each sc to corner, work 3 sc in corner, sc in each of next 2 (2, 4, 6, 6, 8) sc, ch 2, sk next 2 sc, [sc in each of next 8 (8, 8, 9, 9, 9) sc, ch 2, sk next 2 sc] 5 times, sc in each rem sc working 2 sc in each corner neckline and 3 sc in rem bottom corner, join in beg sc, do not turn.

Rnd 4: Ch 1, sc in each sc and each ch around, working 3 sc in each front bottom corner and 2 sc in each neckline corner, join in beg sc, do not turn.

Rnd 5: Ch 1, sc in same sc as joining, ch 2, [reverse sc in next sc, ch 2] rep around, join in beg sc, fasten off.

ARMHOLE EDGING

Make 2

Rnd 1: Attach 2 strands of natural at underarm seam, ch 1, sc evenly sp around armhole opening, join in beg sc, do not turn.

Rnds 2–4: Ch 1, sc in each sc around, join in beg sc, do not turn.

Rnd 5: Ch 1, sc in same sc as joining, ch 2, [reverse sc in next sc, ch 2] rep around, join in beg sc, fasten off. ■

FUCHSIA FANTASY RIPPLE PULLOVER ▶ CONTINUED FROM PAGE 54

FRONT

Rep the same as for back to shoulder shaping.

Shoulder shaping

Maintaining striped pat and carrying unused color loosely across shoulder, rep Row 1 of back shoulder shaping 2 (2, 4, 4, 6, 6) times. At the end of last rep, turn.

First neck shaping

Row 1: Ch 3, 3-dc dec, dc in each of next 22 (26, 26, 30, 30, 34) sts, 2-dc dec, turn.

Row 2: Ch 3, dc in each st across to last 4 sts, 4-dc dec, turn.

Row 3: Ch 3, 3-dc dec, dc in each st across to last 2 sts, 2-dc dec, turn.
[Rep Rows 2 and 3] 4 (5, 5, 6, 6, 7) times. At the end of last rep, fasten off.

Second neck shaping

Row 1: Sk center 59 (67, 67, 75, 75, 83)

sts, attach yarn in next st, ch 2, dc in next dc (beg dec), dc in each of next 22 (26, 26, 30, 30, 34) sts, 4-dc dec, turn.

Row 2: Ch 3, 3-dc dec, dc in each rem st across, turn.

Row 3: Ch 2, dc in each st across to last 4 sts, 4-dc dec, turn.
[Rep Rows 2 and 3] 4 (5, 5, 6, 6, 7) times. At the end of last rep, fasten off.

SLEEVE

Make 2

Row 1 (RS): With size 1 hook and fuchsia, ch 64 (68, 72, 76, 78, 82), dc in 4th ch from hook, dc in each rem ch across, turn. (62, 66, 70, 74, 76, 80 dc)

Row 2 (inc row): Ch 3, dc in same dc as beg ch-3, dc in each st across to last st, 2 dc in last st, turn.

Row 3: Ch 3, dc in each st across, turn.

[Rep Rows 2 and 3] 34 times. (132, 136, 140, 144, 146, 150 dc)
Rep Row 3 until sleeve measures 19½ inches from beg, fasten off.

Note: Sleeve will have 78 rows.

ASSEMBLY

Sew shoulder seams. Matching center of sleeve to shoulder seam, sew sleeve to body of pullover. Sew sleeve and side seams.

NECKLINE TRIM

Rnd 1: With hook size 3, attach fuchsia at shoulder seam, ch 1, sc evenly sp around neckline opening, join in beg sc.

Rnd 2: Ch 1, sc in same sc as beg ch-1, sc in each sc around, join in beg sc.

Rnd 3: Ch 1, sc in same sc as beg ch-1, ch 3, sk next st, [sc in next st, ch 3, sk next st] rep around, join in beg sc, fasten off. ■

COTTON CANDY CAPELET SET ▶ CONTINUED FROM PAGE 57

Row 2: Ch 1, working in back lps only, sc in each st across, turn.

Rows 3–173 (185, 201, 221): Rep Row 2. At the end of last rep, leaving a length, fasten off.
Using care not to twist, sew opposite side of foundation ch and last row tog.

Cape body

Rnd 1 (RS): Attach yarn to ribbing at seam (center back), ch 1, working in side edge of ribbing rows, sc in end of each row around, mark st 87 (93, 101, 111), join in beg sc, turn. (173, 185, 201, 221 sc)

Rnd 2: Work Pat rnd 1.

Note: Beg with Rnd 3, mark the first post st of every rnd throughout.

Rnd 3: Ch 1, *[blsc in next st, flsc in next st] 37 (40, 44, 49) times, blsc in next st *, fptr around post of st 2 rows below (mark this post st), [blsc in next st, flsc in next

st] 4 times, fpdtr around post of marked st 2 rnd below, flsc in next st, fptr around post of same marked st, flsc in next st, fpdtr around post of same marked st, [flsc in next st, blsc in next st] 4 times, fptr around post of st 2 rnds below, rep from * to *, join in beg st, turn.
Work Pat rnds (beg with Pat rnd 1) until 9½ (10, 10½, 11) inches from beg, at the same time, work 4 st dec on next rnd and then every 8th rnd 4 times. Last rnd will have 153 (165, 181, 201 sts).

Shaping

Continue working pat rnds for 16 (16, 16, 17) more rnds, at the same time, [work 4 st dec on next rnd] 9 (6, 2, 0) times, [work 8 st dec on next rnd] 7 (10, 14, 17) times. Last rnd will have 61 (61, 61, 65) sts.

Collar

Rnd 1: Ch 1, sc in each st around, join

in beg st, turn.

Rnds 2–4: Ch 1, sc in each st around, join in beg st, turn.
At the end of last rep, leaving a long length, fasten off.
Roll collar down (if lower neckline is desired, roll farther down in front than on sides), sew collar in place.

GAUNTLETS

Row 1: Ch 51, sc in 2nd ch from hook, sc in each rem ch across, turn. (50 sc)

Row 2: Working in bl only, sc in each st across, turn.

Rows 3–36 (36, 40, 40): Rep Row 2. At the end of last rep, leaving a long length, fasten off.
Sew opposite side of foundation ch and last row tog. ■

CHAPTER 3

Beautiful hand-crocheted pieces have long been handed down from generation to generation to become treasured family heirlooms valued for their legacy and appreciated for their artistry. Exquisite thread designs claim a special place among the priceless and precious

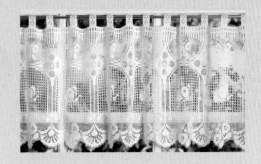

HEIRLOOM MASTERPIECES

creations lovingly stitched and passed to us by our grandmothers and great-grandmothers. Through these gifts, the beloved craft of crochet reaches across and connects the generations. We hope the inspired designs presented here become cherished heirlooms that will long be part of your family tradition.

RENAISSANCE BEAUTY DOILY

The aura of old-world beauty in this airy, delicate design provides a dramatic accent that never goes out of style. Lacy trefoils and old-fashioned roses alternate to create the deep, lavish border of this large and lovely doily.

GAUGE

Rnds 1–6 of center motif = 2¼ inches in diameter

Check gauge to save time.

PATTERN NOTES

Weave in loose ends as work progresses.

Join rnds with a sl st unless otherwise stated.

Make shamrocks and small circles first and set aside.

PATTERN STITCH

3-tr cl: *Yo hook twice, insert hook in indicated st, yo, draw up a lp, [yo, draw through 2 lps on hook] twice, rep from * twice, yo, draw through all 4 lps on hook.

SHAMROCKS

Make 10

Rnd 1 (RS): With natural, ch 7, join to form a ring, ch 1, 18 sc in ring, join in beg sc. (18 sc)

Rnd 2: Ch 1, *sc in each of next 4 sc, ch 3, sl st in 3rd ch from hook (for p), sc

ADVANCED ●○○

SIZE 21 inches in diameter

MATERIALS
- Crochet cotton size 10: 700 yds natural, 200 yds delft blue
- Size 7 steel crochet hook or size needed to obtain gauge

2nd sc before p, in ch-10 sp work 18 sc, rep from * around, join in beg sc.

Rnd 3: Sl st in next sc, *sc in first sc of 18-sc group, [ch 2, sk next sc, dc in next sc] 4 times, ch 2, dc in same sc, [ch 2, sk next sc, dc in next sc] 3 times, ch 2, sk next sc, sc in last sc, sl st in next sc on ring, rep from * around, join in beg sc.

Rnd 4: *Sc in next sc, [2 sc in next ch-2 sp, sc in next dc] 8 times, 2 sc in next ch-2 sp, sc in next sc, sl st in sl st, rep from * around.

Rnd 5: *Sk next sc, [sc in each of next 2 sc, sc in next sc, ch 3, sl st in 3rd ch from hook (for p)] 8 times, sc in each of next 2 sc, sl st in sl st, rep from * twice, join, fasten off. Set aside.

SMALL CIRCLES

Make 10

Rnd 1: With natural, ch 6, join to form a ring, ch 1, 12 sc in ring, join. (12 sc)

Rnd 2: Ch 5 (counts as first dc, ch 2), [dc in next sc, ch 2] rep around, join in 3rd ch of beg ch-5, fasten off. (12 dc; 12 ch-2 sps)

Rnd 3: Attach delft blue in any ch-2 sp, ch 1, [sc, 2 dc, sc] in each ch-2 sp around, join in beg sc. (12 petals)

Rnd 4: Ch 1, sc behind and between the 2 petals at joining, ch 3, [sc behind and between next 2 petals, ch 3] rep around, join in beg sc, fasten off. (12 ch-3 sps)

Rnd 5: Attach natural in any ch-3 sp, ch 1, [sc, 3 dc, sc] in each ch-3 sp around, join in beg sc. (12 petals)

Rnd 6: Ch 1, sc behind and between the 2 petals at joining, ch 4, [sc behind and between next 2 petals, ch 4] rep around, join in beg sc. (12 ch-4 sps)

Rnd 7: Sl st into ch-4 sp, ch 1, [sc, hdc, 3 dc, hdc, sc] in each ch-4 sp around, join in beg sc, fasten off. Set aside.

CENTER MOTIF

Rnd 1 (RS): With natural, ch 7, join to form a ring, ch 1, 20 sc in ring, join in beg sc. (20 sc)

Rnd 2: Ch 1, sc in each sc around, join in beg sc. (20 sc)

Rnd 3: Ch 5 (counts as first dc, ch 2, [dc in next sc, ch 2] rep around, join in 3rd ch of beg ch-5, fasten off. (20 dc; 20 ch-2 sps)

Rnd 4: Attach delft blue in any ch-2 sp, ch 1, [sc, 2 dc, sc] in each ch-2 sp around, join in beg sc. (20 petals)

Rnd 5: Ch 1, sc behind and between the 2 petals of joining, ch 3, [sc behind and between next 2 petals, ch 3] rep around, join in beg sc, fasten off. (20 ch-3 sps)

Rnd 6: Attach natural in any ch-3 sp, ch 1, [sc, 3 dc, sc] in each ch-3 sp around, join in beg sc. (20 petals)

Rnd 7: Ch 1, sc behind and between the 2 petals of joining, ch 6, [sk next sp between petals, sc behind and between next 2 petals, ch 6] 9 times, join in beg sc. (10 ch-6 sps)

Rnd 8: Ch 1, *sc in ch-6 sp, [ch 4, sc in same sp] twice, [ch 4, turn, sc in first ch-4 sp, ch 4, sc in next ch-4 sp] 8 times (ending with RS facing), fasten off, attach natural in next ch-6 sp, rep from * in each ch-6 sp. (10 arms)

Rnd 9: Attach natural in first sc of first arm, working up side of arm, ch 1, [sc in first sc on arm, {sc in next sp, sc in side of next sc} 4 times, 3 sc in next ch-4 sp, sc in next sc, 3 sc in next ch-4 sp, {sc in side of next sc, sc in next sp} 4 times on opposite side of arm, sc in last sc, sl st in next sc of Rnd 7] 10 times, join in beg sc. (25 sc around each arm)

Rnd 10: *Sk first sc of arm, sc in each of next 8 sc, 3 sc in next sc for a corner, sc in each of next 2 sc, [sc, ch 4, sc] in next sc, sc in each of next 2 sc, 3 sc in next sc for a corner, sc in each of next 8 sc, sl last sc of arm, sk sl st worked in Rnd 7, rep from * around each arm, join in beg sc, fasten off.

FILLER

Make 10

Note: *Fillers are worked between the 10*

arms to join arms together.

*Attach delft blue with sl st in 2nd sc of corner 3-sc group of arm, ch 5, drop lp from hook, insert hook in 2nd sc of corner 3-sc group on previous arm, pick up dropped lp and draw through st on hook, [sc, 3 dc, 2 sc, 3 dc, sc] over ch-5 sp, fasten off. Rep from * until all arms are joined tog.

Rnd 11: Attach natural in any ch-4 sp at tip of arm, *ch 6, tr in 6th ch from hook, ch 6, sl st in 4th ch from hook, ch 5, sl st in same place, ch 7, tr in 6th ch from hook, sc in next ch-4 sp, [ch 14, draw lp through 6th ch from hook, in sp just formed work 11 sc, join in first sc on 11-sc, sl st back along ch to end, sc in same ch-4 sp] twice, rep from * around, fasten off.

Rnd 12: Attach natural in 4th sc of 11-sc ring, ch 3, *yo hook twice, insert hook in same sc as beg ch-3, yo, draw up a lp, [yo, draw through 2 lps on hook] twice, rep from * once, yo, draw through all 3 lps on hook, [ch 7, 3-tr cl in next sc] 4 times, *3 tr cl in 4th sc of next 11-sc ring, [ch 7, 3-tr cl in next sc] 4 times, rep from * around, join in top of beg cl. (80 ch-7 lps)

Rnd 13: Sl st in next 3 chs of ch-7, ch 1, insert hook in last ch-7 sp of Rnd 12, draw up a lp, insert hook in same ch sp as beg ch-1, yo, draw through all 3 lps on hook, *[ch 7, sc in next ch-7 sp] twice **, ch 7, draw up a lp in each of next 2 ch-7 lps, yo, draw through all 3 lps on hook, rep from * around, ending last rep at **, ch 3, tr in beg sc to form last ch-7 lp. (60 ch-7 lps)

Rnds 14–16: Ch 1, sc in same ch sp as beg ch-1, [ch 7, sc in next ch-7 lp] rep around, ending with ch 3, tr in beg sc.

Rnd 17: Ch 10 (counts as first dc, ch 7), [dc in next ch-7 sp, ch 7] rep around, join in 3rd ch of beg ch-10.

Rnd 18: Ch 1, work 6 sc in each ch-7 sp around, join in beg sc. (360 sc)

Rnd 19: Ch 1, sc in each sc around, join in beg sc.

Rnd 20: Ch 4 (counts as first dc, ch 1), sk next sc, [sc in next sc, ch 1, sk next sc] rep around, join in 3rd ch of beg ch-4. (180 dc; 180 ch-1 sps)

Rnd 21: Ch 1, sc in same dc as beg ch-1, sc in next ch-1 sp, [sc in next dc, sc in next ch-1 sp] rep around, join in beg sc. (360 sc)

Note: *Count the sts on Rnd 21, use care that a total of 360 sc are worked in order to complete attaching the 10 shamrocks and 10 small circles correctly.*

Rnd 22: Ch 1, sc in same sc, ch 3, pick up a shamrock, sc in backside of shamrock at 3rd p before joining of 2 petals, *ch 3, sk 3 sc on Rnd 21, sc in next sc, ch 3, sc in next p, ch 3, sk next 3 sc on Rnd 21, sc in next sc, sk next 2 p on shamrock, [ch 3, sc in next p, ch 3, sk next 3 sc on Rnd 21, sc in next sc] twice, ch 3, dc in next p, pick up small circle, dc in center of a petal, [ch 3, sk next 3 sc of Rnd 21, sc in next sc, ch 3, sc in center of next petal] 3 times, ch 3, sk next 3 sc on Rnd 21, sc in next sc, ch 3, dc in center of next petal **, pick up next shamrock, dc in 4th p from joining of 2 petals of shamrock, ch 3, sk next 3 sc on Rnd 21, sc in next sc, ch 3, sc in next p, rep from * around, ending last rep at **, dc in next free p (4th) from joining, ch 3, join in beg sc, fasten off.

BORDER

Rnd 1: With natural, working around the outer edge of joined shamrocks and small circles, *leaving 1 free petal on small circle, sc in center dc of 3-dc on next petal, [ch 7, sc in center dc of next petal] 4 times, ch 3, sk 2 p on shamrock, sc in next p, [ch 7, sk next p, sc in next p] 5 times, ch 3, rep from * around, join in beg sc.

Rnd 2: Ch 1, work 9 sc in each ch-7 sp and 3 sc in each ch-3 sp around, join in beg sc, fasten off.

Rnd 3: Attach delft blue in first sc of previous rnd, ch 1, beg in same sc as beg ch-1, [sc in each of next 4 sc of 9-sc group, ch 5, sl st in 5th ch from hook, ch 5, sl st in same sl st, ch 4, sl st in same sl st, sc in each of next 4 sc, sk last sc of 9-sc group] rep across each 9-sc group, working on each 3-sc group, sc in 2nd sc only of each 3-sc group, rep around, join in beg sc, fasten off. ■

VINTAGE FLORAL LACE DOILY

Sweet beaded flowers, richly textured pineapples and delicate, lacy fans come together in perfect harmony to create this divine doily masterpiece. It blends beautifully with many styles and makes a statement of gracious elegance wherever it's displayed.

GAUGE

Rnds 1–3 = 2¼ inches; 4 shells = 1½ inches

Check gauge to save time.

PATTERN NOTES

Weave in loose ends as work progresses. Join rnds with a sl st unless otherwise stated.

PATTERN STITCHES

Shell: [3 dc, ch 2, 3 dc] in indicated st.

Beg shell: Sl st into ch sp of beg shell, [ch 3, 2 dc, ch 2, 3 dc] in indicated st.

Dtr cl: *Yo hook 3 times, insert hook in indicated st, yo, draw up a lp, [yo, draw through 2 lps on hook] 3 times, rep from * 4 times, yo, draw through all 6 lps on hook.

Beg dtr cl: Ch 4 (counts as first dtr), *yo hook 3 times, insert hook in indicated st, yo, draw up a lp, [yo, draw through 2 lps on hook] 3 times, rep from * 3 times, yo, draw through all 5 lps on hook.

V-st: [Dc, ch 2, dc] in indicated st.

INTERMEDIATE ●◐○

SIZE 16 inches in diameter

MATERIALS

- J. & P. Coats Knit-Cro-Sheen crochet cotton size 10: 325 yds cream #42, 150 yds each peach #161 and spruce #179
- Size 5 steel crochet hook or size needed to obtain gauge
- 9 (7mm) cream pearl shank buttons
- Tapestry needle

Double shell: [3 dc, {ch 2, 3 dc} twice] in indicated sp.

Beg double shell: [Ch 3, 2 dc, {ch 2, 3 dc} twice] in indicated st.

Popcorn (pc): 5 dc in indicated st, draw up a lp, remove hook, insert hook in first dc of 5-dc group, pick up dropped lp and draw through st on hook.

Sc dec: Draw up a lp in each of next 2 sc, yo, draw through all 3 lps on hook.

LARGE FLOWER

Rnd 1 (RS): With peach, ch 5, join to form a ring, ch 7 (counts as first tr, ch 3), [tr in ring, ch 3] 7 times, join in 4th ch of beg ch-7. (8 tr; 8 ch-3 sps)

Rnd 2: Working around post of tr st, [ch 2, dc, 6 tr, dc, hdc] around post of tr st, ch 2, [{hdc, dc, 6 tr, dc, hdc} around post of next tr, ch 2] rep around, join in 2nd ch of beg ch-2, fasten off. (8 petals)

Rnd 3: Attach spruce in any rem ch-3 sp of Rnd 1, [beg tr cl, ch 4, tr cl] in same ch-3 sp, ch 4, [{tr cl, ch 4, tr cl} in next ch-3 sp, ch 4] rep around, join in top of beg cl, fasten off. (16 leaves)

Rnd 4: Attach cream in any ch-4 sp, [ch 3, 2 dc, ch 2, 3 dc] in same ch sp, *ch 1, V-st in next ch-4 sp, ch 1 **, shell in next ch-4 sp, rep from * around, ending last rep at **, join in 3rd ch of beg ch-3. (8 shells; 8 V-sts)

Rnd 5: Beg shell in ch sp of beg shell, ch 1, *V-st in next V-st, ch 1 **, shell in next shell, ch 1, rep from * around, ending last rep at **, join in 3rd ch of beg ch-3.

Rnd 6: Beg shell in ch sp of beg shell, ch 2, *V-st in next V-st, ch 2 **, shell in next

shell, ch 2, rep from * around, ending last rep at **, join in 3rd ch of beg ch-3.

Rnd 7: Beg shell in ch sp of beg shell, ch 2, *7 tr in next V-st (pineapple base), ch 2 **, shell in next shell, ch 2, rep from * around, ending last rep at **, join in 3rd ch of beg ch-3. (8 pineapple bases)

Rnd 8: Beg shell in ch sp of beg shell, ch 3, *dc in next tr, [ch 1, dc in next tr] 6 times, ch 3 **, shell in next shell, ch 3, rep from * around, ending last rep at **, join in 3rd ch of beg ch-3.

Rnd 9: Sl st into ch sp of beg shell, beg double shell in same ch sp, ch 2, sk next ch-3 sp, [pc, ch 2] in each of next 6 ch-1 sps, sk next ch-3 sp, [double shell in next shell, ch 2, sk next ch-3 sp, {pc, ch 2} in each of next 6 ch-1 sps, sk next ch-3 sp] rep around, join in 3rd ch of beg ch-3. (48 pc; 8 double shells)

Rnd 10: Beg shell in ch sp of first shell, ch 2, shell in next ch-2 sp of shell, ch 3, sk next ch-2 sp, [pc, ch 2] in each of next 4 ch-2 sps, pc in next ch-2 sp, ch 3, sk next ch-2 sp, [shell in next ch-2 sp of shell, ch 2, shell in next ch-2 sp of shell, ch 3, sk next ch-2 sp, {pc, ch 2} in each of next 4 ch-2 sps, pc in next ch-2 sp, ch 3, sk next ch-2 sp] rep around, join in 3rd ch of beg ch-3.

Rnd 11: Beg shell in ch sp of beg shell, ch 2, *V-st in next ch-2 sp, ch 2, shell in next shell, ch 3, sk next ch-3 sp, [pc, ch 2] in each of next 3 ch-2 sps, pc in next ch-2 sp, ch 3, sk next ch-3 sp **, shell in next shell, ch 2, rep from * around, ending last rep at **, join in 3rd ch of beg ch-3. (32 pc; 16 shells; 8 V-sts)

Rnd 12: Beg shell in ch sp of beg shell, *ch 3, V-st in next V-st, ch 3, shell in next shell, ch 4, sk next ch-3 sp, [pc, ch 2] in each of next 2 ch-2 sps, pc in next ch-2 sp, ch 4 **, shell in next shell, rep from * around, ending last rep at **, join in 3rd ch of beg ch-3. (24 pc; 16 shells; 8 V-sts)

Rnd 13: Beg shell in ch sp of beg shell, *ch 4, V-st in next V-st, ch 4, shell in next shell, ch 4, pc in next ch-2 sp, ch 2, pc in next ch-2 sp, ch 4 **, shell in next shell, rep from * around, ending last rep at **, join in 3rd ch of beg ch-3. (16 pc; 16 shells; 8 V-sts)

Rnd 14: Beg shell in ch sp of beg shell, *ch 3, 10 tr in next V-st, ch 3, shell in next shell, ch 3, pc in next ch-2 sp, ch 3 **, shell in next shell, rep from * around, ending last rep at **, join in 3rd ch of beg ch-3.

Rnd 15: Sl st into ch sp of beg shell, ch 3, 2 dc in same ch sp, *ch 3, [{2 tr, ch 2} in next tr] 9 times, 2 tr in next tr, ch 3, 3 dc in next shell **, ch 3, 3 dc in next shell, rep from * around, ending last rep at **, ch 1, hdc in 3rd ch of beg ch-3 to position hook in last ch-3 sp.

Rnd 16: [Ch 3, 2 dc, ch 2, 3 dc] in same

ch sp as joining, ch 2, sk next ch-3 sp, tr in each of next 2 tr, [ch 1, tr in each of next 2 tr] 9 times, ch 2, sk next ch-3 sp, *shell in next ch-3 sp, sk next ch-3 sp, ch 2, tr in each of next 2 tr, [ch 1, tr in each of next 2 tr] 9 times, ch 2, sk next ch-3 sp, rep from * around, join in 3rd ch of beg ch-3, fasten off.

SMALL FLOWER

Make 8

Rnd 1: With peach, ch 5, join to form a ring, ch 5 (counts as first dc, ch 2), [dc in ring, ch 2] 7 times, join in 3rd ch of beg ch-5. (8 dc; 8 ch-2 sps)

Rnd 2: Working around post of each dc st, ch 1, [sc, hdc, 4 dc, hdc, sc] around post of dc st directly below, ch 2, *[sc, hdc, 4 dc, hdc, sc] around post of next dc, ch 2, rep from * around, join in beg sc, fasten off. (8 petals)

Set flowers aside.

EDGING

Rnd 1 (attaching small flowers):

Attach spruce in any ch-2 sp of any shell, ch 1, sc in same sp, ch 1, sc in any ch-2 sp on back of any flower, [ch 4, sc in next ch-2 lp on flower] 7 times, ch 1, sc in ch-2 sp of same shell, ch 4, sc in next ch-2 sp, ch 4, [sc in next ch-1 sp, ch 4] 9 times, sc in next ch-2 sp, ch 4, *sc in next shell, ch 1, sc in any ch-2 sp on back of any flower, [ch 4, sc in next ch-2 sp on flower] 7 times, ch 1, sc in ch-2 sp of same shell, ch 4, sc in next ch-2 sp, ch 4, [sc in next ch-1 sp, ch 4] 9 times, sc in next ch-2 sp, ch 4, rep from * around, join in beg sc.

Rnd 2: Sl st to center of next ch-4 sp, ch 1, sc in same ch sp, ch 4, [sc in next ch sp, ch 4] 5 times, sk next lp, [sc in next ch sp, ch 4] 10 times, sk next lp, *[sc in

next ch sp, ch 4] 6 times, sk next lp, [sc in next ch sp, ch 4] 10 times, sk next lp, rep from * around, join in beg sc.

Rnd 3: Sl st to center of next ch-4 sp, ch 1, sc in same sp, ch 5, [sc in next ch sp, ch 5] 4 times, sk next lp, [sc in next ch sp, ch 5] 9 times, sk next lp, *[sc in next ch sp, ch 4] 5 times, sk next lp, [sc in next sp, ch 5] 9 times, sk next lp, rep from * around, join in beg sc.

Rnd 4: Sl st to center of middle ch-5 sp at top of flower, ch 1, *[sc, ch 7, sl st in top of last sc worked] in ch-5 sp, ch 2, [dc, ch 2, dc] in next sp, ch 1, [tr, ch 2, tr] in next sp, ch 1, sk 1 sp, [dtr, ch 2, dtr] in next sp, sk 1 sp, ch 2, [dc, ch 2, dc] in next sp, ch 5, sk 1 sp, [sc, ch 13, sl st in last sc worked] in next sp, sk 1 sp, ch 5, [dc, ch 2, dc] in next sp, ch 2, sk 1 sp, [dtr, ch 2, dtr] in next sp, ch 1, sk 1 sp, [tr, ch 2, tr] in next sp, ch 1, [dc, ch 2, dc] in next sp, ch 2, rep from * around, join in beg sc.

Rnd 5: Sl st into ch-7 sp, ch 1, *[13 sc in ch-7 sp, sl st in first sc worked on lp], sc in each st and ch to next ch-13 lp, [21 sc in ch-13 lp, sl st in first sc of same lp] sc in each sc and each ch st across to next ch-7 lp, rep from * around, join in beg sc.

Note: *On Rnd 6, adjust st placement as necessary to maintain shape.*

Rnd 6: Ch 1, sc in same sc, ch 3, sk 1 sc, [sc in next sc, ch 3, sk 1 sc] rep around lp to last sc, sc dec, ch 3, sk next 2 sts, [sc in next sc, ch 3, sk next 2 sc, sc in next sc] rep across to last sc before lp, sc dec, *ch 3, sk 1 sc, [sc in next sc, ch 3, sk 1 sc] rep around lp to last sc, sc dec, ch 3, sk 2 sts, [sc in next sc, ch 3, sk 2 sc, sc in next sc] rep across to last sc before lp, sc dec, rep from * around, ending draw up a lp in last sc, sl st to top of first sc, fasten off. ∎

DESIGN BY
HARTMUT HASS

BUTTERFLIES IN FLIGHT VALANCE

The graceful elegance of butterflies in flight is masterfully captured in the exquisite pattern of this stunning filet valance that adds the perfect touch of old-world charm to a cozy, contemporary setting.

GAUGE

21 sps = 4 inches; 21 rows = 4 inches
Check gauge to save time.

PATTERN NOTES

Weave in loose ends as work progresses.
Graph-reading knowledge is necessary.
Ch-3 at beg of a row counts as first dc.
Ch-5 at beg of a row counts as first
dc, ch 2.

Filet crochet is a method of forming designs with solid and openwork
squares called blocks (bl) and spaces
(sp). A bl is made with 3 dc, and a sp
is ch 2, dc. A bl will appear to have 4
dc; the first dc of the bl is the dc that
defines the sp preceding the bl. A group
of 3 bl will have 9 dc plus 1 dc of sp
preceding bl. The foundation ch is 3
times the number of sps in the first row
plus 5 if the row beg with a sp 9 dc in
8th ch from hook, or plus 3 if row beg
with a bl (dc in 4th ch from hook and
next 2 ch). On following rows ch 5 if
a row begins with a sp, or ch 3 if row
begins with a bl.

Graphs show the sts as they appear on

SIZE Each section is approximately
8½ inches long x 17¾ inches deep
MATERIALS
• Crochet cotton size 20 (50g
  per ball): 5 balls white (makes 7
  sections)
• Size 9 steel crochet hook or size
  needed to obtain gauge
• Tapestry needle

the RS of work. Work first row of graph
from right to left and crochet in that
direction.

When the first row is completed, turn
and follow the 2nd row from left to right.

PATTERN STITCHES

Bl: 3 dc.
Sp: Ch 2, dc in next dc.
Bar: Ch 5, sk 5 sts, dc in next dc.
Bar over lacet: Ch 5, dc in next dc.
Lacet: Ch 3, sk 2 sts, sc in next st, ch
3, sk 2 sts, dc in next dc.
Lacet over bar: Ch 3, sk 2 sts, sc in
next st, ch 3, sk 2 sts, dc in next dc.
Inc sp at beg of a row: Ch 7, dc in

first dc of previous row.

Inc sp at end of row: Ch 2, yo hook 3
times, draw up a lp in turning ch where
last dc was worked, [yo, draw through 2
lps on hook] 4 times.

Dec sp at beg of row: Ch 1, sl st in 3
sts across, sl st in next dc, ch 5.

Dec at end of row: Leave 3 sts at end
of row unworked.

VALANCE

Row 1 (RS): Ch 272, dc in 8th ch from
hook, dc in each rem ch across, turn. (1
sp; 88 bl)

Row 2: Ch 3, dc in each of next 3 dc
(beg bl), [ch 2, sk next 2 dc, dc in next
dc] twice (2 sps over bls made), dc in
each of next 3 dc (bl over bl made), [ch
2, sk next 2 dc, dc in next dc] 8 times
(8 sp over bls made), dc in each of next
21 dc (7 bls over bls made), [ch 2, sk
2 dc, dc in next dc] 5 times (5 sps over
bls made), dc in each of next 3 dc (bl
over bl made), ch 2, sk next 2 dc, dc in
next dc (sp over bl made), dc in each
of next 9 dc (3 bls over bls made), ch
2, sk next 2 dc, dc in next dc (sp over

bl made), dc in each of next 3 dc {bl over bl made), [ch 2, sk next 2 dc, dc in next dc] 5 times (5 sps over bls made), dc in each of next 108 dc (36 bls over bls made), [ch 2, sk next 2 dc, dc in next dc] twice, (2 sps over bls made), dc in each of next 18 dc (6 bls over bls made), [ch 2, sk next 2 dc, dc in next dc] twice (2 sps over bls made), dc in each of next 18 dc (6 bls over bls made), ch 2, sk next 2 chs, dc in 3rd ch of turning ch-5 (sp over sp made), turn.

Rows 3–43: Follow graph (page 91), reading all odd-numbered RS rows from right to left, all even-numbered WS rows left to right, inc and dec sps at beg and end of rows as indicated.

Rep Rows 2–43 for each section of valance until valance is desired width, ending with a Row 2 WS row.

Last row (RS): Ch 5, sk next 2 chs, dc in next dc, dc in each dc and 2 dc in each ch-2 sp across, fasten off.

HANGING LOOP
First hanging loop
Row 1 (RS): Working over ends of rows across top of valance, attach thread with sl st in top of end st of Row 5, ch 3, 3 dc over end st of each of next 5 rows, turn. (16 dc)

Row 2: Ch 3, dc in each of next 6 dc, ch 2, sk next 2 dc, dc in each of next 6 dc, dc in 3rd ch of beg ch-3, turn.

Row 3: Ch 3, dc in each of next 3 dc, ch 2, sk next 2 dc, dc in next dc, 2 dc in next ch-2 sp, dc in next dc, ch 2, sk next 2 dc, dc in each of next 3 dc, dc in 3rd ch of beg ch-3, turn.

Row 4: Ch 3, dc in each of next 3 dc, ch 2, sk next ch sp, dc in each of next 4 dc, ch 2, sk next ch sp, dc in each of next 3 dc, dc in 3rd ch of beg ch-3, turn.

Row 5: Ch 3, dc in each of next 3 dc, 2 dc in next ch sp, dc in next dc, ch 2, sk next 2 dc, dc in next dc, 2 dc in next ch sp, dc in each of next 3 dc, dc in 3rd ch of beg ch-3, turn.

Row 6: Ch 3, dc in each of next 6 dc, ch 2, sk next ch sp, dc in each of next 6 dc, dc in 3rd ch of beg ch-3, turn.

Rows 7–17: Rep Rows 3–6, ending last rep with Row 5.

Row 18: Ch 3, dc in each dc and each ch st across, leaving a length of thread, fasten off. (16 dc)

Fold top of hanging lp (Row 18) to back of valance. With tapestry needle and rem length, sew tops of sts of last row to edge of valance.

Second hanging loop
Row 1: Leaving 15 rows free between hanging lps, sk next 19 rows, attach thread with sl st over top of end st of 20th row, ch 3, 3 dc over end st of each of next 5 rows, turn. (16 dc)

Note: *After completing the first row of the hanging lp, you will have 15 rows to the left of working hanging lp that rem unworked.*

Rows 2–18: Rep Rows 2–18 of first hanging lp.

Rem hanging loops
Rows 1–18: Rep Rows 1–18 of 2nd hanging lp as many times as necessary across top of valance, working last hanging lp over last 5 rows of valance. ■

▶ GRAPH ON PAGE 91

ELEGANT EDGINGS

Add a touch of vintage elegance to new or heirloom pillowcases with the delicate beauty of these deep, exquisitely detailed edgings featuring motifs lushly adorned with the always beautiful, always in vogue roll stitch.

GAUGE

Rnd 1 of rolled lace motif = ¾ inch; Rnds 1–3 of radiant blush motif = 1½ inches
Check gauge to save time.

PATTERN NOTES

Weave in loose ends as work progresses.
Join rnds with a sl st unless otherwise stated.
Rolled lace motif requires 30 yds per motif.
Radiant blush motif requires 25 yds per motif.

PATTERN STITCHES

Shell: [2 dc, ch 2, 2 dc] in indicated st.
Beg shell: [Ch 3, dc, ch 2, 2 dc] in indicated st.
Roll st: Yo hook indicated number of times, insert hook in indicated st, yo, draw up a lp, yo, draw through all lps on hook, ch 1 to secure.
Sc dec: [Insert hook in next st, yo, draw up a lp] twice, yo, draw through all 3 lps on hook.

ROLLED LACE

FIRST MOTIF

Rnd 1 (RS): With crystal blue, ch 4,

SIZE Rolled lace motif, 3¼ inches square
Radiant blush motif, 3¼ inches square

MATERIALS

- J. & P. Coats Knit-Cro-Sheen crochet cotton size 10: 1 ball each crystal blue #25 and almond pink #35
- Size 6 steel crochet hook or size needed to obtain gauge

join to form a ring, ch 3 (counts as first dc throughout), 19 dc in ring, join in 3rd ch of beg ch-3. (20 dc)

Rnd 2: Beg shell in same st as joining, *ch 2, sk next st, sc in next st, ch 3, sc in next st, ch 2, sk next st **, shell in next st, rep from * around, ending last rep at **, join in 3rd ch of beg ch-3.

Rnd 3: Sl st into ch-2 sp, beg shell in same ch-2 sp, *working yo hook 12 times for each roll st, work 5 roll sts in next ch-3 sp **, shell in next ch-2 sp of shell, rep from * around, ending last rep at **, join in 3rd ch of beg ch-3.

Rnd 4: Sl st into ch-2 sp, beg shell in same ch-2 sp, *[ch 2, sc in next roll st] twice, ch 2, [sc, ch 3, sc] in next roll st, [ch 2, sc in next roll st] twice, ch 2 **, shell in next ch-2 sp of next shell, rep

from * around, ending last rep at **, join in 3rd ch of beg ch-3.

Rnd 5: Sl st into ch-2 sp, [ch 3, dc, ch 3, 2 dc] in same ch-2 sp, *ch 7, sc in next ch-3 sp, ch 7 **, [2 dc, ch 3, 2 dc] in ch-2 sp of next shell, rep from * around, ending last rep at **, join in 3rd ch of beg ch-3.

Rnd 6: Sl st into corner ch-3 sp, *[sc, ch 2, sc, ch 7, sc, ch 2, sc] in corner ch-3 sp, ch 3, sk next 3 sts, [sc, ch 2, sc] in next ch, ch 1, sk next 2 chs, [sc, ch 2, sc] in next ch, ch 7, sk next 5 sts, [sc, ch 2, sc] in next ch, ch 1, sk next 2 chs, [sc, ch 2, sc] in next ch, ch 3, sk next 3 sts, rep from * around, join in beg sc, fasten off.

REM MOTIFS

Rnds 1–5: Rep Rnds 1–5 of first motif.
Rnd 6: Work the same as for Rnd 6 of first motif, except on joining side, replacing the ch-7 lps of joining sides with [ch 3, sl st in corresponding ch-7 lp on previous motif, ch 3] 3 times on joining side.

TOP EDGING

Row 1 (RS): Attach crystal blue in corner ch-7 lp, [ch 5 (counts as first dc,

ch 2), dc] in ch-7 sp, *ch 3, sk next 2 ch sps, [dc, ch 1, dc] in next ch-2 sp, ch 3, sk next 2 ch sps, [hdc, ch 2, hdc] in next ch-7 sp, ch 3, sk next 2 ch sps, [dc, ch 1, dc] in next ch-2 sp, ch 3, sk next 2 ch sps, [dc, ch 2, dc] in joining, rep from * across, ending with [dc, ch 2, dc] in corner, turn.

Row 2: Sl st into ch-2 sp, ch 1, *3 sc in ch-2 sp, 5 sc in next ch-3 sp, 2 sc in next ch-1 sp, 5 sc in next ch-3 sp, 3 sc in next ch-2 sp, 5 sc in next ch-3 sp, 2 sc in next ch-1 sp, 5 sc in next ch-3 sp, rep from * across, ending with 3 sc in last ch-2 sp, turn.

Row 3: Ch 1, [sc, ch 2, sc] in first sc, [sk next sc, {sc, ch 2, sc} in next sc] rep across, fasten off.

BOTTOM EDGING

Rows 1–3: Rep Rows 1–3 of top edging.

RADIANT BLUSH

FIRST MOTIF

Rnd 1 (RS): With almond pink, ch 5, join to form a ring, ch 3 (counts as first dc throughout), 15 dc in ring, join in 3rd ch of beg ch-3. (16 dc)

Rnd 2: Ch 1, sc in same st as beg ch-1, ch 3, sk next st, [sc in next st, ch 3, sk next st] rep around, join in beg sc.

Rnd 3: Ch 1, [sc in sc, 5 dc in next ch-3 sp] rep around, join in beg sc.

Rnd 4: Ch 1, *[sc, ch 3, sc] in next sc, ch 2, sk next 2 dc, sc in next dc, ch 2, sk next 2 dc, rep from * around, join in beg sc.

Rnd 5: Sl st into ch-3 sp, ch 3, 6 dc in same ch-3 sp, [7 dc in next ch-3 sp] rep around, join in 3rd ch of beg ch-3.

Rnd 6: Ch 1, *[sc in next st, ch 3, sk next st] 3 times, sc in next st, working yo hook 16 times, work roll st around sc directly below in Rnd 4, rep from * around, join in beg sc.

Rnd 7: Sl st into ch-3 sp, ch 1, *5 sc in ch-3 sp, [3 sc, ch 3, 3 sc] in next ch-3 sp, 5 sc in next ch-3 sp, [sc, ch 1, sc] in top of roll st, rep from * around, join in beg sc, fasten off.

REM MOTIFS

Rnds 1–6: Rep Rnds 1–6 of first motif.

Rnd 7: Work the same as for Rnd 7 of first motif, except on joining side replace the ch-3 with ch 1, sl st in corresponding ch-3 sp of previous motif, ch 1.

TOP EDGING

Row 1 (RS): With almond pink, ch 6, sl st in top side ch-3 sp, ch 6, sl st in first ch made, ch 9, sl st in same ch-3 sp as beg, ch 6, sl st in 4th ch of last ch-9 made, *ch 3, sl st in next ch-3 sp, ch 10, sl st in next ch-3 sp, [ch 9, sl st in joining,

ch 6, sl st in 4th ch of last ch-9 made] 3 times, rep from * across, ending with [ch 9, sl st in joining, ch 6, sl st in 4th ch of last ch-9 made] twice, fasten off.

Row 2 (RS): Attach almond pink in ch-3 sp, ch 2 (counts as first hdc), 4 hdc in ch-3 sp, 7 hdc in next ch-3 sp, *15 hdc in next ch-10 sp, 7 hdc in next ch-3 sp, 5 hdc in each of next 2 ch-3 sps, 7 hdc in next ch-3 sp, rep from * across, ending with 5 hdc in last ch-3 sp, fasten off.

Row 3 (RS): Attach almond pink in top of first hdc, ch 1, sc in first hdc, ch 2, sk next hdc, [sc, ch 2, sc] in next hdc, ch 2, sk next hdc, sc dec over next 2 hdc, *ch 2, sk next 2 hdc, [sc, ch 2, sc] in next hdc, ch 2, sc in next 2 hdc, sc dec over next 2 hdc, ch 2, sk next 2 hdc, [sc, ch 2, sc] in next hdc, ch 2, sk next 3 hdc, [sc, ch 2, sc, ch 3, sc, ch 2, sc] in next hdc, ch 2, sk next 3 hdc, [sc, ch 2, sc] in next hdc, ch 2, sk next 2 hdc, sc dec over next 2 hdc, ch 2, sk next 2 hdc, [sc, ch 2, sc] in next hdc, ch 2, sc in next 2 hdc, sc dec over next 2 hdc, ch 2, sk next hdc, [sc, ch 2, sc] in next hdc, ch 2, sk next hdc, [sc, ch 2, sc] in next hdc, ch 3, [sc, ch 2, sc] in next hdc, ch 2, sk next hdc, [sc, ch 2, sc] in next hdc, ch 2, sk next hdc, sc dec over next 2 hdc, rep from * across, ending last rep with sc in last hdc, fasten off. ∎

WAGON WHEELS TABLE RUNNER

Captured in a lacy net of openwork stitches, the old-fashioned motifs in this elegant table runner are created with circles and spokes reminiscent of the wagon wheels that took our pioneer forbearers West in search of a better life.

GAUGE

Rnds 1–4 of first motif = 2¼ inches
Check gauge to save time.

PATTERN NOTES

Weave in loose ends as work progresses.
Join rnds with a sl st unless otherwise stated.

PATTERN STITCHES

Picot (p): [Sc, ch 3, sc] in indicated ch sp.

Joining dc: Yo hook, insert hook in indicated st, yo, draw up a lp, [yo, draw through 2 lps on hook] twice.

CENTER SECTION

Note: Make 55 motifs.

First motif

Rnd 1 (RS): Ch 5, sl st to join to form a ring, ch 6 (counts as first tr, ch 2), [tr, ch 2] 11 times in ring, join in 4th ch of beg ch-6. (12 tr; 12 ch-2 sps)

Rnd 2: Ch 7 (counts as first dc, ch 4), [dc in next tr, ch 4] rep around, join in 3rd ch of beg ch-7.

ADVANCED ● ● ●

SIZE 23 x 64½ inches

MATERIALS

- Crochet cotton size 10: 1,500 yds cream
- Size 9 steel crochet hook or size needed to obtain gauge
- Spray starch
- Tapestry needle

Rnd 3: Ch 3 (counts as first dc), 5 dc in next ch-4 sp, [dc in next dc, 5 dc in next ch-4 sp] rep around, join in 3rd ch of beg ch-3. (72 dc)

Rnd 4: Ch 1, sc in each dc around, join in beg sc, fasten off.

Second–44th motifs

Rnds 1–3: Rep Rnds 1–3 of first motif.

Notes: Use diagram A as a guide, every dc of Rnd 2 of each motif appoints joining st on Rnd 4. There are 12 joining sts on each motif.

Use diagram B as a guide for joining motifs and to work joining sts to previous motifs.

Work second through 19th motifs in a strip, working 2 joining dc to previous motif. Then work rem motifs and joining

dc sts as indicated in diagram B.

Rnd 4: Ch 1, sc in same st as beg ch-1, sc in each of next 5 sts, work joining dc, sc in each of next 6 sts, work joining dc, finish rnd accordingly, join in beg sc, fasten off.

PICOT SECTION

Note: Use diagram B as a guide for Rnd 1 of picot section.

Rnd 1 (RS): After all 55 motifs are joined, attach thread in first free joining st of 55th motif, [ch 10, sc in next joining st] 5 times, ch 15, sc in next free joining st of first motif, [ch 10, sc in next joining st] 5 times, ch 15, sc in next free joining st of 20th motif, [ch 10, sc in next joining st] 5 times, [ch 15, sc in next free joining st of next motif, {ch 10, sc in next joining st} 3 times] 16 times, ch 15, sc in next free joining st of 37th motif, [ch 10 sc in next joining st] 5 times, ch 15, sc in next free joining st of 19th motif, [ch 10, sc in next joining st] 5 times, ch 15, sc in next free joining st of 38th motif, [ch 10, sc in next joining st] 5 times, [ch 15, sc in next free

joining st of next motif, {ch 10, sc in next joining st} 3 times] 16 times, ch 15, sl st to join in beg sc. (164 ch lps)

Rnd 2: Sl st to center of next ch-10 lp, ch 1, p in same ch sp as beg ch-1, ch 10, [p in next ch sp, ch 10] rep around, join in beg sc.

Rnd 3: Turn to WS, sl st to center of last ch sp, turn to RS, [ch 10, p in next ch sp] rep around, join in beg ch.

Rnd 4: Sl st to center of ch-10 sp, ch 1, p in same ch sp as beg ch-1, ch 10, [p in next ch sp, ch 10] rep around, join in beg sc.

Rnd 5: Turn to WS, sl st in next 4 sts, turn to RS, ch 6 (counts as first dc, ch 3), *5 dc in next ch lp, ch 4, [5 dc in next ch lp, ch 5] 13 times, 5 dc in next ch lp, ch 4, [5 dc in next ch lp, ch 3] 67 times **, rep from * around, ending last rep at ** with 4 dc in same ch sp as beg ch-6, sl st to join in 3rd ch of beg ch-6.

Rnd 6: Turn to WS, sl st in next 5 sts, turn to RS, ch 6 (counts as first dc, ch 3), *5 dc in next ch sp, ch 4, 5 dc in next ch sp, ch 5, [5 dc in next ch sp, ch 6] 12 times, 5 dc in next ch sp, ch 5, 5 dc in next ch sp, ch 4, [5 dc in next ch sp, ch 3] 66 times **, rep from * around, ending last rep at **, 4 dc in same ch sp as beg ch-6, sl st to join in 3rd ch of beg ch-3.

Rnd 7: Sl st in next 2 sts, *[3 dc in ch sp, ch 9, sl st in top of last dc, 2 dc in same ch sp, ch 10] 18 times, [5 dc in next ch sp, ch 10] 64 times, rep from * around, join in top of beg dc. (200 ch lps)

Rnd 8: Turn to WS, sl st to center of last ch-10 lp, turn to RS, ch 1, p in same ch sp as beg ch-1, ch 10, [p in next ch sp, ch 10] rep in each ch-9 and ch-10 sp around, join in beg sc.

Rnds 9–11: Turn to WS, sl st to center of last ch-10 lp, turn to RS, ch 1, p in same ch sp as beg ch-1, ch 10, [p in next ch sp, ch 10] rep around, join in beg sc. At the end of Rnd 11, fasten off.

EDGING MOTIF

Notes: *Make a total of 52 motifs.*
Use diagram C as a guide, mark 4 ch lps at center rounded end of Rnd 11.
All edging motifs are joined to Rnd 11 of picot section.

▶ CONTINUED ON PAGE 92

PINEAPPLE SUNSHINE DOILY

A tradition of beauty and gracious hospitality is winningly presented in the pineapple perfection of this time-honored doily design. A soft, sunny yellow color makes it extra warm and welcoming!

GAUGE

Rnds 1–3 = 1½ inches; Rnds 1–10 = 7 inches in diameter; 2 shell rnds = ¾ inch
Check gauge to save time.

PATTERN NOTES

Weave in loose ends as work progresses.
Join rnds with a sl st unless otherwise stated.
Ch-3 counts as first dc throughout.

PATTERN STITCHES

Shell: [3 dc, ch 3, 3 dc] in indicated st.
Beg shell: [Ch 3, 2 dc, ch 3, 3 dc] in indicated st.
Double shell: [3 dc, ch 3] twice and 3 dc in indicated st.
Beg double shell: [Ch 3, 2 dc, {ch 3, 3 dc} twice] in indicated st.
Picot (p): Ch 4, sl st in first ch.

DOILY

Rnd 1 (RS): With maize, ch 7, join to form a ring, ch 3, 23 dc in ring, join in 3rd ch of beg ch-3. (24 dc)
Rnd 2: Ch 4 (counts as first dc, ch 1), [dc in next dc, ch 1] rep around, join in

3rd ch of beg ch-4.
Rnd 3: Ch 1, sc in same st as beg ch-1, sc in next ch-1 sp, [sc in next dc, sc in next ch-1 sp] rep around, join in beg sc. (48 sc)
Rnd 4: Ch 22, dc in 8th ch from hook, [ch 2, sk next 2 chs, dc in next ch] 4 times, ch 2, sk next sc of Rnd 3, sc in each of next 3 sc of Rnd 3, *ch 22, dc in 8th ch from hook, [ch 2, sk next 2 chs, dc in next ch] 4 times, ch 2, sk next sc of Rnd 3, sc in each of next 3 sc of Rnd 3, rep from * around, join with sl st in first ch of beg ch-22. (12 petals)
Rnd 5: Working up side of petal ch 1, 2 sc in ch-2 sp, *sc in base of next dc, [2 sc in next ch sp, sc in base of next dc]

4 times, 8 sc in sp at top of petal, working down opposite side of petal, [sc in next dc, 2 sc in next ch sp] 5 times, sk next sc on center circle, sc in next sc, sk next sc **, 2 sc in first ch sp on next petal, rep from * around, ending last rep at **, join in beg sc. (468 sc)
Rnd 6: Working up side of next petal, sl st in next 2 sc, ch 1, sc in same st as beg ch-1, sc in each of next 14 sc, *[2 sc in next sc] 4 times, sc in each of next 15 sc **, sk next 2 sc on this petal, sk next sc on center circle and next 2 sc on next petal, sc in each of next 15 sc, rep from * around, ending last rep at **, join in beg sc. (456 sc)
Rnd 7: Sl st in each of next 6 sc, ch 1, sc in same st as beg ch-1, sc in each of next 25 sc, *sk next 6 sc on this petal and next 6 sc on next petal, sc in each of next 26 sc, rep from * around, join in beg sc, fasten off. (312 sc)
Rnd 8: Attach maize with sc at top of any petal in 11th sc up side of petal (counting up 11 sc worked in previous rnd), ch 1, sc in same sc, ch 6, *sk next

▶ CONTINUED ON PAGE 93

SWEET VICTORIAN TABLE TOPPER

Whether accenting a small dining table in an intimate setting for two or topping a pretty, round side table, this exquisite lace creation sets the mood for old-fashioned elegance. Roses accented with glittering gold beads add just enough sparkle for the perfect effect.

GAUGE

9 dc = 1 inch; 4 dc rnds = 1 inch
Check gauge to save time.

PATTERN NOTES

Weave in loose ends as work progresses.
Join rnds with a sl st unless otherwise stated.

PATTERN STITCH

Tr cl: Leaving last lp of each tr on hook, tr in each number of indicated ch sps, yo, draw through rem lps on hook.

LARGE MOTIF

Make 16

First motif

Rnd 1 (RS): Thread 8 beads onto pink thread, make a ch-1 lp at end of thread, push all 8 beads close to hook, insert hook into ch-1 lp, yo, draw thread through lp so that beads form a loose circle, [ch 2, sc into thread following next bead] rep around, join. (8 ch-2 sps)

Rnd 2: Ch 1, sc in first ch-2 sp, ch 3,

ADVANCED ●◐○

SIZE 38 inches square

MATERIALS
- DMC Cebelia crochet cotton size 10 (50g per ball): 4 balls ecru, 2 balls pink
- Size 8 steel crochet hook or size needed to obtain gauge
- 128 large gold seed beads
- Beading needle

[sc in next ch-2 sp, ch 3] rep around, join in beg sc.

Rnd 3: Ch 1, [sc, 3 dc, sc] in each ch-3 sp around, join in beg sc. (8 petals)

Rnd 4: Ch 1, [sc behind and between next 2 petals, ch 4] rep around, join in beg sc.

Rnd 5: Ch 1, [sc, hdc, 4 dc, hdc, sc] in each ch-4 sp around, join in beg sc.

Rnd 6: Ch 1, [sc behind and between next 2 petals, ch 5] rep around, join in beg sc, fasten off.

Rnd 7: Attach ecru in any ch-5 sp, ch 3 (counts as first dc throughout), 3 dc in

same ch sp, ch 4, [4 dc in next ch-5 sp, ch 4] rep around, join in 3rd ch of beg ch-3. (32 dc)

Rnd 8: Ch 3, dc in each of next 3 dc, *dc in first ch of ch-4, ch 4, sk next 2 chs, dc in 4th ch of same ch-4 **, dc in each of next 4 dc, rep from * around, ending last rep at **, join in 3rd ch of beg ch-3. (48 dc)

Rnd 9: Ch 3, dc in each of next 4 dc, *dc in first ch of ch-4, ch 4, sk next 2 chs, dc in 4th ch of same ch-4 sp **, dc in each of next 6 dc, rep from * around, ending with last rep at **, dc in each of next 2 dc, join in 3rd ch of beg ch-3. (64 dc)

Rnd 10: Ch 3, dc in each of next 5 dc, *dc in first ch of ch-4, ch 4, dc in 4th ch of same ch-4 sp **, dc in each of next 8 dc, rep from * around, ending last rep at **, dc in each of next 2 dc, join in 3rd ch of beg ch-3. (80 dc)

Rnd 11: Ch 3, dc in each of next 6 dc, *dc in first ch of ch-4 p, ch 5, dc in 4th

► CONTINUED ON PAGE 94

DESIGN BY
DOT DRAKE

ISLAND IN THE SKY DOILY

With delicate stitch patterns that emulate the graceful look of cro-tatting, this gorgeous doily is stunning in a two-color combination, but would be equally as beautiful worked in a single color to complement a special decor.

GAUGE

Center = 2½ inches in diameter; blue ring = 5¼ inches in diameter before sides, after sides 5¼ x 8 inches
Check gauge to save time.

PATTERN NOTES

Weave in loose ends as work progresses. Join rnds with a sl st unless otherwise stated.

PATTERN STITCHES

Picot (p): Ch 4, sl st in 4th ch from hook.

Tr cl: [Yo hook twice, insert hook into ch-4 sp, yo, draw up a lp, {yo, draw through 2 lps on hook} twice] twice in same ch-4 sp, yo, draw through rem 3 lps on hook.

BLUE RING

Rnd 1 (RS): With delft blue, [ch 12, draw up a lp through first ch of 12, in ring work 5 sc, *ch 4, sl st in 4th ch from hook for p, 2 sc in ring, rep from * 4 times, 3 sc in ring, sl st in first sc of 5-sc, ch 18, sc in middle p on last ring] 12 times, join to joining of first ring.

ADVANCED ●●●

SIZE 14 x 17 inches

MATERIALS

- Crochet cotton size 10 (350 yds per ball): 1 ball each white and delft blue
- Size 9 steel crochet hook or size needed to obtain gauge

Rnd 2: *Working in next ch-18 sp, work 8 sc, p, 16 sc, in next ch-18 sp, work 16 sc, p, 8 sc, [8 sc, p, 8 sc, p, 8 sc] in each of next 4 ch-18 sps, rep from * once, join in beg sc, fasten off.

CENTER

Rnd 1 (RS): With white, ch 5, join to form a ring, ch 1, 12 sc in ring, join in beg sc. (12 sc)

Rnd 2: Ch 5 (counts as first dc, ch 2), [dc in next sc, ch 2] rep around, join in 3rd ch of beg ch-5.

Rnd 3: Ch 1, sc in same st as joining, 2 sc in next ch-2 sp, [sc in next dc, 2 sc in next ch-2 sp] rep around, join in beg sc. (36 sc)

Rnd 4: Ch 1, sc in same sc as beg ch-1, ch 4, sk next 2 sc, [sc in next sc, ch 4, sk next 2 sc] rep around, join in beg sc. (12 ch-4 sps)

Note: Rnd 5 attaches the center in the center of the blue ring.

Rnd 5: Sl st into ch-4 sp, ch 1, sc in same ch-4 sp, *ch 4, tr cl in same ch-4 sp, ch 1, sc in 5th picot on blue ring, ch 1, sl st in top of tr cl, ch 4, sc in same ch-4 sp **, sc in next ch-4 sp, rep from * around, ending last rep at **, join in beg sc, fasten off.

SIDE

Note: Side is worked on each end of blue ring.

With delft blue, sl st in 9th sc of 24 on blue ring, ch 14, draw lp through 5th ch of ch-14, ch 4, draw lp through 8th sc of previous 16, in ch-4 sp work 5 sc, 15 sc in lp, 5 sc in ch-4 sp, sl st in beg sc, ch 10, draw lp back through 9th sc of 15, ch 6, draw lp back through 7th sc of same 15, ch 10, draw lp back through beg of same 15, in sp just made work [4 sc, {p, 2 sc} twice, p, 4 sc], in

► CONTINUED ON PAGE 95

DESIGNS BY
BRENDA STRATTON

HERITAGE LACE COVERLET & DOILY

The simple elegance of this beautifully rendered floral lace design brings to mind the quiet beauty and old-fashioned charm of Grandmother's house. Shimmering pearl bead accents add a sophisticated touch to this exquisite vintage design.

GAUGE

Motif = 6¼ inches square
Check gauge to save time.

PATTERN NOTES

Weave in loose ends as work progresses.
Join rnds with a sl st unless otherwise stated.
Motifs are joined tog as work progresses.

PATTERN STITCHES

Tr cl: [Yo hook twice, insert hook in indicated st, yo, draw up a lp, {yo, draw through 2 lps on hook} twice] twice, yo, draw through all lps on hook.

Anchoring tr cl: Yo hook twice, insert hook in indicated st, yo, draw up a lp, yo, draw through 2 lps on hook, pick up a lp on back of petal in front of petal currently being worked, yo, draw through 3 lps on hook, yo hook twice, insert hook in indicated st, yo, draw up a lp, [yo, draw through 2 lps on hook] twice, yo, draw through all 3 lps on hook.

V-st: [Dc, ch 2, dc] in indicated st.

Dc lp: Sc in indicated st, ch 3, dc in top of sc.

ADVANCED

SIZE Coverlet: 54 x 85 inches
Single: 79 x 110¼ inches
Double: 97¾ x 110¼ inches
Queen: 104 x 122¾ inches
California King: 116½ x 122¾ inches
King: 122¾ x 122¾ inches

MATERIALS

- J. & P. Coats Knit-Cro-Sheen crochet cotton size 10 (325 yds per ball): 30 (60, 71, 84, 94, 99) balls white #1
- Size 3 steel crochet hook or size needed to obtain gauge
- 104 (204, 255, 304, 342, 361) 6mm pearl beads
- 2 (6mm) pearl beads for doily
- White sewing thread
- Sewing needle

Joining dc lp: Sc in indicated st, ch 1, sl st in ch-3 of corresponding dc lp of opposing motif, ch 1, dc in top of last sc on working motif.

Ch-4 corner lp: Sc in indicated st, ch 4, dc in top of last sc.

Ch-5 corner lp: Sc in indicated st, ch 5, dc in top of last sc.

Joining ch-5 corner lp: Ch 2, sl st in ch-5 sp at corner of opposing motif, ch 2.

COVERLET

Note: Make 104 (204, 255, 304, 342, 361) motifs.

First motif

Rnd 1 (RS): Beg at center, ch 4, sl st to join to form a ring, ch 1, 8 sc in ring, join in front lp of first sc. (8 sc)

Rnd 2 (front petals): Working in front lps for this rnd only, [ch 3, tr cl in same st, ch 3, sl st in same st, sl st in next st] 8 times, join in back lp of first sc of Rnd 1. (8 petals)

Rnd 3 (back petals): Working in rem back lps of Rnd 1, [ch 3, anchoring tr cl in same st, ch 3, sl st in same st, sl st in next st] 8 times. (8 petals)

Rnd 4: Working in back petals of Rnd 3 only, sl st in each of first 3 chs at beg of Rnd 3, sl st in top of tr cl, ch 1, sc in same st as beg ch-1, ch 6, [sc in top of next tr cl, ch 6] 7 times, join in beg sc. (8 ch-6 sps)

Rnd 5: Sl st into ch-6 sp, ch 1, 9 sc in

each ch-6 sp around, join in beg sc. (72 sc)

Rnd 6: Sl st across 4 sc, ch 1, 3 sc in same st as beg ch-1, sc in each of next 3 sc, sk next 2 sc, sc in each of next 3 sc, [3 sc in next sc, sc in each of next 3 sc, sk next 2 sc, sc in each of next 3 sc] rep around, join in beg sc. (72 sc)

Rnd 7: Sl st into next sc, *[ch 3, tr cl, ch 3, sl st in same sc] 3 times, ch 7, sk next 8 sc, sl st in next sc, ch 7, sk next 8 sc, rep from * around, join in same st as first sl st.

Rnd 8: Sl st in each of next 3 chs, sl st into top of first tr cl, ch 1, sc in same st as beg ch-1, ch 5, [sc in next tr cl, ch 5] twice, [sc in next sp, ch 5] twice, *[sc in next tr cl, ch 5] 3 times, [sc in next sp, ch 5] twice, rep from * around, join in beg sc.

Rnd 9: Sl st in next 2 chs, ch 1, sc in same ch sp, ch 7, sc in next ch sp, ch 5, sc in next ch sp, ch 3, V-st in next ch-5 sp, ch 3, sc in next ch sp, ch 5, *sc in next ch sp, ch 7, sc in next ch sp, ch 5, sc in next ch sp, ch 3, V-st in next ch-5 sp, ch 3, sc in next ch sp, ch 5, rep from * around, join in beg sc.

Rnd 10: Sl st into next ch-7 sp, ch 1, [11 sc in ch-7 sp, 5 sc in next ch sp, 3 sc in next ch sp, 2 sc in next ch sp, 3 sc in next ch sp, 5 sc in next ch sp] 4 times, join in beg sc. (116 sc)

Rnd 11: Sl st in next 5 sc, ch 6 (counts as first dc, ch 3), dc in same st as beg ch-6, dc in each of next 28 sc, *[dc, ch 3, dc] in next sc, dc in each of next 28 sc, rep from * around, join in 3rd ch of beg ch-6. (120 dc)

Rnd 12: Sl st into next ch-3 sp, [ch 3, dc, ch 2, 2 dc] in same sp, dc in each of next 30 dc, *[2 dc, ch 2, 2 dc] in next ch-3 sp, dc in each of next 30 dc, rep from * around, join in 3rd ch of beg ch-3. (136 dc)

Rnd 13: Sl st into next ch-2 sp, ch 1, [5 sc in ch-2 sp, sc in each dc across to next corner ch sp] rep around, join in beg sc. (156 sc)

Rnd 14: Sl st to center sc of corner 5-sc group, ch 1, [ch-4 corner lp, dc lp] in same sc, sk next 2 sc, [dc lp in next sc, sk next 2 sc] rep across, *[ch-4 corner lp, dc lp] in center sc of corner, sk next 2 sc, [dc lp in next sc, sk 2 sc] rep across, rep from * around, join in beg sc. (56 lps)

Rnd 15: Sl st into ch-4 of next ch-4 corner lp, ch 1, [ch-4 corner lp, dc lp] in same lp, [dc lp in ch-3 of next dc lp] rep across, *[ch-4 corner lp, dc lp] in ch-4 of next ch-4 corner lp, [dc lp in ch-3 of next dc lp] rep across, rep from * around, join in first sc.

Rnd 16: Sl st into ch-4 of next ch-4 corner lp, ch 1, [ch-5 corner lp, dc lp] in same lp, [dc lp in ch-3 of next dc lp] rep across, *[ch-5 corner lp, dc lp] in ch-4 of next ch-4 corner lp, [dc lp in ch-3 of next

dc lp] rep across, rep from * around, join in beg sc, fasten off. (64 dc lps)

With sewing needle and thread, sew a bead to center of Rnd 1 of motif.

Second and all rem motifs

Rnds 1–15: Rep Rnds 1–15 of first motif.

Rnd 16: Rep Rnd 16, replacing dc lp with joining dc lps on sides of motifs to be joined and working joining ch-5 lp at each corner.

Assembly

Join motifs as work progresses for coverlet, 8 x 13 motifs; single, 12 x 17 motifs; double, 15 x 17 motifs; queen, 16 x 19 motifs; California king, 18 x 19 motifs; and king, 19 x 19 motifs.

Edging

Rnd 1: Attach white in any corner ch-5 sp, ch 1, *[ch 4 corner lp, dc lp] in next corner lp, [dc lp in ch-3 of next dc lp] rep across, rep from * around, join in first sc.

Rnds 2 & 3: Sl st into next corner lp, ch 1, *[ch-4 corner lp, dc lp] in same lp, [dc lp in ch-3 of next dc lp] rep across, rep from * around, join in first sc.

Rnd 4: Sl st into next corner lp, ch 5

(counts as first dc, ch 2), dc in same sp, ch 5, [dc, ch 2] twice in same sp, [dc in next lp, ch 2] rep across to next corner, *[dc, ch 2, dc] in corner sp, ch 5, [dc, ch 2] twice in same corner lp, [dc in next lp, ch 2] rep across to next corner, rep from * around, join in 3rd ch of beg ch-5.

Rnd 5: Sl st into ch-5 sp, [ch 3, 2 dc, ch 2, 3 dc] in same ch-5 sp, 2 dc in each ch-2 sp across to next corner, *[3 dc, ch 2, 3 dc] in next ch-5 sp, 2 dc in each ch-2 sp across to next corner, rep from * around, join in 3rd ch of beg ch-3.

Rnd 6: Sl st to next ch-2 sp, [ch 3, 2 dc, ch 2, 3 dc] in same ch-2 sp, dc in each dc across to next corner, *[3 dc, ch 2, 3 dc] in next corner ch-2 sp, dc in each dc across to next corner, rep from * around, join in 3rd ch of beg ch-3.

Rnd 7: Sl st into next ch-2 sp, [ch 3, tr cl, ch 3, sl st in same sp] 4 times, ch 4, sk next 3 dc, sc in next dc, ch 4, sk next 3 dc, [{sl st, ch 3, tr cl, ch 3, sl st in next dc} 3 times, ch 4, sk next 3 dc, sc in next dc, ch 4, sk next 3 dc] rep across to next corner, *[sl st, ch 3, tr cl, ch 3, sl st in

ch-2 sp] 4 times, ch 4, sk next 3 dc, sc in next dc, ch 4, sk next 3 dc, [{sl st, ch 3, tr cl, ch 3, sl st in next dc} 3 times, ch 4, sk next 3 dc, sc in next dc, ch 4, sk next 3 dc] rep across to next corner, rep from * around, join in base of beg ch-3.

Rnd 8: Sl st in each ch of first ch-3, sl st into top of first tr cl, ch 1, sc in same st, ch 5, [sc in next tr cl, ch 5] twice, sc in next tr cl, dc in next sp, ch 1, dc in next sp, [{sc in next tr cl, ch 5} twice, sc in next tr cl, dc in next sp, ch 1, dc in next sp] rep across to next corner, *sc in top of first tr cl at corner, ch 5, [sc in next tr cl, ch 5] twice, sc in next tr cl, dc in next sp, ch 1, dc in next sp, [{sc in next tr cl} twice, sc in next tr cl, dc in next sp, ch 1, dc in next sp] rep across to next corner, rep from * around, join in first sc, fasten off.

DOILY

Make 2 motifs, joining 2nd motif to side of first motif.

Edging

Rep Rnds 1–8 of coverlet edging. ■

BUTTERFLIES IN FLIGHT VALANCE ► CONTINUED FROM PAGE 77

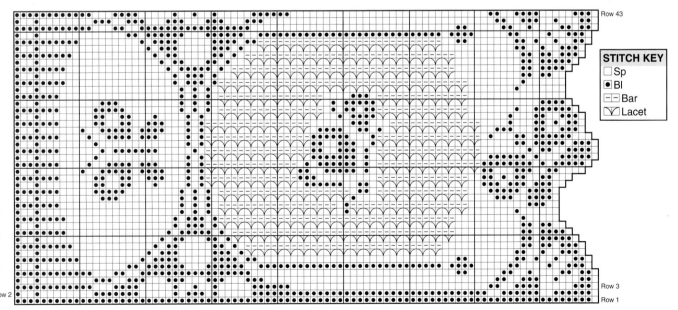

Butterfly Valance Chart

STITCH KEY
☐ Sp
⬤ Bl
⊟ Bar
Y Lacet

First edging motif

Rnds 1–3: Rep Rnds 1–3 of center section motif. (72 dc)

Rnd 4: Ch 1, sc in next 5 sts, insert hook in first marked ch-10 lp of Rnd 11 of picot section, *draw up a lp, yo, draw through 2 lps on hook, sc in each of next 6 sts **, insert hook in next ch-10 lp, rep from * to ** 3 times, sc in each rem st around, join in beg sc, fasten off.

Second & third edging motifs

Rnds 1–3: Rep Rnds 1–3 of center section motif. (72 dc)

Rnd 4: Ch 1, sc in next 5 sts, yo, insert hook in 2nd free joining st (counted from picot area) of previous edging motif, complete joining dc, sc in each of next 6 sts on working motif, yo, insert hook in next joining st of previous motif, complete joining dc, sc in next 6 sts on working motif, [insert hook in next ch-10 lp of Rnd 11, draw up a lp, yo, draw through 2 lps on hook, sc in each of next 6 sts on working motif] 3 times, sc in each rem st around, join in beg sc, fasten off.

Fourth–24th edging motifs

Rnds 1–3: Rep Rnds 1–3 of center section motif. (72 dc)

Rnd 4: Ch 1, sc in each of next 5 sts, yo, insert hook in 2nd free joining st (counted from picot area) of previous edging motif, complete joining dc, sc in next 6 sts, yo, insert hook in next free joining st of previous edging motif, complete joining dc, sc in next 6 sts, [insert hook in next ch-10 lp of Rnd 11, draw up a lp, yo, draw through 2 lps on hook, sc in next 6 sts] 4 times, sc in each rem st around, join in beg sc, fasten off.

For 25th and 26th edging motifs, rep the same as for 2nd edging motif.

For 27th edging motif, rep the same as for 4th–24th edging motifs.

For 28th and 29th edging motifs, rep the same as for 2nd and 3rd edging motifs.

For 30th–50th edging motifs, rep the same as for 4th–24th edging motifs.

For 51st edging motif, rep the same as for 2nd edging motif.

52nd edging motif

Rnds 1–3: Rep Rnds 1–3 of center section motif. (72 dc)

Rnd 4: Ch 1, sc in next 5 sts, yo, insert hook in 2nd joining st (counted from picot area) of previous edging motif, complete joining dc, sc in next 6 sts on working motif, yo, insert hook in first free joining st, complete joining dc, sc in next 6 sts, [insert hook in next ch-10 lp, draw up a lp, yo, draw through 2 lps on hook, sc in next 6 sts] 3 times, yo, insert hook in first free joining st (counted from picot area) of first edging motif, complete joining dc, sc in next 6 sts, joining dc in next joining st, sc in each rem st around, join in beg sc, fasten off.

BORDER

Rnd 1 (RS): Attach thread with sc in first free joining st of first edging motif, [{ch 10, sc in next joining st} 4 times, ch 15, sc in first joining st on next edging motif] rep around for except 2nd, 3rd, 25th, 26th, 28th, 29th, 51st and 52nd edging motifs, work [{ch 10, sc in next joining st} 3 times, ch 15, sc in first free joining st on next motif, join in beg sc.

Rnds 2–4: Sl st to center of ch-10 lp, [ch 10, {sc, ch 3, sc} in same ch lp] rep around, join in first ch of beg ch-10. At the end of Rnd 4, fasten off.

Rnd 5: Attach thread in center of any ch-10 lp, ch 7 (counts as first dc, ch 4), [5 dc in next ch-10 lp, ch 4] rep around, ending with 4 dc in same ch-10 lp as beg ch-7, join in 3rd ch of beg ch-7.

Rnd 6: Sl st in next 2 sts, ch 3 (counts as first dc), 4 dc in same ch sp, ch 4, [5 dc in next ch-4 sp, ch 4] rep around, join in 3rd ch of beg ch-3.

Rnd 7: Sl st in next 5 sts, ch 3, 4 dc in same ch sp, ch 5, [2 tr, 2 dc] in top of last dc of 5-dc group, [5 dc in next ch-4 sp, ch 5 {2 tr, 2 dc} in top of last dc of 5-dc group] rep around, join in 3rd ch of beg ch-3, fasten off.

Spray runner with starch and place runner on a flat surface to dry. ∎

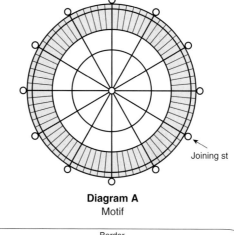

Diagram A
Motif

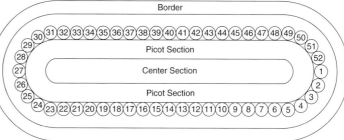

Border
Picot Section
Center Section
Picot Section

Diagram C
Edging Motifs

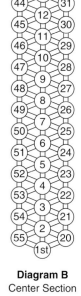

Diagram B
Center Section

4 sc, sc in next sc, ch 9, sk next 3 sc on same petal, sl st in next sc, ch 3, sc in 7th sc on next petal, ch 4, drop lp from hook and insert hook in 5th ch of previously worked ch-9, draw lp through, ch 4, sk next 3 sc on working petal **, sc in next sc, ch 6, rep from * around, ending last rep at **, join in beg sc. (36 ch lps)

Rnd 9: Ch 6 (counts as first dc, ch 3), dc in next sp, ch 3, dc in next sc, ch 3, dc in next sp, ch 3, dc in next sp, ch 3, *[dc in next sc, ch 3, dc in next sp, ch 3] twice, dc in next sp, ch 3, rep from * around, join in 3rd ch of beg ch-6. (60 ch lps)

Rnd 10: Sl st into next ch sp, ch 2 (counts as first hdc), 2 hdc in same sp, [3 hdc in next ch sp] rep around, join in 2nd ch off beg ch-2. (180 hdc)

Rnd 11: Ch 1, sc in same st as beg ch-1, ch 5, sk next 4 hdc, [sc in next hdc, ch 5, sk next 4 hdc] rep around, join in beg sc. (36 ch sps)

Rnd 12: Sl st into next ch sp, beg shell in same ch sp, shell in each ch sp around, join in 3rd ch of beg ch-3. (36 shells)

Rnd 13: Sl st into ch sp of shell, beg shell in same ch sp, ch 1, [shell in next shell, ch 1] rep around, join in 3rd ch of beg ch-3. (36 shells)

Rnd 14: Sl st into ch sp of shell, beg shell in same ch sp, ch 2, [shell in next shell, ch 2] rep around, join in 3rd ch of beg ch-3.

Rnd 15: Sl st into ch sp of shell, beg shell in same ch sp, *ch 4, sc in next ch sp of next shell, ch 3, shell in next ch-2 sp between shells, ch 3, sc in next ch sp of next shell, ch 4 **, shell in next shell, rep from * around, join in 3rd ch of beg ch-3. (24 shells; 24 sc)

Rnd 16: Sl st into ch sp of next shell, beg shell in same sp, *ch 7, [3 dc, ch 5, 3 dc] in next shell, ch 7 **, shell in next shell, rep from * around, ending last rep at **, join in 3rd ch of beg ch-3. (12 ch-5 sp; 12 shells)

Rnd 17: Sl st into ch sp of next shell, beg

shell in same sp, *ch 5, sk next ch-7 sp, 12 tr in next ch-5 sp, ch 5 **, shell in next shell, rep from * around, ending last rep at **, join in 3rd ch of beg ch-3. (12 pineapple bases; 12 shells)

Rnd 18: Sl st into ch sp of shell, beg shell in same ch sp, *ch 4, [tr in next tr, ch 1] 11 times, tr in next tr, ch 4 **, shell in next shell, rep from * around, ending last rep at **, join in 3rd ch of beg ch-3.

Rnd 19: Sl st into ch sp of shell, *ch 4, [sc in next ch-1 sp, ch 3] 10 times, sc in last ch-1 sp, ch 4 **, shell in next shell, rep from * around, ending last rep at **, join in 3rd ch of beg ch-3.

Rnd 20: Sl st into ch sp of shell, beg shell in same ch sp, *ch 5, [sc in next ch-3 sp, ch 3] 9 times, sc in next ch-3 sp, ch 5 **, shell in next shell, rep from * around, ending last rep at **, join in 3rd ch of beg ch-3.

Rnd 21: Sl st into ch sp of shell, beg shell in same ch sp, *ch 5, [sc in next ch-3 sp, ch 3] 8 times, sc in next ch-3 sp, ch 5 **, shell in next shell, rep from * around, ending last rep at **, join in 3rd ch of beg ch-3.

Rnd 22: Sl st into ch sp of shell, beg shell in same ch sp, *ch 5, [sc in next ch-3 sp, ch 3] 7 times, sc in next ch-3 sp, ch 5 **, shell in next shell, rep from * around, ending last rep at **, join in 3rd ch of beg ch-3.

Rnd 23: Sl st into ch sp of shell, beg double shell in same ch sp, *ch 5, [sc in next ch-3 sp, ch 3] 6 times, sc in next ch-3 sp, ch 5 **, double shell in next shell, rep from * around, ending last rep at **, join in 3rd ch of beg ch-3.

Rnd 24: Sl st into first ch sp of double shell, beg shell in same ch sp, shell in next ch sp of next shell, *ch 5, [sc in next ch-3 sp, ch 3] 5 times, sc in next ch-3 sp, ch 5 **, [shell in next shell] twice, rep from * around, ending last rep at **, join in 3rd ch of beg ch-3.

Rnd 25: Sl st into ch sp of shell, beg

shell in same ch sp, *ch 3, shell in next shell, ch 5, [sc in next ch-3 sp, ch 3] 4 times, sc in next ch-3 sp, ch 5 **, shell in next shell, rep from * around, ending last rep at **, join in 3rd ch of beg ch-3.

Rnd 26: Sl st into ch sp of shell, beg shell in same ch sp, *ch 2, shell in next ch-3 sp between shells, ch 2, shell in next shell, ch 5, [sc in next ch-3 sp, ch 3] 3 times, sc in next ch-3 sp, ch 5 **, shell in next shell, rep from * around, ending last rep at **, join in 3rd ch of beg ch-3.

Rnd 27: Sl st into ch sp of shell, beg double shell in same sp, *ch 2, shell in next shell, ch 2, double shell in next shell, ch 5, [sc in next ch-3 sp, ch 3] twice, sc in next ch-3 sp, ch 5 **, double shell in next shell, rep from * around, ending last rep at **, join in 3rd ch of beg ch-3.

Rnd 28: Sl st into ch sp of shell, beg shell in same ch sp, shell in next shell, *ch 3, shell in next shell, ch 3, [shell in next shell] twice, ch 5, sc in next ch-3 sp, ch 3, sc in next ch-3 sp, ch 5 **, [shell in next shell] twice, rep from * around, ending last rep at **, join in 3rd ch of beg ch-3.

Rnd 29: Sl st into ch sp of shell, beg shell in same ch sp, *[ch 3, shell in next shell] 4 times, ch 5, sc in next ch-3 sp, ch 5 **, shell in next shell, rep from * around, ending last rep at **, join in 3rd ch of beg ch-3.

Rnd 30: Sl st into ch sp of shell, beg shell in same sp, *ch 4, shell in next shell, ch 4, double shell in next shell, [ch 4, shell in next shell] twice **, shell in next shell, rep from * around, ending last rep at **, join in 3rd ch of beg ch-3.

Rnd 31: Ch 1, sc in same st as beg ch-1, [sc in each dc, 3 sc in each ch-4 sp between shells and {2 sc, p, 2 sc} in each ch sp of each shell] rep around, join in beg sc, fasten off.

Starch lightly and press. ■

ch of same ch-4 sp **, dc in each of next 10 dc, rep from * around, ending last rep at **, dc in each of next 3 dc, join in 3rd ch of beg ch-3. (96 dc)

Rnd 12: Ch 3, dc in each of next 6 dc, *ch 7, dtr in 3rd ch of ch-5 sp, ch 7, sk first dc of next dc group **, dc in each of next 10 dc, rep from * around, ending last rep at **, dc in each of next 3 dc, join in 3rd ch of beg ch-3.

Rnd 13: Ch 3, dc in each of next 5 dc, *ch 7, 2 sc in next ch-7 sp, sc in dtr, 2 sc in next ch-7 sp, ch 7, sk first dc **, dc in each of next 8 dc, rep from * around, ending last rep at **, dc in each of next 2 dc, join in 3rd ch of beg ch-3.

Rnd 14: Ch 3, dc in each of next 4 dc, *ch 7, sc in next ch-7 sp, sc in each of next 2 sc, [sc, ch 3, sc] in next sc, sc in each of next 2 sc, sc in next ch-7 sp, ch 7, sk next dc **, dc in each of next 6 dc, rep from * around, ending last rep at **, dc in next dc, join in 3rd ch of beg ch-3.

Rnd 15: Ch 3, dc in each of next 3 dc, *ch 8, sc in first sc, ch 10, sk next 3 sc, sk next ch-3 sp and next 3 sc, sc in next sc, ch 8, sk first dc **, dc in each of next 4 dc, rep from * around, ending last rep at **, join in 3rd ch of beg ch-3.

Rnd 16: Sl st into 2nd dc, ch 3, dc in next dc, *[ch 3, dtr in next ch-10 sp] 8 times, ch 3 **, sk 1 dc, dc in each of next 2 dc, rep from * around, ending last rep at **, join in 3rd ch of beg ch-3, fasten off.

Rnd 17: Attach pink in first dtr of any 8-dtr group and beg in same st, ch 1, [{sc in dtr, 3 sc in next ch-3 sp} 7 times, sc in next dtr, 2 sc in next ch sp, sk next dc, sc in next dc, 2 sc in next ch sp] rep around, join in beg sc.

Rnd 18: Ch 1, beg in same sc as beg ch-1, *[{sc, ch 3, sc} in next sc, sc in each of next 3 sc] 7 times, [sc, ch 3, sc] in next sc, sc in next sc, sk next sc, [sc, ch 3, sc] in next sc, sc in next sc, sk next sc, rep from * around, join in beg sc, fasten off.

Rem large motifs

Rnds 1–18: Rep Rnds 1–18 of first motif, joining motifs 4 x 4 squares, joining motifs to previous motif in 18th rnd.

Use photo as a guide for joining to previous ch-3 sps as needed. From 2nd motif on in Rnd 18 work as for first motif except on the 4th and 5th ch-3 sps of 6 instead of making the ch-3 sp, ch 1, sc in corresponding ch-3 sp on adjacent motif, ch 1, continue in pattern. On the next half circle, join the 2nd and 3rd ch-3 sps of 6 in same manner.

FILL-IN MOTIF

Make 9

Rnd 1: With ecru, ch 5, join to form a ring, ch 1, work 12 sc in ring, join in beg sc. (12 sc)

Rnd 2: Ch 1, sc in same sc, ch 3, sk next sc, [sc in next sc, ch 3, sk next sc] rep around, join in beg sc. (6 ch-3 sps)

Rnd 3: Sl st into ch-3 sp, ch 1, [sc, hdc, 3 dc, hdc, sc] in each ch-3 sp around, join in beg sc, sl st behind petals. (6 petals)

Rnd 4: Ch 1, [sc behind and between next 2 petals, ch 4] rep around, join in beg sc. (6 ch-4 sps)

Rnd 5: Sl st into ch-4 sp, ch 1, [sc, dc, ch 1, 7 tr, ch 1, dc, sc] in each ch-4 sp around, join in beg sc. (6 petals)

Note: *Each of the 6 petals of Rnd 5 has 11 sts not counting the 2 ch-1 sps of each petal for a total of 66 sts. On the following rnd, work ch lps catching a thread of indicated st as you will be working 8 ch lps on the 6 petals.*

Rnd 6: Ch 1, sc behind first sc, [ch 5, sk next 7 sts, sc behind next st of petal] 7 times, ch 5, join in beg sc. (8 ch-5 lps worked on 6 petals)

Rnd 7: Sl st into ch sp, ch 3, 5 dc in same ch sp, ch 2, [6 dc in next ch sp, ch 2] rep around, join in 3rd ch of beg ch-3. (48 dc)

Rnd 8: Ch 3, dc in each of next 5 dc, dc in next ch, ch 2, dc in next ch, [dc in each of next 6 dc, dc in next ch, ch 2, dc in next ch] rep around, join in 3rd ch of beg ch-3. (64 dc)

Rnd 9: Ch 3, dc in each of next 6 dc, *dc in next ch, ch 2, dc in next ch **, dc in each of next 8 dc, rep from * around, ending last rep at **, dc in next dc, join in 3rd ch of beg ch-3. (80 dc)

Rnd 10: Ch 3, dc in next 2 dc, *ch 3, sl st in top of last dc (for p), dc in each of next 5 dc, dc in next ch, ch 2, pick up where 4 motifs join, sc in 2nd ch-3 sp from joining of 2 motifs, ch 2, dc in next ch on working motif, dc in each of next 5 dc, rep from * around, join in 3rd ch of beg ch-3, fasten off.

BORDER

Rnd 1: With pink, working in corner large motif, dc in first free ch-3 sp from joining of 2 motifs, *ch 7, tr in 7th ch from hook *, dc in next ch-3 sp, [rep from * to * 3 times, sk next 5 ch-3 sps, dc in next ch-3 sp, {ch 7, tr in 7th ch from hook, dc in next ch-3 sp} 3 times] rep around, join in beg dc.

Rnd 2: Sl st into center of ch-7 sp, *ch 7, sc in next ch sp *, [rep between *s to 3rd sp of last group of 3 ch-7 sps, dc in 3rd sp, tr cl over next 3 ch-7 sps, dc in next sp] rep around, join.

Rnd 3: Sl st to center of ch-7 sp, ch 10, sc in next sp, *ch 7, sc in next ch sp *, rep from * around, except ch 5, tr cl in 2 ch-7 sps above joining of each of 2 motifs, ch 5, sc in next sp, join in 3rd ch of beg ch-10.

Rnd 4: Sl st to center of next ch sp, ch 1, sc in same ch sp, [ch 7, sc in next ch sp] rep around, ending with ch 3, tr in beg sc.

Rnd 5: Ch 1, sc in same ch sp as joining, [ch 7, sc in next ch sp] rep around, ending with ch 3, tr in beg sc.

Rnd 6: Rep Rnd 5.

Rnd 7: Ch 1, sc in same ch sp as joining, ch 7, [sc in next ch sp, ch 7] rep around, join in beg sc.

Rnd 8: Sl st into ch sp, ch 1, *[4 sc, ch 4, sl st in 4th ch from hook, 4 sc in ch-7 sp] twice, 7 sc in next ch-7 sp, ch 7, drop lp from hook, insert hook in 4th previous sc, pick up dropped lp, draw through st on hook, in ch-7 lp just made work 4 sc, ch 4, sl st in 4th ch from hook and 4 sc, work 3 sc in same ch-7 lp as previous beg 7 sc, rep from * around, join in beg sc, fasten off. ■

ISLAND IN THE SKY DOILY ▸ CONTINUED FROM PAGE 87

ch-6 sp make 2 sc, p, sc, dc, p, dc, sc p 2 sc, in ch-10 sp work [4 sc, {p, 2 sc} twice, p, 4 sc], join, fasten off.

BORDER

Rnd 1: With white, working *in 3rd sc from p on first ch-18 sp with 2 p, [tr, ch 5, working next 2 tr tog, make tr in same place as last tr and next tr in next 4th sc, ch 5, tr in same place, ch 5, working next 2 tr tog, tr in 3rd sc following next picot

and tr in 3rd sc before next picot, ch 5] twice, tr, ch 5, working next 2 tr tog make tr in same place as last tr and next tr in 4th sc, ch 5, tr in same place, [ch 5, tr in 5th ch from hook] 3 times, tr in first sc of ch-6 sp at tip of sides, [ch 5, tr in 5th ch from hook] 3 times, tr in ch-6 sp on opposite side, [ch 5, tr in 5th ch from hook] 3 times, rep from * around, join.

Rnd 2: Ch 9, always working tr tog, tr in same place, [tr, ch 5, tr] in next set of joined tr, [tr, ch 5, tr] in next tr, work in this manner around, rep [tr, ch 5, tr] in 3rd ch of each ch-5 in the open areas and in each tr of 2 around ends at sides, join to 5th ch of beg ch-9.

Rnds 3–6: Work [tr, ch 5, tr] in each set of joined tr around, join to 5th ch of ch-9. At the end of Rnd 6, fasten off.

Rnd 7: Attach delft blue in any ch-5 sp, ch 1, beg in same ch sp [4 sc over next

ch-5 sp, ch 7, draw lp through top of previous sc, in ch sp just made, work 11 sc over sp, 4 sc in same ch-5 sp] rep around, join in beg sc, fasten off.

Rnd 8: With white, ch 10, draw lp through first ch, in sp make 5 sc, ch 3, 5 sc, ch 1, sc in 6th sc of blue lp made in Rnd 7, ch 1, 5 sc, ch 3, 5 sc in same sp, join to first sc, [ch 22, draw lp through 10th ch from hook, in sp just made work 5 sc, ch 3, 5 sc, ch 1, sc in 6th sc of blue lp made in Rnd 7, ch 1, 5 sc, ch 1, sc in last ch-3 sp on previous lp, ch 1, 5 sc in same sp, join to first sc] rep around, after last lp, ch 12, join in top of first lp.

Rnd 9: *Work 15 sc in ch-12 sp, 5 sc in next sp, ch 7, draw lp through 10th sc of previous 15 sc, in sp just made, work [3 sc, ch 3] 3 times, 3 sc in same sp, 10 sc in same sp as previous worked 5-sc, rep from * around, join in beg sc, fasten off. ∎

It's a foregone conclusion that everyone's own bundle of joy is the winner in the world of beautiful babies—with all prejudice aside, of course. And naturally the best all-around baby needs fashions and accessories that pack pizzazz! A new life is truly something to celebrate, and these precious designs

BEST-IN-SHOW BABIES

created for babies from newborn to toddler do it with style. From a darling dress, sweet little shoes, and a jazzy jacket and hat set to a snuggly snowsuit, snazzy sweaters and beautiful blankets, you're sure to find the perfect winning designs for your own best baby!

DESIGNS BY
JO ANN BURRINGTON

BABY SNOWSUIT AND PATCHWORK BLANKET

This adorable Eskimo-style snowsuit and quilted-look blanket are double-layered to make them extra-plush and cozy. The snowsuit hood is accented with faux fur, and the sleeves feature pull-off mitts. For a feminine touch, add pretty ribbon bows and dainty embroidered flowers!

BABY SNOWSUIT

GAUGE

With 2 strands of yarn, 18 dc = 4 inches; 9 dc rows = 4 inches; with 1 strand of yarn, 20 dc = 4 inches; 10 dc rows = 4 inches
Check gauge to save time.

PATTERN NOTES

Weave in loose ends as work progresses.
Join rnds with a sl st unless otherwise stated.
Ch-3 counts as first dc throughout.
To sew all seams, with RS of both pieces facing you, lay pieces side by side. With tapestry needle and matching yarn, sew edges tog by running needle in and out through one edge then through other edge and draw snug so pieces touch but do not form a ridge.

OUTER BACK

Make 2
Row 1: Holding 2 strands of mint tog,

INTERMEDIATE ●●●
SIZE Fits infant up to 27 inches long
MATERIALS
- Mary Maxim Baby Soft 3-ply baby yarn: 12 oz each mint #253006 and lemon #253005
- Size E/4 crochet hook or size needed to obtain gauge
- 50 inches ³/₁₆-inch wide green satin ribbon
- 1 yd ¹/₈-inch-wide elastic
- 3 x 16-inch piece white fake fur
- 1 yd gold narrow cord
- 2 yds iridescent white narrow flat cord
- ½-inch flat button
- 2 white or matching color 14-inch zippers
- Straight pins
- Stitch markers
- Sewing needle and thread
- Tapestry needle

beg at ankle, ch 34, dc in 4th ch from

---

hook, dc in each rem ch across. (32 dc)
Row 2: Ch 3, dc in each st across, turn.
Row 3: Rep Row 2.
Rows 4 & 5: Ch 3, 2 dc in next st, dc in each st across to last 2 sts, 2 dc in next st, dc in last st, turn. (36 dc)
Row 6: Rep Row 2.
Row 7: Ch 3, dc in each st across to last 2 sts, 2 dc in next st, dc in last st, turn. (37 dc)
Note: *As work progresses, place a st marker in the last st on Row 18 for center back seam.*
Rows 8–26: Rep Row 2.
Row 27: Ch 3, dc in each st across, ch 23 for sleeve, turn.
Row 28: Dc in 4th ch from hook, dc in each of next 19 chs, dc in each dc across, turn. (58 dc)
Row 29: Ch 3, dc in each dc across to last 2 sts, 2 dc in next st, dc in last st, turn.
Rows 30–32: Rep Row 2.
Row 33: Ch 3, dc in each st across to

last 3 sts, dc dec over next 2 sts, dc in last st, turn. (58 dc)

Row 34: Ch 1, sk first st, sl st in each of next 2 sts, sc in next st, hdc in next st, dc in each rem sts across, turn. (55 sts)

Row 35: Ch 3, dc in each st across to last 4 sts, hdc in next st, sc in next st, leaving last 2 sts unworked, turn. (53 sts)

Rows 36–41: Rep Rows 34 and 35. (38 sts)

Row 42: Ch 1, sl st in next 2 sts, sc in each of next 2 sts, hdc in each of next 2 sts, dc in each of next 24 sts, dc dec over next 2 sts, dc in next st, leaving rem 5 sts unworked for neck edge, turn. (29 sts)

Row 43: Ch 3 (mark beg ch-3 with st marker for shoulder seam), dc dec over next 2 sts, dc in each st across to last 5 sts, hdc in next st, sc in next st leaving last 3 sts unworked, turn. (25 sts)

Row 44: Ch 1, sl st in next 2 sts, sc in next st, hdc in next st, dc in each of next 12 sts, hdc in next 2 sts, sc in next 2 sts leaving last 5 sts unworked across shoulder, fasten off.

Sew center back seam from Row 18 to neck edge.

INNER BACK
Make 2

Rep outer back with 1 strand of lemon yarn.

OUTER FRONT
Rows 1–18 (first leg): With 2 strands of mint, rep Rows 1–18 of outer back. At the end of Row 18, fasten off.

Rows 1–18 (second leg): With 2 strands of mint, rep Rows 1–18 of outer back. At the end of Row 18, do not fasten off.

Row 19 (body): Ch 3, dc in each st across 2nd leg, with WS of last row on first leg facing, dc in each st across, turn. (74 dc)

Rows 20–28: Ch 3, dc in each st across, turn.

Row 29: Ch 3, [dc dec over next 2 sts] rep across to last st, dc in last st, turn. (38 dc)

Row 30: Ch 3, dc dec over next 2 sts, dc in each st across to last 3 sts, dc dec

over next 2 sts, dc in last st, turn. (36 dc)

Row 31: Ch 2, sk next dc, dc in each st across, turn. (35 dc)

Rows 32–46: Ch 2, dc in each st across leaving ch-2 of previous row unworked, turn. At the end of last rep, fasten off. (20 dc)

INNER FRONT

Rep outer front with 1 strand of lemon yarn.

OUTER SLEEVE FRONT
Make 2

Row 1: With 2 strands mint, ch 6, dc in 2nd ch from hook, dc in each of next 3 chs, [dc, sl st] in end ch, turn. (5 dc)

Rows 2 & 3: Ch 3, sk sl st, dc in next dc, 2 dc in each st across, turn. (20 dc)

Row 4: Ch 3, dc in each st across, turn.

Row 5: Rep Row 4.

Rows 6 & 7: Ch 3, 2 dc in next st, dc in each st across to last 3 sts, 2 dc in next st, dc in last st, turn. (24 dc)

Row 8: Rep Row 4.

Row 9: Ch 3, dc in each of next 2 sts, ch 18 (hand opening), sk next 18 sts, dc in each of next 3 dc, turn.

Row 10: Ch 3, dc in each dc and each ch across, turn. (24 dc)

Rows 11 & 12: Rep Row 4.

Rows 13–18: Ch 3, 2 dc in next st, dc in each rem st across, turn. (30 dc)

Row 19: Rep Row 4.

Row 20: Ch 3, 2 dc in next st, dc in each of next 20 sts, sc in next 8 sts, fasten off, turn. (31 sts)

Note: Place a st marker in end of last row for underarm seam.

Row 21: Sk first 8 sts, attach yarn with sl st in next dc, ch 1, sc in each of next 2 sts, hdc in next st, dc in each st across to last 3 sts, 2 dc in next st, dc in next st, leaving last st unworked, turn. (23 sts)

Row 22: Ch 3, dc in each of next 17 sts, hdc in next st, sc in next 2 sts, turn. (21 sts)

Row 23: Ch 1, sk first st, sc in next st, hdc in next st, dc in each st across to last 2 sts, 2 dc in next st, dc in last st, turn. (21 sts)

Row 24: Ch 3, dc in each st across to

last 5 sts, hdc in next st, sc in each of next 2 sts, turn. (19 sts)

Row 25: Ch 1, sk first st, sl st in next st, sc in next st, hdc in next st, dc in each rem st across, turn. (17 sts)

Rows 26 & 27: Rep Rows 24 and 25. (13 sts)

Row 28: Rep Row 24. (11 sts)

Row 29: Ch 1, sc in first st, hdc in next st (place a st marker on this last hdc for top of zipper), dc in each rem st across, turn. (11 sts)

Row 30: Ch 3, dc in each of next 7 sts, 3 dc in next st, turn. (11 sts)

Row 31: Ch 3, 2 dc in next st, dc in each st across to last 2 sts, 2 dc in next st, dc in last st, turn. (13 sts)

Row 32: Ch 1, sc in each of next 4 sts, hdc in next st, dc in each of next 6 sts, 2 dc in next st, dc in last st, turn. (14 sts)

Row 33: Ch 3, dc in each of next 4 sts, hdc in next st, sc dec over next 2 sts, leaving last 6 sts unworked for neck edge, turn. (7 sts)

Row 34: Ch 1, sk first st, [sl st, ch 3] in next st, dc in each of next 3 sts, 2 dc in next st, dc in last st, turn. (7 sts)

Rows 35–38: Ch 3, dc in each st across, turn. At the end of last rep, fasten off.

To sew shoulder seam, matching marker on Row 20 to outer back at last st before sleeve ch, sew edges of outer sleeve front to sleeve and shoulder of outer back. Rep with other outer sleeve front on other side of outer back.

INNER SLEEVE FRONT
Make 2

Rep outer sleeve front with 1 strand of lemon yarn and sew to inner back.

OUTER BOOTIE
Make 2

Rnd 1: Beg with sole, with 2 strands of mint, ch 18, dc in 3rd ch from hook, dc in each of next 14 chs, 3 dc in last ch, working on opposite side of foundation ch, dc in each of next 15 chs, join in top of beg ch. (34 dc)

Rnd 2: Ch 3, dc in same st as beg ch-3, dc in each of next 16 sts, 3 dc in next st, dc in each of next 16 sts, dc in same st as beg ch-3, join in 3rd ch of beg ch-3. (38 dc)

Rnd 3: Ch 3, dc in next st, [2 dc in next st, dc in next st] rep around, join in 3rd ch of beg ch-3. (56 dc)

Rnd 4: Ch 1, sc in each st around, join in beg sc.

Rnd 5: Working in back lps for this rnd only, ch 3, dc in each of next 23 sts, [dc dec over next 2 sts] 5 times across toe, dc in each rem st around, join in 3rd ch of beg ch-3. (51 dc)

Rnd 6: Ch 3, dc in each of next 22 sts, [dc dec over next 2 sts] 3 times, dc in each rem st around, join in 3rd ch of beg ch-3. (48 dc)

Rnds 7–11: Ch 3, dc in each dc around, join in 3rd ch of beg ch-3.

Rnd 12: Ch 1, sc in each st around, join in beg sc, fasten off.

INNER BOOTIE
Make 2

Rep outer bootie with 1 strand of lemon yarn.

FINISHING & ASSEMBLY

On outer front, embroider three 1-inch 5-petal flowers with iridescent white narrow flat cord using lazy-daisy st with first flower over center of Rows 39 and 40, 2nd flower on each end of Rows 35 and 36, about 1 inch in from the edge. With gold narrow cord, embroider a French knot at center of each flower.

With WS tog, hold inner front behind outer front, matching sts of last rows and working through both layers, attach a strand of mint with sc in first st of last row, sc in each st across, fasten off.

On each zipper, fold both top tabs to the back, tack in place with sewing needle and thread. With top of first zipper even with last rows on fronts, insert zipper between layers with inner front on WS of zipper and outer front on RS and edges of fronts ⅛-inch from teeth of zipper, pin top of zipper in place. Taking care not to stretch or gather either piece and keeping edges of fronts ⅛-inch from teeth of zipper, pin bottom of zipper to same rows on inner front and outer front. Pin remainder

of edges in place. With sewing needle and thread, taking care that sts do not show, sew pinned edge of zipper in place through all layers. Rep on opposite side of front with 2nd zipper.

With WS tog and matching edges, place inner back and sleeve fronts inside outer back and sleeve fronts, pin sleeve edges tog all around.

To join inner and outer hand openings, matching chs and chs, working through both layers, with Row 1 on sleeve fronts away from you, working in sps between sts worked into ch-18, join a strand of lemon with a sc in first sp, sc in each sp across, fasten off.

With Row 1 on sleeve fronts toward you, join a strand of lemon with a sl st in side of first st worked into ch-18, sc in next 18 sk sts, sl st in side of last st worked into ch-18, fasten off.

Cut 2 pieces elastic each 6 inches long. Stretching slightly, pin first piece across center back between inner and outer layers even with underarm ch, taking care that sts do not show, sew in place through all layers using sewing needle and thread. Sk next row upward and sew 2nd length of elastic piece to next row in similar manner.

On each side, matching ends of rows, sew inner front and inner back tog up to bottom of zipper; rep with outer front and outer back.

On each side of back and sleeves, insert zipper between layers with inner sleeve front on WS of zipper and outer sleeve front on RS. Pin top of zipper to marked sts on Row 29 of sleeve fronts; place edges of sts ⅛-inch from teeth of zipper and pin bottom of zipper to same rows on inner back and outer back. Pin rem edges in place. With sewing needle and thread, taking care that sts do not show, sew pinned edge of zipper in place through all layers.

On left sleeve, working through both layers, join a strand of mint yarn with sc in base of last worked st on Row 33 at neck edge, sc in ends of rows across to corner, 3 sc in corner, sc in each st across Row 38, 3 sc in corner, sc in ends

of rows across to top of zipper at front, fasten off.

On right sleeve, joining at top of zipper and ending at neck edge, rep as for left sleeve.

Cut 2 pieces elastic each 8 inches long. With each length of elastic, sew ends tog to form a ring.

With RS of both pieces facing out, with toes matching, place inner bootie inside outer bootie, place first elastic ring between layers, sew tops of Rnd 11 on inner and outer booties tog through the elastic.

To attach bootie to leg, with toes pointing toward front of snowsuit, gathering starting ch of inner leg to fit, sew top of Rnd 12 on inner bootie to starting ch of inner leg, rep in same manner sewing outer bootie on outer leg. Rep in same manner to attach 2nd bootie.

BOW
Make 5

Cut a 10-inch piece of green ribbon, run under a st on outer layer, with ends of ribbon even in length, tie a 2-inch bow leaving ends for streamers, trim ends. Tie a bow at center front of each bootie and a bow just below each flower on front.

OUTER HOOD
Center panel
Row 1: With 2 strands of mint, ch 16, dc in 4th ch from hook, dc in each rem ch across, turn. (14 dc)

Rows 2–33: Ch 3, dc in each dc across, turn.

Row 34: Ch 1, sc in each dc across, fasten off.

Side panel
Make 2

Row 1: With 2 strands of mint, ch 23, dc in 4th ch from hook, dc in each rem ch across, turn. (21 dc)

Note: *Place a st marker in sk ch-3 of Row 1 for back edge.*

Row 2: Ch 3, dc in each dc across, turn.

Row 3: Ch 3, 2 dc in next dc, dc in each rem dc across, turn. (22 dc)

Rows 4–13: Rep Rows 2 and 3. (27 dc)

► CONTINUED ON PAGE 120

TUNISIAN TAPESTRY JACKET & HAT

A colorful mix of sport weight yarn worked in Tunisian crochet creates the bright, tweedlike pattern in this adorable jacket and hat. Its classic style makes this set a versatile and always fashionable addition to a little girl's wardrobe!

GAUGE

With hook size H, 20 sts = 4 inches; 16 rows = 4 inches
Check gauge to save time.

PATTERN NOTES

Weave in loose ends as work progresses. Join rnds with a sl st unless otherwise stated.

To change color at the left edge, form the turning ch at the beg of the return row with the new color. When the color is changed at the left edge at the beg of every R Row, preserve the ch selvedge by inserting the hook under the last thread and drawing the new color thread up from under the current color and laying it over the hook before drawing a lp through as usual.

PATTERN STITCHES

Tunisian simple st (tss): F Row: Row is worked from right to left in which all lps are picked up onto hook by inserting hook under front vertical bar of each st. At the end of the row, insert hook under last vertical bar along with the st just behind it. End every F Row this way

ADVANCED ● ● ●

SIZE 6 months (12 months, 18 months, 2 years)
Chest: 21½ (22½, 23½, 24) inches
Length: 9 (9½, 10, 10¾) inches
Hat: 15 (16, 17, 18) inches in diameter

MATERIALS

- Zitron Polo Skacel sport weight yarn (1¾ oz per ball): 3 (3, 5, 5) balls turquoise #76 (MC), 2 balls each mint green #4 (A), yellow #46 (B) and pink #52 (C)
- Size H/8 afghan crochet hook or size needed to obtain gauge
- Sizes G/6 and H/8 crochet hooks
- 5 (⅝-inch) daisy buttons
- 1½-inch daisy button
- 1 yd ⅞-inch-wide yellow ribbon (optional)
- Stitch marker
- Straight pins
- Tapestry needle

regardless of pattern st.

R Row: Row is worked from left to right in which sts are discarded, beg with a ch 1, and followed by [yo, draw through 2 lps on hook] rep across until 1 lp

remains. This rem st counts as the first st of the next row. This is always the R Row, regardless of the pattern st.

Tunisian purl st (tps): Bring yarn to front with hook, insert into vertical bar as usual, yo and draw up a lp.

Cross 2: Sk 1 st, tss in next st, tss in sk st.

Tss dec: Work tss in 2 vertical bars at one time.

Tss inc: Insert hook into bump behind next st, draw up a lp.

Bind off: Working under vertical thread, sl st or sc in each st across.

TWIST ST PATTERN

Forward row: *1 tps, cross 2, rep from * across row, ending with tss in last st.

Return row: Ch 1 in new color and complete row as usual.

COLOR SEQUENCE

Work 1 R and F Row in MC between each CC R and F Row,
2 sets of R and F Rows with A, [2 sets of R and F Rows with B, 1 set of R and F Rows with C, 3 sets of R and F Rows with A] rep for pattern.

JACKET

BACK

Foundation row: With afghan hook and MC, ch 56 (59, 61, 62), draw up 1 lp in the back lp of 2nd ch from hook and in each ch across. R Row (A), ch 1, *yo, draw through 2 lps, rep from * across. Continue to follow twist st pattern, work 4½ inches or desired length to underarm.

Armhole shaping

Sl st in pattern over 5 (5, 6, 6) sts, work in pattern to within 5 (5, 6, 6) sts, turn and complete R Row as usual. Continue to work even in pattern st as established on 46 (49, 49, 50) sts until back measures 8 (8½, 9, 9¾) inches.

Neck shaping

Maintaining pattern, work across 13 (14, 14, 14) sts, turn and complete R Row as usual. On next F Row, work across 11 (12, 12, 12) sts, tss dec, turn and complete R Row as usual. (12, 13, 13, 13 sts) For next F Row, work across 10 (11, 11, 11) sts, tss dec, turn and complete R Row as usual. (11, 12, 12, 12 sts) For next F Row, bind off shoulder sts in pattern. Sl st along right neckline edge and across 20 (21, 22, 22) sts of center back, then completing F Row as usual on rem 13 (14, 14, 14) sts, turn and complete R Row as usual. For the next 2 F Rows, tss dec and complete entire rows as usual. For next F Row, bind off 11 (12, 12, 12) shoulder sts.

RIGHT FRONT

With afghan hook and MC, ch 44 (47, 49, 50) and work as for back, dec along center front edge as follows: At the beg of every other F Row, bind off 2 sts 12 (13, 13, 13) times, tss dec 4 (4, 5, 6) times. (11, 12, 12, 12 sts) *At the same time,* bind off for right armhole the same as for back. Work even until front measures the same as back from beg foundation ch.

LEFT FRONT

Work as for right front, reversing center front edge as follows: at the end of every other F Row, leave 2 sts unworked 12 (13, 13, 13) times, tss dec 4 (4, 5, 6)

times. (11, 12, 12, 12 sts) *At the same time,* bind off for left armhole the same as for back. Work even until front measures the same as back.

SLEEVE

Make 2

With afghan hook size H and MC, ch 32 (32, 33, 33), work in tss, inc 1 st each end of every 3rd row 0 (0, 12, 16) times and every 4th row 8 (10, 0, 0) times. (48, 52, 57, 65 sts)

Work even until sleeve measures 8 (9½, 10¼, 11) inches, bind off.

FINISHING

Sew shoulder seams. Set sleeve into armhole opening. Sew side and sleeve seams closed.

Edging

Note: When working Rnd 1, add sts where you need them by occasionally working ch 1 between sc sts to prevent sts from elongating.

Rnd 1 (RS): With hook size H, attach MC to bottom edge of sweater at side seam with a sl st, ch 1, work sc around lower, front and neckline edges, working an extra sc at corners. Lap right front over left front and mark 5 button positions, first ½ inch from top at point of overlapped fronts and last ½ inch from bottom edge and the rem 3 evenly sp between, join, fasten off, turn.

Rnd 2 (WS): Attach B, ch 3 (counts as first dc), [sl st in next st, dc in next st] rep around, *at the same time,* work buttonholes at marked sts on right front edge with [sl st in next st, ch 3, sk next 2 sts, sl st in next st] rep from each buttonhole at marked st, join in same st as beg ch-3, fasten off.

Sew buttons to correspond with buttonholes.

Sleeve Edging

Make 2

Rnd 1 (RS): With hook size H, attach MC in opposite side of foundation ch at sleeve seam, ch 1, sc evenly sp around sleeve opening, join in beg sc, fasten off, turn.

► CONTINUED ON PAGE 121

SWEET SUMMER SHOES

Dress up a pretty summer frock with these adorable, ankle-strap shoes adorned with ribbon ties. Stitched in size 10 thread in a lacy, open pattern, they'll keep your baby girl's feet cool and chic on warm-weather outings!

GAUGE

10 sc = 1 inch; 9 sc rows = 1 inch
Check gauge to save time.

PATTERN NOTES

Weave in loose ends as work progresses.
Join rnds with a sl st unless otherwise stated.
Ch-3 counts as first dc throughout.

SOLE

Rnd 1: Beg at toe end of sole, with white, ch 12, sc in 2nd ch from hook, sc in each rem ch across, turn. (11 sc)

BEGINNER ●●○

SIZE Newborn (3 months, 6 months)

MATERIALS

- Crochet cotton size 10:100 yds each pink and white
- Size 5 steel crochet hook or size needed to obtain gauge
- 25 (27, 29) inches ⅛-inch-wide white ribbon
- Stitch marker
- Tapestry needle

Rows 2–5 (2–6, 2–7): Working in back lps only, ch 1, 2 sc in first sc, sc in each sc across to last sc, 2 sc in last sc, turn. (19, 21, 23 sc)

Rows 6–12 (7–16, 8–20): Working in back lps only, ch 1, sc in each st across, turn.

Rows 13 & 14 (17 & 18, 21 & 22): Ch 1, working in back lps only, ch 1, sc dec over next 2 sc, sc in each sc across to last 2 sc, sc dec over next 2 sc, turn. (15, 17, 19 sc)

Rows 15–21 (19–27, 23–33): Working

► CONTINUED ON PAGE 123

HIS & HER GINGHAM AFGHANS

DESIGNS BY
KAREN RIGSBY

Flowers for her, balloons for him … one enchanting design can be made for boy or girl with a change of colors, different embellishments, and a ruffled or plain border. Gingham and lattice patterns are superbly combined for a look that's uniquely different!

GAUGE

Center section, 14 sts = 4 inches; 14 sc rows = 4 inches; gingham section, 16 sts = 4 inches; 14 rows in sc = 4 inches Check gauge to save time.

PATTERN NOTES

Weave in loose ends as work progresses. Join rnds with a sl st unless otherwise stated.

The center section and gingham section of these afghans are crocheted the same, hers with soft antique rose and white, and his with powder blue and white. Pattern will indicate her color, simply use powder blue for his. Each afghan has a different border.

AFGHAN CENTER SECTION

Row 1: With soft antique rose, ch 72, sc in 2nd ch from hook, sc in each rem ch across, turn. (71 sc)

Rows 2–72: Following Diagram 1, reading RS rows from right to left and WS

SIZE Hers: 47 x 48 inches
His: 46 x 48 inches

MATERIALS

- Phentex Merit 3-ply weight yarn (50g per ball): Hers: 9 balls white #00101, 8 balls soft antique rose #11425, 2 balls glacier #00750, small amounts of each purple, mauve, powder blue and dark rose; His: 10 balls white #00101, 8 balls powder blue #00820, 2 balls glacier #00750, small amounts of each purple, mauve, blue, apple green and lime green
- Size H/8 crochet hook or size needed to obtain gauge
- 2²/₃ yds ³/₈-inch-wide aqua picot-edged ribbon (hers), powder blue ribbon (his)
- 1¹/₃ yds ¹/₈-inch-wide aqua ribbon (hers)
- Yarn needle

rows from left to right, ch 1, work sc in each st across working with both soft antique rose and white across each row,

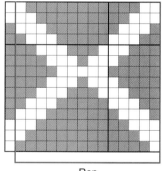

Rep

Diagram 1

STITCH & COLOR KEY
☐ 1 sc with white
▨ 1 sc with rose (hers) or blue (his)

changing colors as diagram indicates and working over color not in use, turn at the end of each row.

Row 73: Ch 1, with soft antique rose, sc in each st across, fasten off.

Trim

Rnd 1 (RS): Attach glacier in top left corner, ch 1, reverse sc in first st, [ch

1, sk next st, reverse sc in next st] rep across edge, *working along side edge, [ch 1, reverse sc] for every 2 row ends *, working across opposite side of foundation ch, ch 1, reverse sc in first ch, [ch 1, sk next ch, reverse sc in next ch] rep across, rep from * to * across rem side edge of rows, join in beg sc, fasten off.

AFGHAN GINGHAM SECTION

Note: When working a solid color row, carry the unused color across the back to be in place for next row. Work over unused yarn in each row and the unused yarn of the ch sp in the previous row.

Row 1: With white, ch 162, 1 sc in 4th from hook (counts as first sc, ch-1 sp), [ch 1, sk next ch, sc in next ch] rep across, turn. (80 sc)

Row 2: Ch 1, sc in first ch sp, ch 1, sc in next ch sp, *with soft antique rose, [ch 1, sc in next ch sp] 4 times **, with white, [ch 1, sc in next ch sp] 4 times, rep from * across, ending last rep at **, turn. (10 groups each color)

Row 3: With white, ch 3 (counts as first sc, ch-1 sp), sc in next ch sp, [ch 1, sk next sc, sc in next ch sp] rep across, ending with ch 1, sc in last sc, turn.

Rows 4 & 5: Rep Rows 2 and 3.

Row 6: Rep Row 2.

Row 7: With soft antique rose, rep Row 3.

Row 8: Starting with white, rep Row 2.

Rows 9–12: Rep Rows 7 and 8.

Row 13: Rep Row 3.

Rows 14–17: Rep Rows 2 and 3

Row 18: Rep Row 2.

Rows 19–24: Rep Rows 7–12.

Rows 25–30: Rep Rows 13–18.

Right edge gingham section

Continue in pattern as established, working over 5 squares only (39 sts), turn. (20 sc; 19 ch-1 sps)

Work in pattern until 72 rows are completed on this section, fasten off.

Left edge gingham section

With RS facing, attach soft antique rose in 39th st from left edge (this is a ch-1 sp), continue in pattern until the same length as right edge, fasten off.

Top edge gingham section

With RS facing, attach soft antique rose and work across 39 sts in pattern, ch 81, work across the last 39 sts, placing the first sc in the first ch sp. At the end of the row, attach white, turn.

Work in pattern across the row, taking care to work into the back of the ch sts and not allowing them to twist. Work 28 more rows in pattern, fasten off.

JOINING SECTIONS

Note: The center section is 71 sts wide, while the opening in the gingham section is 81 sts wide. To ensure a flat joining, sk 10 sts evenly sp along gingham section on top and bottom edges.

With WS facing, using soft antique rose, sl st center section to gingham section, when seen from the front, the joining sts will be under the glacier trim worked around the center section.

OUTER TRIM

Rnd 1: Rep Rnd 1 of trim the same as for afghan center section.

HER BORDER

Rnd 1: Attach white in ch sp at any corner of outer trim, ch 3 (counts as first dc), [dc, ch 2, 2 dc] in same ch sp, ch 1, sk next ch sp, [[2 dc, ch 2, 2 dc} shell in next ch sp, ch 1, sk next ch sp] rep around, join in 3rd ch of beg ch-3. (147 shells)

Rnd 2: Sl st into ch-2 sp of shell, [ch 3, dc, ch 2, 2 dc] in same ch-2 sp, ch 1, [{2 dc, ch 2, 2 dc} shell in next ch-2 sp of shell, ch 1] rep around, working in center corner ch-1 sp of each corner, ch 1, shell in ch-1 sp, ch 1 to keep work flat, join in 3rd ch of beg ch-3.

Rnds 3 & 4: Sl st into ch-2 sp of shell, [ch 3, dc, ch 2, 2 dc] in same ch-2 sp of shell, ch 1, [{2 dc, ch 2, 2 dc} in next ch-2 sp of next shell, ch 1] rep around, join in 3rd ch of beg ch-3. At the end of Rnd 4, fasten off.

Rnd 5 (RS): Attach soft antique rose in first dc of any corner shell, ch 1, sc in same dc, *2 sc in next dc, ch 3, sl st in first ch of ch-3, 2 sc in next dc, 1 sc in

next dc, ch 1 **, sc in next dc, rep from * around, ending last rep at **, join in beg sc, fasten off.

HIS BORDER

Rnd 1: Attach white in any corner ch sp, ch 1, [sc, ch 1, sc] in same corner ch sp, ch 1, [sc in next ch sp, ch 1] rep around, working [sc, ch 1, sc] in each corner ch-1 sp, join in beg sc.

Rnd 2: Ch 2 (counts as first hdc throughout), hdc in same st as beg ch-2, 3 hdc in corner ch sp, 2 hdc in next st, [hdc in next ch sp, hdc in next st] rep around, working 2 hdc in first st of corner, 3 hdc in corner ch sp, 2 hdc in next st, join in 2nd ch of beg ch-2.

Rnds 3 & 4: Ch 2, hdc in each hdc around, working 2 hdc in first hdc of corner, 3 hdc in center hdc of each corner and 2 hdc in 3rd hdc of corner, join in 2nd ch of beg ch-2.

Rnds 5–7: Ch 2, hdc in each st around, working at each corner, dc in first st of corner, 3 dc in center st, dc in next st of corner, join in 2nd ch of beg ch-2. At the end of last rep, fasten off.

Rnd 8: Attach powder blue in first dc before corner 3-dc group, ch 1, sc in same st, hdc in next st, dc in next st, ch 3, sl st in first ch of ch-3, *dc in next st, hdc in next st **, sc in each of next 2 sts, hdc in next st, dc in next st, ch 3, sl st in first ch of ch-3, rep from * around, ending last rep at **, sc in next st, join in beg sc, fasten off.

HER FINISHING
Flower

Note: Make 5 flowers for each corner in the following colors, 1 each purple, mauve and powder blue and 2 dark rose.

Rnd 1: Ch 5, join to form a ring, [ch 3, 2 tr in ring, ch 3, sl st in ring] 5 times, leaving a length of yarn, fasten off.

Leaf
Make 8

Rnd 1: With glacier, ch 10, tr in 4th ch from hook, dc in each of next 2 chs, hdc in each of next 2 chs, sc in each of next 2 chs, ch 1, working on opposite

► CONTINUED ON PAGE 122

DESIGN BY
ROSEANNE KROPP

SUNDAY-BEST BIB

For any dress-up occasion, this lacy bib featuring sweet filet hearts and pretty ribbon bows is the perfect accessory for a Sunday-best outfit. It's dainty and delightful in size 10 thread and makes a classy gift for a special baby girl!

GAUGE

9 dc = 1 inch; 4 dc rows = 1 inch
Check gauge to save time.

PATTERN NOTES

Weave in loose ends as work progresses.
Join rnds with a sl st unless otherwise
stated.
Graph-reading knowledge is necessary.

BIB

Row 1: Starting at bottom of bib with
white, ch 40, 2 dc in 4th ch from hook,
dc in each of next 35 chs, 3 dc in last ch,
turn. (41 dc)

Row 2: Ch 3, 2 dc in first dc, dc in each
dc across to last dc, 3 dc in last dc, turn.
(45 dc)

Row 3: Ch 3, 2 dc in first dc, dc in each
of next 8 dc, ch 1, sk 1 dc, dc in each of
next 34 dc, 3 dc in last dc, turn.

Row 4: Ch 3, 2 dc in first dc, dc in each
of next 34 dc, ch 1, sk 1 dc, dc in next
dc, dc in ch-1 sp, dc in next dc, ch 1, sk
1 dc, dc in each of next 8 dc, 3 dc in last
dc, turn.

Row 5: Ch 3, 2 dc in first dc, dc in each
of next 8 dc, ch 1, sk 1 dc, dc in next dc,
dc in ch-1 sp, dc in each of next 3 dc, dc
in next ch-1 sp, dc in next dc, ch 1, sk 1

BEGINNER ●●●
SIZE 8½ x 11 inches

MATERIALS

- J. & P. Coats Knit-Cro-Sheen
  crochet cotton size 10: 300 yds
  white #1, 100 yds shaded pinks
  #15, small amounts each mid rose
  #46A and mint green #28
- Size 7 steel crochet hook or size
  needed to obtain gauge
- 1½ yds ¼-inch-wide pink picot-
  edged ribbon
- Sewing needle and thread

dc, dc in each of next 34 dc, 3 dc in last
dc, turn.

Row 6: Ch 3, 2 dc in first dc, dc in each
of next 34 dc, ch 1, sk 1 dc, dc in next
dc, dc in next ch-1 sp, dc in each of next
7 dc, dc in next ch-1 sp, dc in next dc, ch
1, sk 1 dc, dc in each of next 8 dc, 3 dc
in last dc, turn.

Rows 7–28: Working in basic pattern of
previous rows, follow graph as indicated,
turn at the end of each row, beg each row
with ch 3.

Neck shaping

Row 29: Ch 3, dc in each of next 15
dc, [yo, draw up a lp in next st, yo, draw
through 2 lps on hook] 3 times, yo, draw

through all 4 lps on hook (ending bl
dec), turn.

Row 30: Ch 2, [yo, draw up a lp in next
st, yo, draw through 2 lps on hook] twice,
yo, draw through all 3 lps on hook (beg bl
dec), dc in each of next 14 dc, turn.

Row 31: Ch 3, dc in each of next 11 dc,
ending bl dec, turn.

Rows 32 & 33: Ch 3, dc in each dc
across, turn.

Row 34: Ch 3, dc in each of next 9 dc,
ending bl dec, turn.

Row 35: Beg bl dec, dc in each of next 8
dc, fasten off.

With WS of Row 28 facing, sk next 23
dc of Row 28, attach white in next dc, ch
2, work beg bl dec, dc in each of next 16
dc, turn. Finish opposite neckline shaping
to correspond.

Edging

Row 1: With RS facing, attach white to
top of beg ch-3 of row just finished, ch 4
(counts as first dc, ch 1), [sk next dc, dc
in next dc, ch 1] 4 times, [dc, ch 1, dc] in
end of row, working along side of bib, ch
1, dc in end of each row, work 2 extra sps
along bottom curve to turn corner, dc in
first ch of opposite side of foundation ch,
[ch 1, sk next ch, dc in next ch] 18 times,
work along left side of bib to correspond,
attach shaded pinks, fasten off white, turn.

Row 2: Ch 1, sc in same st, *ch 1, sk
next ch-1 sp, [tr, ch 1] 4 times in next ch-
1 sp **, sk next dc and ch-1 sp, sc in next
dc, ch 2, sc in next dc, rep from * around
outer edge of bib, ending last rep at **, sc
under beg ch-4 of Row 1 of edging, turn.

Row 3: Ch 1, sc in same sc, p of ch 3,
hdc in 3rd ch from hook, *[dc in next tr, p]
4 times, sc in next sc **, sl st in next ch-
2 sp, sc in next sc, p, rep from * around
outer edge of bib, ending last rep at **,
fasten off.

TIES & NECKLINE EDGING

With WS of bib facing, attach mid rose
to sc at end of Row 3 of edging on right
edge of bib, ch 1, sc in same st, work 2
sc evenly at the end of each row on neck
edge and 1 sc in each st, ending with sc in

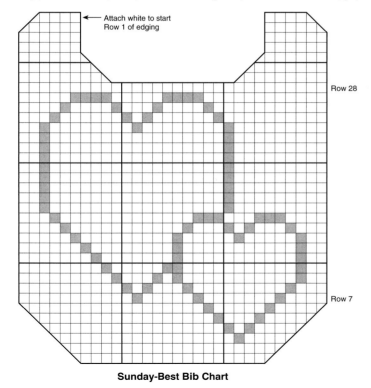

Attach white to start
Row 1 of edging

Row 28

Row 7

Sunday-Best Bib Chart

▶ CONTINUED ON PAGE 122

DESIGNS BY
SHARON HATFIELD

FAST & FUN HOODED SWEATERS

Simplicity with style is the focus of these two adorable sweaters that work up easily in worsted weight yarn using a variety of simple stitch patterns. By simply changing hooks, they can each be made in three different sizes from 6 to 18 months!

RED, WHITE & BLACK SWEATER

GAUGE

7 dc with hook size G = 2 inches; 3 dc with hook size H = 1 inch, 5 dc with hook size I = 2 inches
Check gauge to save time.

PATTERN NOTES

Weave in loose ends as work progresses.
Join rnds with a sl st unless otherwise stated.

Ch-3 counts as first dc throughout.

Use hook size G for size 6 months, hook size H for size 12 months and hook size I for size 18 months.

PATTERN STITCHES

Shell: 5 dc in indicated st.
Beg shell: Ch 3, 4 dc in same st.

SWEATER

Row 1: Beg at neckline with hook size G (H, I) and cherry red, ch 40, dc in 4th

BEGINNER ○●●

SIZE 6 (12, 18) months
Finished chest: 20 (22, 24) inches

MATERIALS
- Coats & Clark Red Heart Super Saver worsted weight yarn: 7 oz cherry red #319, 4 oz black #312, 2 oz white #311
- Sizes G/6 (H/8, I/9) crochet hooks or sizes needed to obtain gauge
- 6 (¾-inch) white buttons
- 3-inch cardboard
- Sewing needle and thread
- Yarn needle

ch from hook, dc in each of next 4 chs (front), shell in next ch, dc in each of next 4 chs (sleeve), shell in next ch, dc in each of next 14 chs (back), shell in next ch, dc in each of next 4 chs (sleeve), shell in next ch, dc in each of next 6 chs (front), turn. (54 dc)

Rows 2–4: Ch 3, [dc in each dc to center dc of next shell, shell in center dc of shell] 4 times, dc in each rem dc across

front, turn. (102 dc)

Row 5: Ch 3, dc in each of next 14 dc, sk next 20 dc (sleeve), dc in each of next 32 dc, sk next 20 dc (sleeve), dc in each of next 15 dc, turn. (62 dc)

Row 6: Ch 3, dc in next dc, [2 dc in next dc, dc in each of next 2 dc] rep across, turn. (82 dc)

Row 7: Ch 3, dc in each dc across, turn.

Rows 8–14: Rep Row 7. At the end of Row 14, fasten off.

Row 15: With white, rep Row 7, fasten off.

Row 16: With black, rep Row 7, fasten off.

Row 17: With white, rep Row 7, fasten off.

Row 18: Attach cherry red, ch 1, sc in each sc across, dec 1 sc at back of sweater, turn. (81 sc)

Row 19: Ch 3, sk next sc, shell in next sc, sk next sc, [sc in next sc, sk next sc, shell in next sc, sk next sc] rep across, ending with dc in last sc, fasten off. (20 shells)

SLEEVE

Make 2

Rnd 1 (RS): Working in rem sk sts of Row 4, attach cherry red at underarm in side edge of Row 5, ch 3, dc in same st, dc in each of next 20 dc of Row 4, 2 dc in side edge of Row 5, join in 3rd ch of beg ch-3, turn. (24 dc)

Rnd 2: Ch 3, dc in each dc around, join in 3rd ch of beg ch-3.

Rnds 3–5: Rep Rnd 2. At the end of Rnd 5, fasten off.

Rnd 6: With white, rep Rnd 2, fasten off.

Rnd 7: With black, rep Rnd 2, fasten off.

Rnd 8: With white, rep Rnd 2, fasten off.

Rnd 9: Attach cherry red, ch 1, sc in same dc as beg ch-1, sc dec over next 2 dc, [sc in next dc, sc dec over next 2 dc] 7 times, join in beg sc. (16 sc)

Rnd 10: Beg shell in same st as joining, sk next sc, sc in next sc, sk next sc, [shell in next sc, sk next sc, sc in next sc, sk next sc] 3 times, join in 3rd ch of beg ch-3, fasten off. (4 shells)

RIGHT FRONT TRIM

Row 1 (RS): Attach black at bottom right front in side edge of Row 19, ch 1, 2 sc in same sp as beg ch-1, 2 sc in next row,

[sc, ch 2, sc] in next row, [2 sc in each of next 2 rows, {sc, ch 2, sc} in next row] 5 times, 2 sc in next row, fasten off. (38 sc; 6 ch-2 sps)

LEFT FRONT TRIM

Row 1 (RS): Attach black at top edge in side edge of Row 1, ch 1, work 2 sc over each row to bottom edge, fasten off. (38 sc)

HOOD

Row 1 (RS): Working in opposite side of foundation ch at neckline, attach cherry red, ch 1, work 36 sc evenly sp across neckline opening, turn. (36 sc)
Row 2: Ch 3, [2 dc in next sc, dc in next sc] 17 times, 2 dc in last sc, turn. (54 dc)
Row 3: Ch 3, dc in each dc across, turn.
Rows 4–14: Rep Row 3. At the end of Row 14, leaving a length of yarn, fasten off. Fold Row 14 in half and matching sts, sew hood seam closed.

Hood trim
Row 1 (RS): Attach black in side edge of Row 1 of hook, ch 1, work 38 sc evenly sp around hood opening, fasten off, turn.
Row 2: Attach white, ch 1, sc in each st across, fasten off.
Roll hood edge back.

Pompom
Wrap 1 strand each white and black around the 3 inch cardboard 40 times, slide strands off cardboard and tie a length of yarn around center of bundle tightly, clip loops, trim pompom as needed. Sew pompom to center back point of hood.

FINISHING

Sew buttons opposite buttonholes.

VARIEGATED & RED SWEATER

GAUGE

7 dc with hook size G = 2 inches; 3 dc with hook size H = 1 inch; 5 dc with hook size I = 2 inches
Check gauge to save time.

PATTERN NOTES

Weave in loose ends as work progresses.

SIZE 6 (12, 18) months
Finished chest: 20 (22, 24) inches
MATERIALS
- Coats & Clark Red Heart Super Saver worsted weight yarn: 7 oz mexicana #950, 3 oz hot red #390
- Sizes G/6 (H/8, I/9) crochet hooks or sizes needed to obtain gauge
- 5 (¾-inch) yellow buttons
- Sewing needle and thread
- Yarn needle

Join rnds with a sl st unless otherwise stated. Ch-3 counts as first dc throughout. Use hook size G for size 6 months, hook size H for size 12 months and hook size I for size 18 months.

PATTERN STITCHES

Shell: 5 dc in indicated st.
Beg shell: Ch 3, 4 dc in same st.

SWEATER

Rows 1–6: With mexicana, rep Rows 1–6 of red, white and black sweater. (82 dc)
Rows 7–13: Ch 3, dc in each dc across, turn. At the end of Row 13, fasten off.
Row 14 (WS): Attach hot red, ch 3, [fpdc around next dc, bpdc around next dc] rep across, ending with dc in last st, turn.
Row 15 (RS): Ch 3, fpdc around each fpdc, bpdc around each bpdc across row, ending with dc in last st, do not turn.

RIGHT FRONT BUTTON EDGE

Row 1 (RS): Ch 1, work 29 sc evenly sp up right front, turn. (29 sc)
Rows 2 & 3: Ch 1, sc in each of next 29 sc, turn. At the end of Row 3, fasten off.

LEFT FRONT BUTTONHOLE EDGE

Row 1 (RS): Attach hot red at neckline in side edge of Row 1, ch 1, work 29 sc evenly sp down left front, turn. (29 sc)
Row 2: Ch 1, sc in each of next 2 sc, [ch 2, sk next 2 sc, sc in each of next 4 sc] 4 times, ch 2, sk next 2 sc, sc in last sc, turn. (5 buttonholes)

Row 3: Ch 1, sc in each sc and 2 sc in each ch-2 sp across, fasten off.

SLEEVE

Make 2
Rnd 1 (RS): With cherry red, rep Rnd 1 of red, white and black sweater. (24 dc)
Rnds 2–6: Ch 3, dc in each dc around, join in 3rd ch of beg ch-3. At the end of Rnd 6, fasten off.
Rnd 7: Attach mexicana, ch 3, [fpdc around next dc, bpdc around next dc] rep around, join in 3rd ch of beg ch-3.
Rnd 8: Ch 3, [fpdc around fpdc, bpdc around bpdc] rep around, join in 3rd ch of beg ch-3, fasten off.

HOOD

Row 1 (RS): Sk the 3 rows of right front edge and working in opposite side of foundation ch of neckline, attach mexicana, ch 1, sc in same st as beg ch-1, sc in each of next 6 sts, [2 sc in next st, sc in next st] 11 times, sc in each of next 7 sts, do not work across 3 rows of left front edge, turn. (47 sc)
Row 2: Ch 3, dc dec over next 2 sts, dc in each st across to last 3 sts, dc dec over next 2 sts, dc in last st, turn. (45 dc)
Rows 3–5: Rep Row 2. (39 dc)
Rows 6–13: Ch 3, dc in each dc across, turn. At the end of Row 13, leaving a length of yarn, fasten off.
Fold Row 13 of hood in half, with rem length, sew seam closed.

Hood trim
Row 1 (RS): Attach hot red in side edge of Row 1 of hood, ch 1, work 50 sc evenly sp around hood opening, turn.
Row 2: Ch 3, dc in each sc across, turn.
Row 3: Ch 3, [fpdc around next dc, bpdc around next dc] rep across, ending with dc in last st, turn.
Row 4: Ch 3, fpdc around each fpdc, bpdc around each bpdc across, ending with dc in last st, fasten off.
Fold hood trim back.

FINISHING

Sew buttons opposite buttonholes. ∎

DESIGN BY
KATHLEEN POWER JOHNSON

HYACINTH'S PARTY DRESS

A swish of pretty fabric topped with a dainty crocheted bodice makes this sweet and simple party frock a fun, easy project. Match favorite colors of crochet thread to any fabric print for a coordinated look to suit any holiday or special occasion!

GAUGE

16 sts = 2 inches; 9 rows = 2 inches
Check gauge to save time.

PATTERN NOTE

Weave in loose ends as work progresses.

PATTERN STITCHES

P: Sc, ch 3, sl st in top of sc.
Extended dc: Work dc in corresponding st 2 rows below.

BODICE PATTERN

Row 1 (RS): With MC, ch 2, 3 dc in 3rd sc, [ch 1, sk 3 sts, 3 dc in next st] rep across, ending with 2 dc in last st, turn.
Row 2: With MC, ch 2, [dc in next ch-1 sp, extended dc in center sk sc, dc in same ch-1 sp, ch 1] rep across, ending with 2 dc in top of ch-2, change color, turn.
Row 3: Ch 2, [dc in next ch-1 sp, extended dc into center dc 2 rows below, dc in same ch-1 sp, ch 1] rep across, ending with 2 dc in top of ch-2, turn.

BEGINNER ○●●
SIZE 6 months (12 months, 2, 4, 6)
Chest: 19 (20, 23, 25, 27) inches
Bodice length: 5 (5½, 6, 7, 7¼) inches
Back neck to hem: 14½ (17, 20, 22½, 24½) inches

MATERIALS

- DMC Pearl cotton size 5 (27.3 yds per skein): 7 (8, 10, 11, 13) skeins snow white #B5200 (MC), 3 (4, 4, 5, 5) skeins each periwinkle #341 (A) and celery #3348 (B)
- Size 7 steel crochet hook or size needed to obtain gauge
- ½ (½, ¾, ¾, ¾) yd 44/45 inches wide cotton or cotton blend fabric, preshrunk
- 6 (6, 8, 8, 8) ³/₈-inch heart shape buttons
- Matching thread and needle or sewing machine
- Straight pins

Rep Row 3 for bodice pattern, working color sequence of MC, MC, A and B unless otherwise stated.

BODICE BACK

Foundation row: With MC, ch 80 (84, 96, 104, 112), sc in 2nd ch from hook, sc in each rem ch across, turn. (79, 83, 95, 103, 111 sc)
Maintaining color sequence, work in bodice pattern for 1 inch, ending with a RS row.

Armhole shaping
Row 1 (WS): Sl st in next 5 sts, ch 2, work in bodice pattern across, leaving last 4 sts unworked and ending with dc in ch-1 sp, hdc into center dc 2 rows below, turn. (71, 75, 87, 95, 103 sts)
Row 2: Sl st in first 3 sts, ch 2, dc in ch-1 sp, ch 1, continue in bodice pattern across, do not ch 1 and ending with hdc in center dc, leaving last 2 sts unworked turn. (67, 71, 83, 91, 99 sts)
Row 3: Sl st in first st, ch 3, starting in next ch sp, work in bodice pattern across, ending with dc in ch sp, hdc into center dc 2 rows below, leaving last 2 sts unworked, turn. (63, 67, 79, 87, 95 sts)
For size 2 only, rep Row 2 of back bodice once. (75 sts)

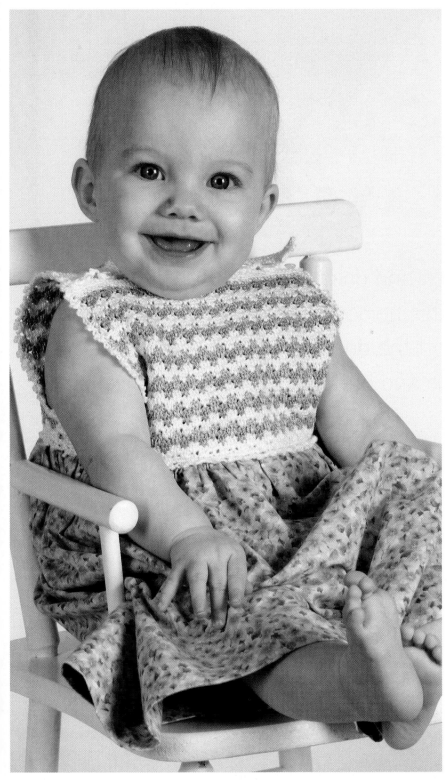

each rem st across, turn. (19, 19, 23, 23, 27 sc)

Rep Row 2 of first neck and shoulder shaping until 2nd shaping measures the same as first shaping.

BODICE FRONT

Rep bodice back and armhole shaping until front bodice measures 3½ (3¾, 4, 5, 5¼) inches.

First neck & shoulder shaping

Rep first neck and shoulder shaping the same as for back bodice until bodice measures 5 (5½, 6, 7, 7¼) inches.

Last row: Ch 3, [sk 2 sts, p in next st, ch 3] rep across, adjusting sts as necessary to end with sc in last st, fasten off.

Second neck & shoulder shaping

Rep second neck and shoulder shaping the same as for back bodice until bodice measures 5 (5½, 6, 7, 7¼) inches.

Last row: Ch 3, [sk 2 sts, p in next st, ch 3] rep across, adjusting sts as necessary to end with sc in last st, fasten off.

Sew back and front bodice side seams tog.

BODICE EDGING

Note: Work bodice edging around oppo-site side of foundation ch of bodice front and back, armhole and neckline edges. Attach MC, ch 3, [sk 2 sts, p in next st, ch 3] rep across, adjusting as necessary to end even.

Sew buttons to back bodice shoulder area aligning with ch-3 of edging on front bodice.

SKIRT

Cut fabric to 15 (17½, 20, 21½, 23¼) inches long.

With RS tog, sew a ½-inch back seam and press open. Fold bottom hem under to desired length and press. Hem skirt with sewing needle and thread.

For waistline edge, sew a row of basting sts about ½ inch from edge, gather edge to fit opening of bodice. With seam at center back of bodice, lap bodice over gathered edge, adjusting gathers, pin in place. Sew skirt to bodice. ■

For sizes 4 and 6, rep Rows 2 and 3 of bodice back once. (79, 87 sts)

Work even in bodice pattern until bodice measures 4¾ (5¼, 5¾, 6¾, 7) inches. (63, 67, 75, 79, 87 sts)

First neck & shoulder shaping

Row 1: With MC, ch 1, sc in each of next 19 (19, 23, 23, 27) sts, turn.

Row 2: Ch 1, sc in each sc across, turn. (19, 19, 23, 23 27 sc)

Rep Row 2 until bodice measures 5¼ (5¾, 6¼, 7¼, 7½) inches, fasten off.

Second neck & shoulder shaping

Row 1: Sk center 25 (29, 29, 33, 33) sts for neckline opening, attach yarn in next st, ch 1, sc in same st as beg ch-1, sc in

DESIGN BY
BRENDA STRATTON

PRETTY POSIES LAYETTE

A lacy, textured stitch and dainty, floral accents create the beautiful design in this heirloom-quality ensemble. Soft cotton yarn shows off the delicate pattern and makes this set both comfortable and pretty!

GAUGE

With hook size F, 3 shell patterns = 3½ inches; with hook size G, 5 shell patterns = 6 inches
Check gauge to save time.

PATTERN NOTES

Weave in loose ends as work progresses.
Join rnds with a sl st unless otherwise stated.
Use hook size F for sweater, bonnet and booties, hook size G for afghan and steel hook for flowers and leaves.
WS of shell row is always RS of work.

PATTERN STITCHES

Picot (p): [Sc, ch 2, sc] in last sc worked.
Shell: [{Dc, ch 1} 3 times and dc] in indicated st.
Shell Pattern: Sc in st indicated, shell in next st indicated.
Tr cl: Holding back last lp of each st on hook, 3 tr in indicated st, yo, draw through all 4 lps on hook.

INTERMEDIATE ●●●

SIZE 6 months
MATERIALS
- Patons Bumblebee baby cotton yarn (1¾ oz per skein): 16 skeins lily of the valley #02005, 1 skein each wild rose #02414 and sweet grass #02712
- Sizes F/5 and G/6 crochet hooks or sizes needed to obtain gauge
- Size 3 steel crochet hook
- Straight pins
- Sewing needle and thread
- Stitch marker
- Yarn needle

SWEATER
Yoke

Row 1: Beg at neckline edge with hook size F and lily of the valley, ch 61 loosely, sc in 2nd ch from hook, sc in each rem ch across, turn. (60 sc)
Row 2: Ch 1, sc in each of next 12 sc (front), 3 sc in next sc, sc in each of next 4 sc (sleeve), 3 sc in next sc, sc in each of next 24 sc (back), 3 sc in next sc, sc in each of next 4 sc (sleeve), 3 sc in next sc, sc in each of next 12 sc (front), turn. (68 sc)
Row 3: Ch 1, sc in each st across, turn.
Row 4: Ch 1, sc in each sc across front, 3 sc in center sc of 3-sc group, sc in each sc across sleeve, 3 sc in center sc of 3-sc group, sc in each sc across back, 3 sc in center sc of 3-sc group, sc in each sc across sleeve, 3 sc in center sc of 3-sc group, sc in each sc across front. (76 sc)
Rows 5–10: Rep Rows 3 and 4. (100 sc)
Row 11: Rep Row 3. (100 sc)
Row 12 (beg of pattern, WS): Sc in next sc, [sk next sc, shell in next sc, sk next sc, sc in next sc] rep across, turn. (25 shell sts)
Row 13: Ch 5 (counts as first dc, ch 2 throughout), sc in center ch-1 sp of shell, ch 2, dc in next sc, [ch 2, sc in center ch-1 sp of next shell, ch 2, dc in next sc] rep across, turn.
Row 14: Ch 1, sc in next dc, [shell in next sc, sc in next dc] rep across, end-

ing with sc in 3rd ch of ch-5, turn.

Row 15: Rep Row 13.

Right front

Row 16: Ch 1, sc in next dc, *shell in next sc, sc in next dc, rep from * 3 times, turn.

Row 17: Ch 5, sc in center ch-1 sp of next shell, ch 2, dc in next sc, *ch 2, sc in center ch-1 sp of next shell, ch 2, dc in next sc, rep from * twice, turn.

Rows 18–21: Rep Rows 16 and 17.

Row 22: Rep Row 16, fasten off.

Back

Note: *Sk next 4 shells, attach lily of the valley in next dc.*

Rows 16–22: Working across 9 shells, rep Rows 16–22 of right front.

Left front

Sk next 4 shells, attach lily of the valley in next dc, rep Rows 16–22 of right front. At the end of last rep, do not fasten off.

Joining

Row 23: Ch 5, sc in center ch-1 sp of next shell, ch 2, dc in next sc, *ch 2, sc in center ch-1 sp of next shell, ch 2, dc in next sc *, rep from * to * twice, ch 3, dc in next sc on back section, rep from * to * 9 times, ch 3, dc in next sc on left front section, rep from * to * 4 times, turn.

Row 24: Ch 1, sc in next dc, shell in next sc, sc in next dc, rep from * to * 3 times, shell in 2nd ch of ch-3, rep from * to * 9 times across back, shell in 2nd ch of ch-3, rep from * to * 4 times across front, turn.

Rows 25–40: Continue in established pattern. At the end of Row 40, fasten off. Turn sweater WS out.

SLEEVE

Make 2

Rnd 1: Attach lily of the valley in center st of underarm, starting with shell row in pattern, ch 1, sc in joining, work 2 shell patterns on edge of armhole to yoke, work 4 shell patterns across 4 shell patterns on sleeve, work 2 shell patterns down other edge of armhole, join in beg sc, turn.

Rnd 2: Ch 5, sc in center ch-1 sp of shell, ch 2, dc in next sc, ch 2, [sc in center ch-1 sp of next shell, ch 2, dc in next sc, ch 2] rep around, join in 3rd ch of beg ch-5, turn.

Rnd 3: Ch 1, sc in joining, shell in next

sc, [sc in next dc, shell in next sc] rep around, join in beg sc, turn.

Rnds 4–18: Rep Rnds 2 and 3.

Rnd 19: Sl st into ch-2 sp, ch 1, 2 sc in ch-2 sp, [sk next sc, 2 sc in next ch-2 sp] rep around, ending with sc in last ch-2 sp, sc in 3rd ch of ch-5 at beg of Rnd 18, turn. (32 sc)

Rnds 20–22: Ch 1, sc in each sc around, join in beg sc, turn.

Rnd 23: Ch 1, p in same sc as beg ch-1, sk next sc, [p in next sc, sk next sc] rep around, join in beg sc, fasten off.

Neck beading & trim

With RS facing, attach lily of the valley in right neck edge, ch 4, sk 1 st, dc in next st, [ch 1, sk next st, dc in next st] rep across neck edge, ch 1, working down front of sweater, [p in next row, sk next row] rep to bottom edge, sl st in each st across bottom edge, [p in next row, sk next row] rep up front of sweater and across top of beading row, adjusting placement of p as necessary to maintain shape of garment, fasten off.

TIE

With lily of the valley, ch 171, sl st in 2nd ch from hook, sl st in each rem ch across, fasten off. Weave through ch-1 sps of beading at neckline edge.

With lily of the valley make 1-inch pompoms and attach to each end of tie.

FLOWER

Make 2

Rnd 1: With steel hook size 3 and wild rose, ch 5, join to form a ring, ch 1, 6 sc in ring, join in front lp only of beg sc. (6 sc)

Rnd 2: [Ch 5, sl st in front lp only of next st] rep around, join in front lp only of beg sc.

Rnd 3: Sl st into back lp of same st, [ch 5, sl st in back lp only of next st] rep around, join in beg sc, fasten off.

LEAF

Make 2

Rnd 1: With steel hook size 3 and sweet grass [ch 4, tr cl, ch 3, sl st in top of tr cl, ch 4, sl st in ring] 3 times, fasten off. (3-leaf group)

Using photo as a guide, sew a leaf group to each side of sweater yoke, position a flower on top of leaf group and sew in place.

BONNET

Rnd 1: Beg at center of crown with hook size F and lily of the valley, ch 2, 6 sc in 2nd ch from hook, do not join rnds, use a st marker to mark rnds. (6 sc)

Rnd 2: 2 sc in each sc around. (12 sc)

Rnds 3–12: Sc around, inc 6 sc evenly sp around. (72 sc)

Rnd 13: Sc in each sc around, join in beg sc, turn. (72 sc)

Row 14: WS of work, beg of pattern, sc in next sc, *sk next sc, shell in next sc, sk next 2 sc, sc in next sc, rep from * 11 times, turn. (12 shell sts)

Row 15: Ch 5, sc in center ch-1 sp of next shell, ch 2, dc in next sc, *ch 2, sc in center ch-1 sp of next shell, ch 2, dc in next sc, rep from * across, turn.

Row 16: Ch 1, sc in next dc, *shell in next sc, sc in next dc, rep from * across, ending with sc in 3rd ch of beg ch-5 of previous row, turn.

Rows 17–30: Rep Rows 15 and 16. At the end of last row, fasten off.

Fold front of bonnet back over top so that 2 rows of shell pattern are showing, pin in place on both sides.

Neck edge

Row 1: Starting at left side of bonnet, attach lily of the valley through both thicknesses, ch 1, sc in same st as beg ch-1, work 48 sc evenly sp across, turn. (49 sc)

Row 2 (beading row): Ch 4 (counts as first dc, ch 1), sk next sc, dc in next sc, [sk next sc, dc in next sc] rep across, turn. (25 dc)

Row 3: Ch 1, sc in each dc and each ch-1 sp across, fasten off. (49 sc)

FLOWER & LEAF TRIM

Making a flower and a leaf, rep flower and leaf trim as for sweater. Sew leaf group to center back of right side of bonnet, position flower at center of leaf group and sew in place.

TIE

With F hook and lily of the valley, ch 121, sl st in 2nd ch from hook, sl st in each rem ch across, fasten off.

Weave tie through beading row. With lily of the valley, make 1-inch pompoms and attach to each end of tie.

BOOTIE

Make 2

Rnd 1: With hook size F and lily of the valley, ch 14, 3 sc in 2nd ch from hook, sc in each of next 11 chs, 3 sc in last ch, working on opposite side of foundation ch, sc in each of next 11 chs, do not join rnds, use a st marker to mark rnds. (28 sc)

Rnd 2: [2 sc in each of next 3 sc, sc in each of next 11 sc] twice. (34 sc)

Rnd 3: [Sc in next sc, 2 sc in next sc] 3 times, sc in each of next 12 sc, 2 sc in next sc, [sc in next sc, 2 sc in next sc] twice, sc in each of next 11 sc. (40 sc)

Rnds 4 & 5: Sc around, inc 3 sc evenly sp at each end. (52 sc)

Foot

Rnds 1–6: Sc in each sc around. At the end of Rnd 6, continue to sc to center st at next end, work 4 sc beyond center sc, sl st in next sc, turn.

Instep

Rows 1–10: Ch 1, sc in each of next 9 sc, sl st in next st of foot, turn. At the end of Row 10, fasten off.

Cuff

Rnd 1: With heel end of bootie facing, attach lily of the valley at center back, ch 1, sc in each sc around, join in beg sc.

Rnd 2 (beading rnd): Ch 4, sk next sc, [dc in next sc, ch 1, sk next sc] rep around, join in 3rd ch of beg ch-4. (21 dc)

Rnd 3: Ch 1, sc in same st as beg ch-1, sc in each st around, join in beg sc, turn.

Rnd 4: Ch 1, sc in same sc, sk next 2 sc, shell in next sc, sk next 2 sc, [sc in next sc, sk next 2 sc, shell in next sc, sk next 2 sc] rep around, join in beg sc, turn. (7 shells)

Rnd 5: Ch 5, sc in center ch-1 sp of next shell, ch 2, [dc in next sc, ch 2, sc in center ch sp of next shell, ch 2] rep around, join in 3rd ch of beg ch-5, turn.

Rnds 6–8: Rep Rnds 4 and 5, ending last rep with Rnd 4, fasten off.

TIE

Make 2

With hook size F and lily of the valley, ch 71, sl st in 2nd ch from hook, sl st in each rem ch across, fasten off. Starting at center front of bootie, weave tie through beading rnd. With lily of the valley make 4 (1-inch) pompoms and attach to each end of each tie.

FLOWER & LEAF TRIM

Make 2

Follow instruction for flower and leaf as for sweater. Sew a leaf group and flower to the instep of each bootie.

AFGHAN

Row 1: With hook size G and lily of the valley, ch 115, sc in 2nd ch from hook, sk next 2 chs, [shell in next ch, sk next 2 chs, sc in next ch] rep across, turn. (19 shells)

Rows 2–80: Rep Rows 15 and 16 of bonnet. At the end of Row 80, turn.

Border

Rnd 1: With RS facing, ch 1, 3 sc in same sp (beg corner), sc in next sc, [2 sc in next ch-2 sp, sc in next dc, 2 sc in next ch-2 sp, sc in next sc] rep across to corner, 5 sc in next sp for corner, *sc in side of next row, [2 sc in next sp, sc in side of next row] rep across to corner *, 5 sc in next sp for corner, sc in base of next shell, [2 sc in next ch-2 sp, sc in base of next shell] rep across to next corner, 5 sc in next sp for corner, rep from * to *, 2 sc in same st as beg corner, join in beg sc.

Rnd 2: Ch 3, 4 dc in same sc, dc in each sc across to center st of next corner, [5 dc in center sc of next corner, dc in each dc across to center st of next corner] rep around, join in 3rd ch of beg ch-3.

Rnds 3 & 4: Sl st into center dc of corner, ch 3, 4 dc in same st as beg ch-3, dc in each dc across to center dc of next 5-dc group, [5 dc in center corner dc, dc in each dc across to center dc of next 5-dc group] rep around, join in 3rd ch of beg ch-3.

Note: *Adjust sts as necessary to allow a shell to fall in center dc of 5-dc group at each corner.*

Rnd 5: Sl st to center dc of 5-dc group at corner, turn, [ch 4, {dc, ch 1} twice and dc] in same dc, [sk next 2 dc, shell in next dc, sk next 2 dc, sc in next dc] rep across to next corner, *shell in center dc of corner, sc in next dc, [sk next 2 dc, shell in next dc, sk next 2 dc, sc in next dc] rep across to next corner, rep from * around, join in 3rd ch of beg ch-4.

Rnd 6: Sl st to center ch-1 sp at corner, turn, ch 1, sc, ch 3, sc in same ch-1 sp, ch 2, dc in next sc, [ch 2, sc in center ch-1 sp of next shell, ch 2, dc in next dc] rep across, ch 2, *[sc, ch 3, sc] in center sp at corner, ch 2, dc in next sc, [ch 2, sc in center ch-1 sp of next shell, ch 2, dc in next sc] rep across, ch 2, rep from * around, join in beg sc.

Rnd 7: Sl st into corner ch-3 sp, [ch 4, {dc, ch 1} 4 times and dc] in same sp, sc in next dc, [shell in next sc, sc in next dc] rep across to next corner, *in center sp of corner work [{dc, ch 1} 5 times and dc] in same dc, sc in next dc, [shell in next sc, sc in next dc] rep across to next corner, rep from * around, join in 3rd ch of beg ch-4.

Rnd 8: Sl st to center ch-1 sp of corner, turn, ch 1, [sc, ch 3, sc] in same sp, ch 3, dc in next sc, [ch 2, sc in center ch-1 sp of next shell, ch 2, dc in next sc] rep across to next corner, ch 3, *[sc, ch 3, sc] in center corner sp, ch 3, dc in next sc, [ch 2, sc in center ch-1 sp of shell, ch 2, dc in next sc] rep across to next corner, ch 3, rep from * around join in beg sc.

Rnd 9: Sl st into corner ch-3 sp, [ch 5, {tr, ch 1} 7 times and tr] in same sp, sc in next dc, [shell in next sc, sc in next dc] rep across to next corner ch-3 sp, *[{tr, ch 1} 8 times and tr] in ch-3 sp, sc in next dc, [shell in next sc, sc in next dc] rep across to next corner sp, rep from * around, join in 4th ch of beg ch-5, fasten off.

Flower & Leaf

Follow instruction for flower and leaf as for sweater and make 4 each. Place a leaf and flower in each corner and sew in place.

Block afghan to size. ■

Rows 14–17: Rep Row 2.

Row 18: Ch 3, dc in each st across to last 3 sts, dc dec over next 2 sts, dc in last st, turn. (26 dc)

Row 19: Ch 3, dc dec over next 2 sts, dc in each rem st across, turn. (25 dc)

Rows 20 & 21: Rep Rows 18 and 19. (23 dc)

Row 22: Ch 3, dc in each st across to last 7 dc, [dc dec over next 2 dc] 3 times, dc in last dc, fasten off. (20 dc)
Mark last st made with st marker for back edge. Long straight edge is face edge.

INNER HOOD

Rep center panel and side panels of outer hood with 1 strand of lemon yarn.

FINISHING & ASSEMBLY

To join outer panels, pin first st of Row 22 on a side panel to end of last row on long edge of center panel. Pin marked st of Row 22 on side panel to end of Row 24 of center panel. Pin marked st of Row 1 of side panel to Row 1 of center panel. Working through both layers, attach a strand of matching color yarn with sc in first pinned st, matching edges, sp sts evenly so edges lie flat, sc across to next marker at end of Row 24 of center panel, sc across to last pinned st, fasten off. Rep in same manner to attach 2nd side panel to center panel.

Join inner side panels to inner center panel in same manner as outer panels. To attach hood to snowsuit, match front bottom corners of outer hood to unworked area on neck edge of outer back and sleeves, easing in fullness to fit, with matching yarn, sew tog through both layers. Rep with inner hood, back and sleeves.

Working through both layers around face edge of hood, join a strand of mint with sl st in sc worked into Row 33 on right edge, spacing sts evenly so edges lie flat, sc in ends of rows and in sts across face

edge of hood, sl st in st worked into Row 33 on left edge, fasten off.
Cut fake fur to fit face opening of hood and sew in place through all layers. Sew button to center of Row 37 on left sleeve at center front neck edge. On right sleeve for buttonhole at neck edge, spread sts at center of Row 37 to fit button; with sewing needle and thread, sew in place.

PATCHWORK BLANKET

GAUGE

Each block = 4½ x 5½ inches; 5 dc = 1 inch; 3 dc rows = 1 inch
Check gauge to save time.

PATTERN NOTES

Weave in loose ends as work progresses.
Join rnds with a sl st unless otherwise stated.
Ch-3 counts as first dc throughout.
Cut 36 pieces of quilt batting each 4 x 4½ inches. Set aside.

BLOCK

Note: Make 36 each mint and lemon.
Row 1: Ch 21, dc in 4th ch from hook, dc in each rem ch across, turn. (19 dc)

Rows 2–14: Ch 3, dc in each dc across, turn. At the end of last rep, fasten off.

Rnd 15: Working around outer edge, attach white in first st, [ch 3, 2 dc] in same st, [sk next st, dc in next st, working in front of dc just made, dc in sk st] rep across to corner, 3 dc in corner, [dc in bottom of next row, working in front of dc just made, dc in top of same row] 13 times across edge, working in opposite side of foundation ch, 3 dc in corner, [sk next ch, dc in next ch, working in front of last dc made, dc in sk ch] rep across, 3 dc in corner st, [dc in top of next row, working in front of dc just made, dc in bottom of same row] 13 times, join in 3rd ch of beg ch-3, fasten off.

BEGINNER ●●●

SIZE 28 x 34 inches

MATERIALS
- Mary Maxim Baby Soft 3-ply baby yarn: 5 oz each lemon #253005 and mint #253006
- Coats & Clark Red Heart Baby Fingering yarn: 5 oz white #001
- Size E/4 crochet hook or size needed to obtain gauge
- Quilt batting
- 12 yds ⅛-inch-wide yellow ribbon
- 12 yds ⅛-inch-wide green ribbon
- 36 small gold beads
- Sewing needle and thread
- Tapestry needle

Rnd 16: Holding 2 blocks tog with piece of batting between, working through both thicknesses, attach white in center st of any corner, ch 1, 3 sc in same st, sc in each st around, working 3 sc in each center corner st, join in beg sc, fasten off. Alternating colors, sl st long edges of 6 blocks tog for 6 rows. Sl st rows tog.

EDGING

Rnd 1: Attach white in any corner sc, ch 1, 3 sc in same st, sc around outer edge of blanket, working 3 sc in each corner, join in beg sc, fasten off.

Rnd 2: Attach lemon in any center corner sc, ch 1, 3 sc in same st, sc in each sc around, working 3 sc in each center corner sc, join in beg sc, fasten off.

Rnd 3: Attach white in any sc, ch 1, reverse sc in each sc around, join in beg sc, fasten off.

FINISHING

Cut ribbon into 14-inch lengths.
On one side of blanket, tie each yellow ribbon in bow around st in center of each mint block and on the other side of blanket, tie green ribbon in bow around st in center of each lemon block. Sew a bead to knot on each bow. ∎

TUNISIAN TAPESTRY
JACKET & HAT ▶ CONTINUED FROM PAGE 104

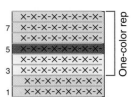

Rnd 2 (WS): Attach B, ch 3, sl st in next st, [dc in next st, sl st in next st] rep around, join in same st as beg ch-3, fasten off.

HAT

CROWN

With afghan hook size H and MC, ch 75 (81, 87, 90) and work as for back until 10th (12th, 12th, 14th) R Row. Work

next row in pattern, binding off in sc. Sew side seam across ends of rows.

TOP

Rnd 1: With hook size G, leaving at slight length at beg, wrap MC around finger once, draw up a lp through center, ch 1, work 7 sc into lp, pull slight length at the beg to tighten and close opening, do not join rnds, use a st marker to mark rnds. (7 sc)

Rnd 2: 2 sc in each st around. (14 sc)

Rnd 3: [Sc in next sc, 2 sc in next sc] rep around. (21 sc)

Rnd 4: [Sc in each of next 2 sc, 2 sc in next sc] rep around. (28 sc)

Rnds 5–10 (11, 12, 13): Sc around, working 1 more sc between sc inc for each rnd. (70, 77, 84, 91 sc) At the end of last rep, sl st in next st, fasten off.

Pin top to last row of crown and sew in place.

BRIM

Rnd 1 (RS): With hook size G, attach MC in bottom edge of crown, ch 1, work

X-X-X-X-X-X-X-X-	
7 X-X-X-X-X-X-X-X-	One-color rep
X-X-X-X-X-X-X-X-	
5 X-X-X-X-X-X-X-X-	
X-X-X-X-X-X-X-X-	
3 X-X-X-X-X-X-X-X-	
X-X-X-X-X-X-X-X	
1 X-X-X-X-X-X-X-X	

Tunisian Jacket
Diagram

75 (81, 87, 90) sc evenly sp around, do not join rnds, use st marker to mark rnds.

Rnd 2: Sc in each st around, inc 7 (8, 9, 10) sc evenly sp around. (82, 89, 96, 100 sc)

Rnds 3 & 4: Sc in each sc around.

Rnds 5–16: Rep Rnds 2–4. (110, 121, 132, 140 sc)

Rnd 17: [Sl st in next st, dc in next st] rep around, ending with join in same st as beg sl st, fasten off.

Mold crown over a bowl using a damp cloth.

Fold up front brim and sew 1½-inch daisy button through both brim and crown layers.

Optional: If you do not use the button, tie ribbon into a bow and tack to the back of hat. ■

side of foundation ch, sl st in next ch, sc in next ch, hdc in next ch, dc in each

of next 2 chs, tr in each of next 2 chs, ch 3, sl st in next ch, leaving a length of yarn, fasten off.

Using photo as a guide, sew 5 flowers and leaves to afghan.

Cut ⅜-inch-wide aqua ribbon into 4 equal lengths. Tie each length into a bow. Cut ⅛-inch-wide aqua ribbon into 4 equal lengths. Fold ribbon length in half and tack to center back of bow. Tack finished bow to afghan.

HIS FINISHING
Balloon

Note: *Make 6 for each corner in the following colors: 1 each, purple, mauve, apple green and lime green and 2 blue.*
Rnd 1: Ch 4, join to form a ring, ch 2

(counts as first hdc), 11 hdc in ring, join in 2nd ch of beg ch-2. (12 hdc)
Rnd 2: Ch 2, hdc in same st as beg ch-2, 2 hdc in each rem hdc around, join in 2nd ch of beg ch-2. (24 hdc)
Row 3: Ch 2, 2 hdc in same st as beg ch-2, leaving a 12-inch length, fasten off. For balloon string, draw rem length back through center hdc of 3-hdc group of Row 3.

Using photo as a guide and a separate length of yarn, sew balloons at each corner. Cut ⅜-inch powder blue ribbon into 4 equal lengths. Holding string from each balloon in a group, tie a small bow around strings. Tack bow to afghan. Cut balloon strings even. ■

end of Row 3 of edging, ch 80, hdc in 2nd ch from hook, hdc in each rem ch across, sc in each sc across neck edge, ch 80, hdc in 2nd ch from hook, hdc in each rem ch across, sl st in next sc, fasten off.

FLOWER

With mid rose, ch 6, sl st in first ch of beg ch-6 to form petal, [ch 5, sl st in first ch of beg ch-6 to form next petal] 5 times, fasten off.
Leaf
Attach mint green to back of flower in

any sl st, [ch 6, sl st in 6th ch from hook] twice, fasten off.

FINISHING
Weave ribbon through ch-1 sps of Row 1 of edging. Secure ends on WS of bib. Cut a 2-inch length of ribbon, fold in half and sew to Row 22 at center of heart. Sew flower over ribbon on Row 22. Make 2 bows and attach 1 to each side edge of Row 27 of bib. ■

in back lps only, ch 1, sc in each st across, turn.

Row 22 (28, 34): Working in back lps only, ch 1, sc dec over next 2 sc, sc in each sc across to last 2 sc, sc dec over next 2 sc, turn. (13, 15, 17 sc)

Row 23 (29, 35): Working in back lps only, ch 1, [sc dec over next 2 sc] twice, sc in each of next 5 (7, 9) sts, [sc dec over next 2 sc] twice, turn. (9, 11, 13 sc)

Row 24 (30, 36): Working in back lps only, ch 1, sc dec over next 2 sc, sc in each sc across to last 2 sc, sc dec over next 2 sc, do not turn. (7, 9, 11 sc)

FOOT

Rnd 1: Ch 1, working around outer edge of sole, work 68 (82, 96) sc, join in beg sc.

Rnd 2: Working in back lps only, sc in each st around, join in beg sc.

Rnd 3: Ch 1, sc in each sc around, join in beg sc, fasten off.

Rnd 4: Working in back lps only, attach pink at center back of foot, ch 3, dc in each sc around, join in 3rd ch of beg ch-3.

Rnd 5: Ch 4 (counts as first dc, ch 1), sk next dc, [dc in next dc, ch 1, sk next dc] rep around, join in 3rd ch of beg ch-4.

(34, 41, 48 dc)

Rnd 6: Ch 3, dc in next ch-1 sp, [dc in next dc, dc in next ch-1 sp] rep around, join in 3rd ch of beg ch-3. (68, 82, 96 dc)

Rnd 7: Ch 4, sk next dc, [dc in next dc, ch 1, sk next dc] 8 (12, 14) times, [dc in next dc, ch 1, sk next 2 dc] 10 (10, 12) times, [dc in next dc, ch 1, sk next dc] rep around, join in 3rd ch of beg ch-4.

Rnd 8: Ch 3, [dc in next ch-1 sp, dc in next dc] 9 (13, 15) times, [dc in next ch-1 sp] 10 (10, 12) times, [dc in next dc, dc in next ch-1 sp] rep around, join in 3rd ch of beg ch-3.

Rnd 9: Ch 4, sk next dc, [dc in next dc, ch 1, sk next dc] 7 (9, 12) times, [dc in next dc, ch 1, sk next 2 dc] 4 (7, 7) times, [dc in next dc, ch 1, sk next dc] rep around, join in 3rd ch of beg ch-4.

Rnd 10: Ch 3, dc in next ch-1 sp, place st marker in last dc, [dc in next dc, dc in next ch-1 sp] rep around, join in 3rd ch of beg ch-3, fasten off.

FOOT TRIM

With top of shoe facing and working in rem free lps of Rnd 3, attach white with sc at center back, ch 3, [sc in next st, ch 3] rep around, join in beg sc, fasten off.

ANKLE STRAP

Row 1: With pink ch 8, dc in 4th ch from hook, ch 2, sk next 2 chs, dc in each of next 2 chs, turn.

Row 2: Ch 3, dc in next dc ch 2, dc in each of next 2 dc, turn.

Rows 3–10, 3–11, 3–11: Rep Row 2.

Row 11 (12, 12): Ch 3, dc in next dc, ch 2, dc in each of next 2 dc, sl st in marked dc and in ch-3 at beg of Rnd 10, turn.

Row 12 (13, 13): Dc in each of next 2 dc of ankle strap, ch 2, dc in each of next 2 dc, turn.

Row 13 (14, 14): Ch 3, dc in next dc, ch 2, dc in each of next 2 dc, sk next st on Rnd 10 of shoe, sl st in next st, turn.

Row 14 (15, 15): Sl st in first dc of previous row, ch 3, dc in next dc, ch 2, dc in each of next 2 dc, turn.

Rows 15–23 (16–25, 16–25): Rep Row 2.

Row 24 (26, 26): Ch 3, dc in next dc, ch 2, dc in each of next 2 dc, fasten off.

FINISHING

Cut individual ribbon length in half, weave ribbon length through ch-2 sps of ankle strap. ■

Crocheted dolls and toys appeal to children of all ages, providing lovable, safe playthings to be enjoyed for years and treasured for a lifetime. With the appealing patterns in this kid-pleasing chapter, ordinary yarns and threads are transformed into cherished playtime

AWARD-WINNING DOLLS & TOYS

friends and captivating toys that are sure to bring smiles of delight to bright, shining little faces. It's hard to know who will enjoy these enchanting creations the most—you as you lovingly stitch them for a treasured child or grandchild, or the lucky little ones who receive them.

LADY IRIS

Decked out in her fancy, flower-trimmed hat and purse and wearing her elegant pearl jewelry, this high-society bear is ready for afternoon tea at the country club. Sitting 20 inches tall and stitched in cuddly-soft, bulky yarn, she's a big, lovable bear who's just as precious without her finery.

GAUGE

With size G hook and worsted weight yarn, 4 sc = 1 inch; 4 rnds = 1 inch
With size H hook and bulky yarn, 5 sc = 1½ inches; piece for head measures approximately 2¼ inches after Rnd 3 of face shaping rnd
Check gauge to save time.

PATTERN NOTES

Weave in loose ends as work progresses. Unless otherwise stated, do not join rnds, mark first st of each rnd with st marker. Where joining is indicated, join with a sl st unless otherwise stated.

PATTERN STITCH

Sc dec: [Insert hook in next st, yo, draw up a lp] twice, yo, draw through all 3 lps on hook.

HEAD

Row 1 (RS): With hook size H and bulky yarn, beg at nose, ch 6, sc in 2nd ch from hook, sc in each rem ch across, turn. (5 sc)
Rows 2 & 3: Ch 1, sc in each sc across, turn.

INTERMEDIATE ○○●

SIZE 20 inches tall, sitting
MATERIALS
- Coats & Clark Red Heart Light & Lofty bulky yarn (6 oz per skein): 5 skeins Café Au Lait #9334
- Coats & Clark Red Heart Classic worsted weight yarn: 4 oz lavender #584, small amount black #12
- Sizes G/6 and H/8 crochet hooks or sizes needed to obtain gauge
- 2 (⅞-inch) round black shank buttons
- Purple, lavender and pink silk flowers
- ¾ yd 1½-inch-wide white double-edge lace ruffle
- ⅓ yd ¾-inch-wide white lace ruffle
- 1⅓ yds ⅞-inch-wide lavender wire-edged ribbon
- 2½ yds ⅜-inch-wide lavender picot-edge ribbon
- Small piece black felt
- Craft glue
- ½-inch pink heart shank button
- Pair costume pearl earrings
- Costume pearl string necklace
- Stitch markers
- Fiberfill
- Sewing needle and white thread
- Yarn needle

Face shaping

Rnd 3: Ch 1, sc in each of next 5 sc of Row 3, sc in end of each of next 3 rows (mark first and 3rd of these sc sts for top edge of nose), sc in each of next 5 chs across opposite side of foundation ch, sc in opposite end of each of 3-sc rows. (16 sc)
Rnd 4: Sc in each of next 5 sc, 2 sc in first marked st, sc in next sc, 2 sc in next marked st, sc in each of next 8 sc. (18 sc)
Rnd 5: Sc in each of next 5 sc, 2 sc in next sc, sc in each of next 3 sc, 2 sc in next sc, sc in each of next 8 sc. (20 sc)
Rnd 6: Sc in each sc around.
Rnd 7: Sc in each of next 8 sc, 2 sc in next sc, sc in each of next 11 sc. (21 sc)
Rnd 8: Rep Rnd 6.
Rnd 9: Sc around, working 2 sc in each corner at bottom edge and 2 sc at each side of nose. (25 sc)

Rnd 10: Sc around, inc 4 sc evenly sp around sides and top of nose, but not over pervious inc sts. (29 sc)

Rnds 11–15: Sc around, inc 5 sc evenly sp around side and top of nose on each rnd, but not over previous inc. (54 sc)

Rnds 16–23: Rep Rnd 6.

Back head shaping

[Sc in each of next 3 sc, sc dec over next 2 sc] rep around continuously until opening is just large enough to stuff head; stuff head firmly. Continue to dec until no sts rem, adding fiberfill as needed. Leaving a length of yarn, fasten off, tack opening closed.

EAR

Make 4

Row 1 (RS): With hook size H and bulky yarn, ch 3, sc in 2nd ch from hook, 3 sc in next ch (top edge of ear), working on opposite side of foundation ch, sc in next ch, turn. (5 sc)

Row 2: Ch 1, sc in first sc, 2 sc in next sc, sc in next sc (mark this as center st of ear), 2 sc in next sc, sc in last sc, turn. (7 sc)

Rows 3–5: Ch 1, sc evenly across, working 1 sc inc in sc on each side of center sc, turn. (13 sc)

At the end of Row 5, fasten off.

For each ear, place 2 ear sections with WS tog and sew tog around. Sew ears to top outside edges of head as shown, rounding each ear slightly.

BODY

Rnd 1: Beg at bottom of body, with hook size H and bulky yarn, ch 2, 6 sc in 2nd ch from hook. (6 sc)

Rnd 2: 2 sc in each sc around. (12 sc)

Rnd 3: [Sc in next sc, 2 sc in next sc] rep around. (18 sc)

Rnd 4: [Sc in each of next 2 sc, 2 sc in next sc] rep around. (24 sc)

Rnd 5: [Sc in each of next 3 sc, 2 sc in next sc] rep around. (30 sc)

Rnd 6: [Sc in each of next 4 sc, 2 sc in next sc] rep around. (36 sc)

Rnd 7: [Sc in each of next 5 sc, 2 sc in next sc] rep around. (42 sc)

Rnd 8: [Sc in each of next 6 sc, 2 sc in next sc] rep around. (48 sc)

Rnd 9: Sc in each sc around.

Rnds 10–15: Rep Rnd 9.

Rnds 16–18: Sc around, inc 2 sc evenly sp around. (54 sc)

Rnds 19–23: Rep Rnd 9. At the end of Rnd 22, place a marker in both first and 28th sts for shoulders of body.

Rnds 24–30: Sc evenly around, working 1 sc dec on each side of each marked st on each rnd (4 decs per rnd). (26 sc) Stuff body firmly with fiberfill and sew neck edge to bottom of head.

ARM

Make 2

Rnds 1–4: Beg at top of arm, rep Rnds 1–4 of body. (24 sc)

Rnds 9–18: Sc around, working 1 sc dec in each rnd. (22 sc)

Rnds 19–23: Rep Rnd 6. At the end of Rnd 23, turn.

Top foot shaping

Row 1 (WS): Ch 1, sc in each of next 11 sc, turn. (11 sc)

Rows 2–7: Ch 1, sc in each sc across, turn. At the end of Row 7, fasten off.

Edging

Attach bulky yarn to Rnd 23 at back center of leg, ch 1, work 3 rnds of sc evenly around edge of leg and piece for top foot shaping. At the end of last rep, fasten off.

Bottom foot section

Row 1: With bulky yarn, ch 14, sc in 2nd ch from hook, sc in each rem ch across, turn. (13 sc)

Rows 2–7: Ch 1, sc in each sc across, turn. At the end of Row 7, fasten off.

Edging

With RS facing, attach bulky yarn at bottom right corner, sc evenly around to bottom left corner, fasten off.

Stuff leg firmly to beg of foot. Place WS of piece for bottom of foot to WS of top of foot and, leaving bottom open, st tog from corner to corner. Stuff foot firmly, then st bottom edge of bottom piece for foot to rem sts on edge of leg.

For bear in sitting position, sew legs to bottom sides of body as shown.

Rnds 5–9: Sc in each sc around.

Rnds 10–17: Sc around, working 1 sc dec in each rnd. At the end of Rnd 17, turn. (16 sc)

Paw back shaping

Row 1 (WS): Ch 1, sc in each of next 8 sc, turn. (8 sc)

Rows 2–7: Ch 1, sc in each of next 8 sc, turn. At the end of Row 7, fasten off.

Edging

With RS facing, attach bulky yarn at bottom right corner, sc evenly around to bottom left corner, fasten off.

Inside paw section

Row 1 (WS): With bulky yarn, ch 8, sc in 2nd ch from hook, sc in each rem ch across, turn. (7 sc)

Rows 2–7: Ch 1, sc in each sc across, turn. At the end of Row 7, fasten off.

Edging

With RS facing, attach bulky yarn at bottom right corner, sc evenly around to bottom left corner, fasten off.

Stuff arm firmly to beg of paw. Place WS of inside piece for paw to WS of back of paw and leaving bottom open, st tog from corner to corner. Stuff paw firmly, then st bottom edge of inside piece to rem sts of Rnd 25 of arm. Sew arms to top side of body.

LEG

Make 2

Rnds 1–4: Rep Rnds 1–4 of body. (24 sc)

Rnd 5: Rep Rnd 4 of body. (32 sc)

Rnd 6: Sc in each sc around.

Rnds 7 & 8: Rep Rnd 6.

NOSE

Row 1 (RS): Beg at bottom of nose, with hook size H and black yarn, ch 3, sc in 2nd ch from hook, sc in next ch, turn. (2 sc)

Row 2: 2 sc in each of next 2 sc, turn. (4 sc)

Row 3: Ch 1, sc in each sc across, do not turn.

Rnd 4: Ch 1, sc in same st as last sc of Row 3, sc in end of next 2 rows, sc in bottom of nose, sc in end of next 2 rows, 2 sc in first sc of Row 3, sc in each of next 3 sc, join in beg sc, leaving a length of yarn, fasten off.

Sew nose to face. With black yarn, embroider mouth as shown. Sew on buttons for eyes as shown, sewing back and forth several times through head between the buttons and pulling yarn tightly to indent eyes slightly.

HAT

Rnd 1: With hook size G and lavender, ch 2, 6 sc in 2nd ch from hook. (6 sc)

Rnd 2: 2 sc in each sc around. (12 sc)

Rnd 3: [Sc in next sc, 2 sc in next sc] rep around. (18 sc)

Rnd 4: [Sc in each of next 2 sc, 2 sc in next sc] rep around. (24 sc)

Rnd 5: [Sc in each of next 3 sc, 2 sc in next sc] rep around. (30 sc)

Rnd 6: [Sc in each of next 4 sc, 2 sc in next sc] rep around. (36 sc)

Rnds 7–11: Sc around, continue to inc 6 sc evenly sp around. (66 sc)

Rnd 12: Working in back lps only, [sc in each of next 9 sc, sc dec over next 2 sc] rep around. (60 sc)

Rnds 13–17: Sc in each st around. At the end of Rnd 17, join in front lp of first sc.

Rnd 18: Working in front lps only, ch 4 (counts as first hdc, ch 2), [hdc in next st, ch 2] rep around, join in 2nd ch of beg ch-4. (60 ch-2 sps)

Rnd 19: Sl st into ch-2 sp, ch 3 (counts as first dc), [dc, ch 2] in same ch-2 sp, [2 dc, ch 2] in each rem ch-2 sp around, join in 3rd ch of beg ch-3.

Rnd 20: Sl st into next ch-2 sp, ch 4 (counts as first hdc, ch 2), [hdc, ch 2] in each rem ch-2 sp around, join in 2nd ch of beg ch-4.

Rnd 21: Ch 1, *[{sc, ch 3} twice, sc, ch 1] in next ch-2 sp, [dc, ch 2, dc, ch 1] in next ch-2 sp, rep from * around, join in beg sc, fasten off.

PURSE

Rnds 1–6: Rep Rnds 1–6 of hat. (36 sc)

Rnd 7: Sc in each sc around.

Rnds 8 & 9: Rep Rnd 7.

Rnd 10: Working in back lps only, sc in each st around.

Rnds 11–18: Rep Rnd 7. At the end of Rnd 18, join in beg sc.

Rnd 19: Ch 4 (counts as first dc, ch 1), sk next sc, [dc in next sc, ch 1, sk next sc] 17 times, join in 3rd ch of beg ch-4. (18 dc; 18 ch-1 sps)

Rnd 20: Work 2 sc in each ch-1 sp around. (36 sc)

Rnd 21: Sc in each st around, join in front lp of beg sc, turn.

Rnd 22: Working in back lps only, ch 1, sk next st, *[{sc, ch 3} twice, sc, ch 1] in next st, sk next st, [dc, ch 2, dc, ch 1] in next st, sk next st, rep from * around, join in beg sc, fasten off.

Bottom ruffle

Rnd 1: Holding purse upside down, attach lavender in rem free lps of Rnd 9, rep Rnd 18 of hat. (36 ch-2 sps)

Rnd 2: Rep Rnd 19 of hat.

Rnd 3: Sl st in next dc, rep Rnd 21 of hat.

Drawstring cord

Make 2

With hook size G and lavender, ch 80, sl st in 2nd ch from hook, sl st in each rem ch across, fasten off.

Weave first drawstring through ch-1 sps of Rnd 19, sew ends tog. Weave 2nd drawstring opposite of first through same rnd, sew ends tog. To draw purse closed, hold each cord at opposite sides of bag and pull closed.

FINISHING

Use photo as a guide for all finishing features. Remove shank from heart button and glue button to center of mouth. From black felt, cut 2 eyelashes. Glue eyelashes behind top edges of button eyes, reversing position for right and left eyes. Attach earrings to ears. Sew double-edge lace ruffle around hat. Cut ⅞-inch-wide lavender wire-edged ribbon in half and glue or sew to inside of hat on each side for ties. Make a large, multi-lp bow from 1¾ yds of ⅜-inch-wide lavender picot ribbon and glue to side of hat at base of brim. Glue flower bouquet to center of bow. Sew single-edge lace around purse along base of bottom ruffle. Tie rem ⅜-inch-wide picot ribbon into a bow and glue to front of purse. Glue small flower bouquet to center of bow. Tie hat on bear's head as shown and hang purse over arm. Place pearl necklace around neck and pearl earrings in ears. ∎

Eyelash
Cut 2

DESIGN BY
ANGELA WINGER

LEOPOLD

The lion may be known as the regal king of beasts, but Leo is just too cute and cuddly to be the majestic-looking monarch! He's stitched in cozy worsted weight yarn, which is then fringed throughout to create his soft "fur" and mane.

GAUGE

With hook size G, 4 sc = 1 inch; 4 sc rnds = 1 inch
Check gauge to save time.

PATTERN NOTES

Weave in loose ends as work progresses.
Do not join rnds unless otherwise stated, use st marker to mark rnds.
When joining rnds, join with a sl st.
Use crochet hook size G throughout.
Size E hook is used to attach fringe.

BODY

Rnd 1: With gold, ch 2, 6 sc in 2nd ch from hook. (6 sc)
Rnd 2: 2 sc in each sc around. (12 sc)
Rnd 3: [Sc in next sc, 2 sc in next sc] 6 times. (18 sc)
Rnd 4: [Sc in each of next 2 sc, 2 sc in next sc] 6 times. (24 sc)
Rnd 5: [Sc in each of next 3 sc, 2 sc in next sc] 6 times. (30 sc)
Rnd 6: [Sc in each of next 4 sc, 2 sc in next sc] 6 times. (36 sc)
Rnd 7: [Sc in each of next 11 sc, 3 sc in next sc] 3 times. (42 sc)
Rnd 8: Sc in each of next 12 sc, 3 sc in next sc, [sc in each of next 13 sc, 3 sc in next sc] twice, sc in next sc. (48 sc)
Rnd 9: Sc in each of next 13 sc, 3 sc

in next sc, [sc in each of next 15 sc, 3 sc in next sc] twice, sc in each of next 2 sc. (54 sc)
Rnd 10: Sc in each of next 14 sc, 3 sc in next sc, [sc in each of next 17 sc, 3 sc in next sc] twice, sc in each of next 3 sc. (60 sc)
Positioning rnd: Sc in each of next 19 sc, place marker and continue.
Rnd 11: Working in back lps for this rnd only, sc in each st around. (60 sc)
Rnd 12: Sc in each sc around.
Rnds 13–15: Rep Rnd 12.
Rnd 16: [Sc in each of next 8 sc, sc dec over next 2 sc] 6 times. (54 sc)

BEGINNER ●●

SIZE Sitting, 14 inches tall
MATERIALS
- Coats & Clark Red Heart Super Saver worsted weight yarn: 14 oz gold #321, 5 oz coffee #365, 1½ oz soft white #316, small amount black #312
- Size G/6 crochet hook or size needed to obtain gauge
- Size E/4 crochet hook
- 2 (15mm) animal eyes
- 7 oz fiberfill
- Stitch marker
- Tapestry needle

Rnds 17–19: Rep Rnd 12.
Rnd 20: [Sc in each of next 7 sc, sc dec over next 2 sc] 6 times. (48 sc)
Rnds 21–23: Rep Rnd 12.
Rnd 24: [Sc in each of next 6 sc, sc dec over next 2 sc] 6 times. (42 sc)
Rnds 25–27: Rep Rnd 12.
Rnd 28: [Sc in each of next 5 sc, sc dec over next 2 sc] 6 times. (36 sc)
Rnds 29–31: Rep Rnd 12.
Rnd 32: [Sc in each of next 4 sc, sc dec over next 2 sc] 6 times. (30 sc)
Rnd 33: [Sc in each of next 3 sc, sc dec over next 2 sc] 6 times. (24 sc)
Rnds 34 & 35: Rep Rnd 12. Stuff body with fiberfill.
Rnd 36: [Sc in each of next 2 sc, sc dec over next 2 sc] 6 times. (18 sc)
Rnd 37: Rep Rnd 12, sl st in next st, fasten off.
Finish stuffing body with fiberfill. Sew a side.

ARM

Make 2

Rnd 1: With gold, ch 6, sc in 2nd ch from hook, sc in each of next 3 chs, 3 sc in last ch, working on opposite side of foundation ch, sc in each of next 3 chs, 2 sc in same ch as beg sc, use st marker to mark rnds. (12 sc)

Rnd 2: [Sc in next sc, 2 sc in next sc] 6 times. (18 sc)

Rnd 3: Sc in each of next 5 sc, [2 sc in next sc] 6 times, sc in each of next 7 sc. (24 sc)

Rnd 4: Working in back lps for this rnd only, sc in each st around. (24 sc)

Rnd 5: Sc in each sc around.

Rnd 6: Rep Rnd 5.

Rnd 7: Sc in each of next 6 sc, [sc dec over next 2 sc] 6 times, sc in each of next 6 sc. (18 sc)

Rnd 8: Sc in each of next 5 sc, [sc dec over next 2 sc] 3 times, sc in each of next 7 sc. (15 sc)

Rnd 9: Sc in each of next 5 sc, [insert hook in next sc, yo, draw up a lp] 3 times, yo, draw through all 4 lps on hook, sc in each of next 7 sc. (13 sc)

Stuff with fiberfill, continue stuffing as work progresses.

Rnds 10–17: Rep Rnd 5.

Rnd 18: Sc in each of next 7 sc, 2 sc in next sc, sc in each of next 5 sc. (14 sc)

Rnd 19–27: Rep Rnd 5. At the end of Rnd 27, sc in each of next 4–6 sc to end rnd at center back.

Row 28: Insert fiberfill as needed into rem of arm, fold top of arm flat across, working through both thicknesses, ch 1, work 7 sc across arm, leaving a length of yarn, fasten off. Sew arm to side of body.

TAIL

Note: Do not stuff tail with fiberfill.

Rnd 1: Rep Rnd 1 of arm. (12 sc)

Rnds 2–16: Sc in each sc around. At the end of Rnd 16, sc in as many sc sts as necessary to end rnd on side of tail.

Row 17: Fold tail flat across, working through both thicknesses, ch 1, work 6 sc across, fasten off.

Sew to center back lower portion of body.

LEG

Make 2

Rnd 1: With gold, ch 10, sc in 2nd ch from hook, sc in each of next 7 chs, 3 sc in end ch, working on opposite side of foundation ch, sc in each of next 7 chs, 2 sc in same ch as beg sc. (20 sc)

Rnd 2: [2 sc in next sc] twice, sc in each of next 5 sc, [2 sc in next sc] 6 times, sc in each of next 5 sc, [2 sc in next sc] twice. (30 sc)

Rnd 3: Sc in each of next 8 sc, [2 sc in next sc] 12 times, sc in each of next 10 sc. (42 sc)

Rnd 4: Sc in each of next 8 sc, hdc in each of next 24 sts, sc in each of next 10 sc. (42 sc)

Rnd 5: Working in back lps for this rnd only, hdc in each st around. (42 sc)

Rnd 6: Sc in each st around.

Rnd 7: Sc in each of next 11 sts, [dc dec over next 2 sts] 12 times, sc in next 7 sts. (30 sts)

Rnd 8: Sc in each of next 11 sts, [dc dec over next 2 sts] 6 times, sc in next 7 sts. (24 sts)

Rnd 9: Sc in each of next 11 sts, [dc dec over next 2 sts] 4 times, sc in each of next 5 sts. (20 sts)

Stuff paw with fiberfill.

Rnd 10: Sc in each of next 10 sts, [dc dec over next 2 sts] twice, sc in each of

next 6 sts. (18 sts)

Rnds 11–18: Rep Rnd 6.

Rnd 19: Sc in each of next 12 sts, [2 sc in next st] twice, sc in each of next 4 sts. (20 sc)

Rnds 20–25: Rep Rnd 6. At the end of Rnd 20, sc in next st.
Finish stuffing with fiberfill.

Row 26: Fold Rnd 25 flat across, working through both thicknesses, work 10 sc across, leaving a length of yarn, fasten off. Attach legs to front of body to pose lion in a sitting position.

MUZZLE

Rnds 1–5: With soft white, rep Rnds 1–5 of body. (30 sc)

Rnds 6–10: Sc in each sc around.

Rnd 11: Sc in each of next 9 sc, [sc dec over next 2 sc] 6 times, sc in each of next 9 sc. (24 sc)

Rnds 12 & 13: Sc in each sc around.
At the end of Rnd 24, fasten off. Stuff muzzle with fiberfill.

HEAD

Rnd 1: Attach gold to center bottom of muzzle, sc in each sc around. (24 sc)

Rnd 2: Sc in each of next 9 sc, [2 sc in next sc, sc in next sc] 6 times, sc in each of next 3 sc. (30 sc)

Note: Inc section of rnds is for face.

Rnd 3: Sc in each of next 10 sc, [2 sc in next sc, sc in next sc] 6 times, sc in each of next 8 sc. (36 sc)

Rnd 4: Sc in each of next 12 sc, [2 sc in next sc, sc in next sc] 9 times, sc in next 6 sc. (45 sc)

Rnd 5: Sc in each st around.

Rnds 6–8: Rep Rnd 5.

Rnd 9: Sc in each of next 21 sc, [2 sc in next sc] 9 times, sc in each of next 15 sc. (54 sc)

Rnds 10–13: Rep Rnd 5.

Rnd 14: [Sc in each of next 7 sc, sc dec over next 2 sc] 6 times. (48 sc)

Rnd 15: Rep Rnd 5.

Rnd 16: [Sc in each of next 6 sc, sc dec over next 2 sc] 6 times. (42 sc)

Rnd 17: Rep Rnd 5.

Rnd 18: [Sc in each of next 5 sc, sc dec over next 2 sc] 6 times. (36 sc)

Rnd 19: Rep Rnd 5. At the end of Rnd 19, draw up a lp, remove hook.

ATTACHING EYES

Attach animal eyes evenly sp apart on face between Rnds 3 and 4 of head.

Rnd 20: [Sc in each of next 4 sc, sc dec over next 2 sc] 6 times. (30 sc)

Rnd 21: [Sc in each of next 3 sc, sc dec over next 2 sc] 6 times. (24 sc)

Rnd 22: [Sc in each of next 2 sc, sc dec over next 2 sc] 6 times. (18 sc) Finish stuffing head with fiberfill.

Rnd 23: [Sc in next sc, sc dec over next 2 sc] 6 times. (12 sc)

Rnd 24: [Sc dec over next 2 sc] 6 times, leaving a length of yarn, fasten off. (6 sc) Sew opening closed.

Nose

Row 1: With black, ch 2, 2 sc in 2nd ch from hook, turn. (2 sc)

Row 2: Ch 1, 2 sc in next sc, sc in next sc, turn. (3 sc)

Row 3: Ch 1, 2 sc in next sc, sc in next sc, 2 sc in next sc, turn. (5 sc)

Row 4: Ch 1, 2 sc in next sc, sc in each of next 3 sc, 2 sc in next sc, turn. (7 sc)

Row 5: Ch 1, sc in each of next 7 sc, fasten off black, turn.

Bridge of nose

Row 6: Attach gold, ch 1, sc in each of next 7 sc, turn. (7 sc)

Rows 7–12: Ch 1, sc in each sc across, turn. At the end of Row 12, leaving a length of yarn, fasten off.
Stuff nose and bridge of nose slightly as work progresses. With a length of black yarn, sew nose over end of snout. While you still have the black on tapestry needle, embroider mouth below nose. With rem length of gold, sew bridge of nose to top of snout.

EAR

Make 2

Rnd 1: With gold, ch 5, sc in 2nd ch from hook, sc in each of next 2 chs, 3 sc in end ch, working on opposite side of foundation ch, sc in next 2 chs, 2 sc in same ch as beg sc, do not join, use st marker. (10 sc)

Rnd 2: 2 sc in first sc, sc in each of next 3 sc, [2 sc in next sc] twice, sc in each of next 3 sc, 2 sc in next sc. (14 sc)

Rnd 3: 2 sc in first sc, sc in each of next 5 sc, [2 sc in next sc] twice, sc in each of next 5 sc, 2 sc in next sc. (18 sc)

Rnd 4: Sc in each of next 18 sc, fold ear flat and working through both thicknesses, sc in each of next 9 sc, leaving a length of yarn, fasten off.
Sew ears to top of head.

FRINGE

Notes: *Use hook size E to attach fringe to lion.*

For each fringe, fold a strand in half, insert hook into st, draw yarn at fold through st on hook to form a lp, draw cut ends through lp on hook, pull gently to secure.

Do not work fringe on Rnds 1–3 of each arm for paws and Rnds 1–4 of each leg for paws.

Mane

Cut coffee yarn in 8-inch lengths. Attach strands of coffee between ears and down around and under the muzzle (this resembles a man's beard). Fill in the back of head the same way. Put same length fringe on tail for approximately 6 rnds.

Muzzle

Cut white yarn in 3-inch lengths. Attach fringe to each white st of muzzle. Do not attach fringe on black portion of nose. For whiskers, when muzzle is completed, remove 3 fringe pieces on each side of muzzle and replace with black fringe.

Body fringe

Cut gold yarn in 3-inch lengths. Attach fringe to each st on rem of lion. Trim ends as desired. ■

GOOSE-CHASE PUZZLE BOOK

A colorful combination of crochet and painting creates this fun, easy puzzle book to entertain little ones as they try to correctly put together the two-sided puzzle pieces that tell the story of a naughty goose who steals a boy's scarf!

GAUGE

15 sc = 5 inches; 17 sc rows = 5 inches
Check gauge to save time.

PATTERN NOTES

Weave in loose ends as work progresses.
Join rnds with a sl st unless otherwise stated.

BEGINNER ●●●

SIZE Book: 12½ inches square
Each puzzle piece: 3 inches square

MATERIALS

- Coats & Clark Red Heart Kids worsted weight yarn (5 oz per skein): 2 skeins white #2001, 3 skeins blue #2845
- Size H/8 crochet hook or size needed to obtain gauge
- Non toxic washable fabric paint: dark blue, yellow, black, iridescent blue, white, purple, brown, green and red
- Paintbrush
- Nontoxic fabric stiffener (optional)
- 2 (9½ inches square) 7-count plastic canvas
- Stitch markers
- Tapestry needle

BLOCK PIECE

Make 36

Row 1: With white, ch 8, sc in 2nd ch from hook, sc in each rem ch across, turn. (7 sc)

Row 2: Ch 1, sc in each sc across, turn.

Rows 3–7: Rep Row 2.

Row 8: Rep Row 2, do not turn.

Row 9: Working in side edge of rows, ch 1, sc in side edge of each row, with 2 sc in side edge of Row 1 (9 sc), working across opposite side of foundation ch, 2 sc in first ch, sc in each of next 5 chs, 2 sc in last ch (9 sc), working up opposite side edge of rows, 2 sc in side edge of Row 1, sc in each of next 7 rows, leaving a length of yarn, fasten off.

Making 9 blocks, stack block pieces in groups of 4 and sew them tog along edges to form block.

BOX

Note: *Make 3 blue and 1 white.*

Row 1: Ch 36, sc in 2nd ch from hook, sc in each rem ch across, turn. (35 sc)

Rows 2–40: Ch 1, sc in each sc across, turn.

Edging

Rnd 1: Ch 1, working around outer edge, work 33 sc evenly sp across each side, with 3 sc in each corner, join in beg sc, fasten off. (144 sc)

Painting

Using diagrams as a guide, paint blocks and white box top as indicated or as desired. Set aside and allow drying time.

BOX SIDE

Make 6

Rnd 1: With blue, ch 112, join with sl st to form a ring, ch 1, 2 sc in first ch, sc in

each of next 27 sc, [3 sc in next ch, place a st marker in center sc of 3-sc group, sc in each of next 27 chs] 3 times, sc in same ch as beg 2-sc group, join in beg sc.

Rnds 2–4: Ch 1, 2 sc in first sc, sc in each sc around, working 3 sc in center marked sc of each corner, ending with 1 sc in same sc as beg 2-sc group, join in beg sc. At the end of Rnd 4, fasten off.

BOX TOP

Stack white box, unpainted side up, 1 piece plastic canvas centered in middle and 1 blue box on opposite side of plastic canvas and with 3 box sides on outer edges of layers. Sew all pieces tog, encasing plastic canvas in middle, sewing around inner edges of box sides. Sew all pieces tog sewing around outer edges of box sides.

BOX BOTTOM

Place 2 blue box pieces tog with plastic canvas sandwiched between layers and rem 3 box sides, assemble the same as box top.

ASSEMBLY

Place box top on box bottom, open box as if opening a book so that box top and bottom are now side by side. Using upper layer of box side on top and bottom, sew top and bottom of box tog along edge.

TIE

Note: *Make 2 each with white and blue.*

Ch 36, sl st in back ridge only of each ch across, fasten off.

Attach white ties to top of box and blue ties to bottom of box in such a way that box can be tied closed.

If desired, spray box with stiffener.

FINISHING

Place the 9 puzzle pieces inside box, close and tie each group of ties in a bow. ■

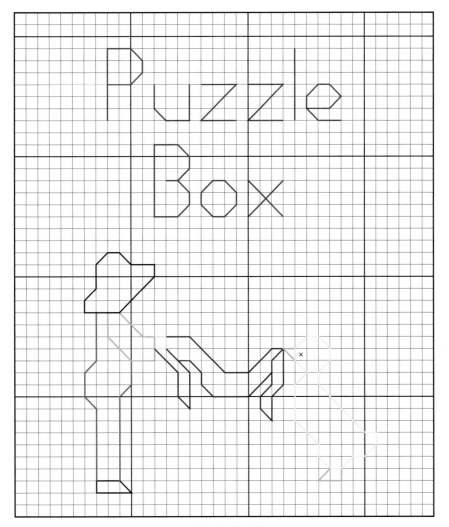

Puzzle Box Top

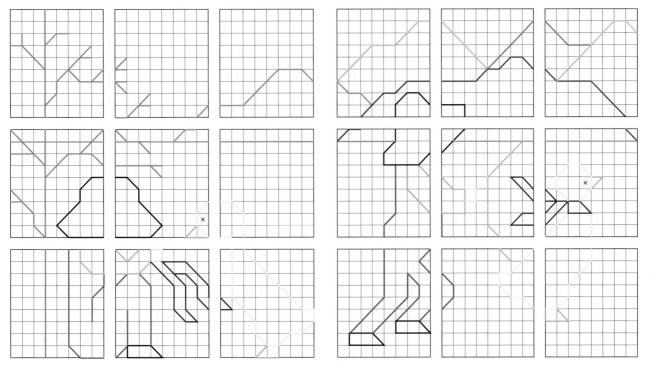

Puzzle Blocks

DESIGN BY
LORI ZELLER

PRETTY PATTI

A creative mix of baby and sport weight yarns combined with size 10 crochet thread creates the darling details in this cuddly-sweet doll. Always ready to share a hug and listen to whispered secrets, Patti is sure to become any little girl's treasured friend and playtime companion!

GAUGE

With D hook, 6 sc = 1 inch; 6 sc rows = 1 inch; with steel hook, 5 dc = ½ inch; 2 dc rows = ½ inch
Check gauge to save time.

PATTERN NOTES

Weave in loose ends as work progresses.
Join rnds with a sl st unless otherwise stated.
Ch-3 counts as first dc throughout.

PATTERN STITCHES

Shell: [2 dc, ch 1, 2 dc] in indicated st.
Beg shell: Sl st into indicated st, [ch 3, 1 dc, ch 1, 2 dc] in indicated st.

DOLL

HEAD & BODY

Rnd 1: With D hook and pink, ch 2, 6 sc in 2nd ch from hook, join in beg sc, turn. (6 sc)
Rnd 2: Ch 1, 2 sc in each sc around, join in beg sc, turn. (12 sc)
Rnd 3: Ch 1, sc in first sc, 2 sc in next sc, [sc in next sc, 2 sc in next sc] rep around, join in beg sc, turn. (18 sc)
Rnd 4: Ch 1, sc in each of next 2 sc, 2

SIZE 12 inches tall

MATERIALS

- Sport weight yarn: 2 oz pink, 1 oz brown, scraps of black and red
- Pompadour baby yarn: 1 oz each aqua and sweet dreams print, small amount baby pink
- Crochet cotton size 10: 100 yds white
- Size D/3 crochet hook or size needed to obtain gauge
- Size 6 steel crochet hook or size needed to obtain gauge
- 3 snap fasteners
- 10 inches ⅛-inch-wide white ribbon
- Fiberfill
- Sewing needle and thread
- Tapestry needle

sc in next sc, [sc in each of next 2 sc, 2 sc in next sc] rep around, join in beg sc, turn. (24 sc)
Rnd 5: Ch 1, sc in each of next 3 sc, 2 sc in next sc, [sc in each of next 3 sc, 2 sc in next sc] rep around, join in beg sc, turn. (30 sc)
Rnd 6: Ch 1, sc in each of next 4 sc, 2

sc in next sc, [sc in each of next 4 sc, 2 sc in next sc] rep around, join in beg sc, turn. (36 sc)
Rnd 7: Ch 1, sc in each sc around, join in beg sc, turn.
Rnd 8: Ch 1, sc in each of next 5 sc, 2 sc in next sc, [sc in each of next 5 sc, 2 sc in next sc] rep around, join in beg sc, turn. (42 sc)
Rnds 9–15: Rep Rnd 7.
Rnd 16: Ch 1, sc in each of next 16 sc, [2 sc in next sc] 4 times, sc in each of next 2 sc, [2 sc in next sc] 4 times, sc in each of next 16 sc, join in beg sc, turn. (50 sc)
Rnds 17 & 18: Rep Rnd 7.
Rnd 19: Ch 1, sc in each of next 23 sc, [sc dec over next 2 sc] twice, sc in each of next 23 sc, join in beg sc, turn. (48 sc)
Rnds 20–22: Rep Rnd 7.
Rnd 23: Ch 1, sc in each of next 15 sc, [sc dec over next 2 sc] 4 times, sc in each of next 2 sc, [sc dec over next 2 sc] 4 times, sc in each of next 15 sc, join in beg sc, turn. (40 sc)
Rnd 24: Ch 1, [sc in each of next 6 sc, sc dec over next 2 sc] rep around, join in beg sc, turn. (35 sc)

Rnd 25: Ch 1, [sc in each of next 3 sc, sc dec over next 2 sc] rep around, join in beg sc, turn. (28 sc)

Rnd 26: Ch 1, [sc in each of next 2 sc, sc dec over next 2 sc] rep around, join in beg sc, turn. (21 sc) Stuff head with fiberfill.

Rnd 27: Ch 1, [sc in each of next 5 sc, sc dec over next 2 sc] rep around, join in beg sc, turn. (18 sc)

Rnds 28 & 29: Rep Rnd 7.

Rnd 30: Ch 1, [sc in next sc, 2 sc in next sc] rep around, join in beg sc, turn. (27 sc)

Rnd 31: Ch 1, [sc in each of next 2 sc, 2 sc in next sc] rep around, join in beg sc, turn. (36 sc)

Rnd 32: Ch 1, [sc in each of next 8 sc, 2 sc in next sc] 4 times, join in beg sc, turn. (40 sc)

Rnds 33–48: Rep Rnd 7.

Rnds 49–51: Rep Rnds 24–26. Stuff body and continue to stuff body as work progresses. (21 sc)

Rnd 52: Ch 1, [sc in next sc, sc dec over next 2 sc] rep around, join in beg sc, turn. (14 sc)

Rnd 53: Ch 1, [sc dec over next 2 sc] 7 times, join in beg sc, leaving a length of yarn, fasten off. (7 sc)

ARM
Make 2

Rnd 1: With D hook and pink, ch 2, 7 sc in 2nd ch from hook, join in beg sc, turn. (7 sc)

Rnd 2: Ch 1, 2 sc in each sc around, join in beg sc, turn. (14 sc)

Rnd 3: Ch 1, [sc in each of next 6 sc, 2 sc in next sc] rep around, join in beg sc, turn. (16 sc)

Rnd 4: Ch 1, sc in each sc around, join in beg sc, turn.

Rnds 5–10: Rep Rnd 4.

Rnd 11: Ch 1, sc dec over next 2 sc, sc in each rem sc around, join in beg sc, turn. (15 sc)

Rnd 12: Rep Rnd 4.

Rnd 13: Rep Rnd 11. (14 sc)

Rnd 14: Ch 1, sc in each of next 6 sc, 2 sc in each of next 2 sc, sc in each of next 6 sc, join in beg sc, turn. (16 sc)

Rnd 15: Rep Rnd 11. (15 sc)

Rnds 16 & 17: Rep Rnds 4 and 11. (14 sc)

Rnd 18: Ch 1, [sc dec over next 2 sc, sc in each of next 5 sc] twice, join in beg sc, turn. (12 sc)

Rnd 19: Rep Rnd 4.

Rnd 20: Ch 1, [sc in each of next 3 sc, 2 sc in next sc] rep around, join in beg sc, turn. (15 sc)

Rnd 21: Ch 1, sc in each of next 7 sc, [sc, ch 3 (for thumb), sc in 2nd ch from hook, sc] in next sc, sc in each of next 7 sc, join in beg sc, turn.

Rnd 22: Ch 1, sc in each of next 10 sc, working on opposite side of thumb ch, sc in each of next 2 chs, sc in each of next 8 sc, join in beg sc, turn. (20 sc)

Rnd 23: Ch 1, sc in each of next 7 sc, sk next 6 sc, sc in next 7 sc, join in beg sc, turn. (14 sc)

Rnd 24: Rep Rnd 4. Stuff with fiberfill.

Rnd 25: Ch 1, [sc in each of next 5 sc, sc dec over next 2 sc] twice, join in beg sc, turn. (12 sc)

Rnd 26: Ch 1, [sc in each of next 4 sc, sc dec over next 2 sc] twice, join in beg sc, leaving a length of yarn, fasten off. (10 sc)

LEG
Make 2

Row 1: Starting with sole, with D hook and pink, ch 3, sc in 2nd ch from hook, sc in next ch, turn. (2 sc)

Row 2: Ch 1, 2 sc in each sc across, turn. (4 sc)

Row 3: Ch 1, sc in each sc across, turn.

Row 4: Rep Row 3.

Row 5: Ch 1, sc in first sc, sc dec over next 2 sc, sc in next sc, turn. (3 sc)

Row 6: Rep Row 3.

Row 7: Ch 1, sc in first sc, sk next sc, sc in last sc, turn.

Rnd 8: Sl st in first sc, 3 sc in next sc, work 19 more sc around sole with 3 sc in opposite side of foundation ch, join in beg sc, turn. (25 sc)

Rnd 9: Ch 1, sc in each sc around, join in beg sc, turn.

Rnd 10: Rep Rnd 9.

Rnd 11: Ch 1, sc in each of next 8 sc, [sc dec over next 2 sc] twice, sc in next sc, [sc dec over next 2 sc] twice, sc in each of next 8 sc, join in beg sc, turn. (21 sc)

Rnd 12: Rep Rnd 9.

Rnd 13: Ch 1, sc in each of next 6 sc, [sc dec over next 2 sc] twice, sc in next sc, [sc dec over next 2 sc] twice, sc in next 6 sc, join in beg sc, turn. (17 sc)

Rnd 14: Ch 1, sc in each of next 4 sc, [sc dec over next 2 sc] twice, sc in next sc, [sc dec over next 2 sc] twice, sc in next 4 sc, join in beg sc, turn. (13 sc)

Rnd 15: Rep Rnd 9.

Rnds 16–18: Ch 1, 2 sc in first sc, sc in each rem sc around, join in beg sc, turn. (16 sc)

Rnd 19: Rep Rnd 9.

Rnd 20: Rep Rnd 16. (17 sc)

Rnd 21: Rep Rnd 9.

Rnd 22: Ch 1, sc in each sc around to last sc, 2 sc in last sc, join in beg sc, turn. (18 sc)

Rnd 23: Rep Rnd 9.

Rnd 24: Ch 1, sc dec over next 2 sc, sc in each of next 3 sc, 2 sc in next sc, sc in each of next 6 sc, 2 sc in next sc, sc in each of next 3 sc, sc dec over next 2 sc, join in beg sc, turn. (18 sc)

Rnd 25: Rep Rnd 9.

Rnd 26: Ch 1, sc dec over next 2 sc, [sc in each of next 4 sc, 2 sc in next sc] twice, sc in each of next 4 sc, sc dec over next 2 sc, join in beg sc, turn. (18 sc)

Rnds 27 & 28: Rep Rnd 9.

Rnd 29: Ch 1, 2 sc in first sc, sc in each rem sc around, join in beg sc, turn. (19 sc)

Rnds 30–32: Rep Rnd 9.

Rnd 33: Ch 1, sc in each of next 4 sc, 2 sc in next sc, sc in each of next 9 sc, sc in next sc, sc in each of next 4 sc, join in beg sc, turn. (21 sc)

Rnds 34–39: Rep Rnd 9.

Rnd 40: Ch 1, [sc in each of next 5 sc, sc dec over next 2 sc] rep around, join in beg sc, turn. (18 sc)

Rnd 41: Ch 1, [sc in next sc, sc dec over next 2 sc] rep around, join in beg sc, turn. (12 sc)

Rnd 42: Ch 1, [sc dec over next 2 sc] rep around, join in beg sc, leaving a length of yarn, fasten off. (6 sc)

HAIR

Rnd 1: With D hook and brown, ch 2, 7 sc in 2nd ch from hook, join in beg sc, turn. (7 sc)

Rnd 2: Ch 1, 2 sc in each sc around, join in beg sc, turn. (14 sc)

Rnd 3: Ch 1, [sc in next sc, 2 sc in next sc] rep around, join in beg sc, turn. (21 sc)

Rnd 4: Ch 1, [sc in each of next 2 sc, 2 sc in next sc] rep around, join in beg sc, turn. (28 sc)

Rnd 5: Ch 1, sc in each sc around, join in beg sc, turn.

Rnd 6: Ch 1, [sc in each of next 3 sc, 2 sc in next sc] rep around, join in beg sc, turn. (35 sc)

Rnd 7: Ch 1, [sc in each of next 4 sc, 2 sc in next sc] rep around, join in beg sc, turn. (42 sc)

Rnds 8–12: Rep Rnd 5.

Rnd 13: Ch 1, [sc in each of next 13 sc, 2 sc in next sc] rep around, join in beg sc, turn. (45 sc)

Rnds 14 & 15: Rep Rnd 5.

Rnd 16: Ch 1, working in back lps only, sc in each st around, join in beg sc, do not turn.

Rnd 17: Ch 1, working in front lps only, ch 1, sc in same st as beg ch-1, ch 6, [sc in next st, ch 6] rep around, join in beg sc, leaving a length of yarn, fasten off.

ASSEMBLY

Sew opening closed at bottom of body. Sew hand seam closed flat and sew opening in side of thumb. Sew opening closed at top of leg. To attach legs, place on each side of body with feet pointing forward and thread a long length of pink on tapestry needle and draw through center of leg at Rnd 37, draw out on opposite side of leg and draw through body from side to side at Rnd 47 and out opposite side of body, through 2nd leg at Rnd 37 and back through same leg, knot and secure end.

Attach arms in same manner working through Rnd 5 of arms and through Rnd 32 of body.

Using photo as a guide, with black, embroider eye over Rnds 14 and 15 of head. With pink, embroider nose over Rnds 16 and 17. With red, embroider smiley mouth centered below nose.

Sew scalp to head. Cut 45 strands of brown yarn each 17 inches long. [Fold a strand in half, insert hook in rem free lp of Rnd 15, draw strand of yarn through at fold to form a lp on hook, draw cut ends through lp on hook and pull gently to secure] rep in each rem lp of Rnd 15.

HAIR TIE

With hook size 6 and white, ch 4, dc in first ch of ch-4, turn, [ch 3, dc in base of ch-3, turn] 57 times, fasten off.

Draw hair up in a ponytail, wrap tie around hair and tie ends in a bow. Trim hair as desired.

CLOTHES

PANTIES
Waistband

Row 1: Beg with waistband, with hook size 6 and white, ch 5, sc in 2nd ch from hook, sc in each rem ch across, turn. (4 sc)

Rows 2–76: Ch 1, working in back lps only, sc in each st across, turn.

Row 77: Holding opposite side of foundation ch to Row 76, working through both thicknesses, sl st in each st across, turn right side out.

Bottom

Rnd 1: Ch 3, work 84 dc evenly sp in side edge of rows, join in 3rd ch of beg ch-3. (85 dc)

Rnds 2–8: Ch 3, dc in each dc around, join in 3rd ch of beg ch-3.

First leg

Rnd 9: Ch 3, sk next 41 dc, sl st in

next dc, ch 3, dc in each of next 42 dc, dc in each of next 3 chs, join in 3rd ch of beg ch-3.

Rnd 10: Ch 1, [sc in each of next 2 sts, sc dec over next 2 sts] rep around, join in beg sc.

Rnd 11: Ch 1, sc in each st around, join in beg sc.

Rnd 12: Ch 1, [sc in next sc, ch 3] rep around, join in beg sc, fasten off.

Second leg

Rnd 9: Attach white in next st of Rnd 8, ch 3, dc in each dc around, dc in each of next 3 crotch chs, join in 3rd ch of beg ch-3.

Rnds 10–12: Rep Rnds 10–12 of first leg.

DRESS

Row 1: With hook size D and aqua, ch 31, sc in 2nd ch from hook, sc in each of next 4 chs, ch 2, sc in each of next 5 chs, ch 2, sc in each of next 10 chs, [ch 2, sc in each of next 5 chs] twice, turn.

Row 2: Ch 3, dc in each of next 4 sc, shell in next ch-2 sp, dc in each of next 5 sc, shell in next ch-2 sp, dc in each of next 10 sc, [shell in next ch-2 sp, dc in each of next 5 sc] twice, turn.

Row 3: Ch 1, [sc in each dc to next ch-1 sp, {sc, ch 2, sc} in next ch-1 sp of shell] 4 times, sc in each rem dc, turn.

Row 4: Ch 3, dc in each sc and shell in each ch-2 sp across, turn.

Row 5: Ch 1, working in front lps only, sc in each dc and each ch across, turn. (74 sc)

Row 6: Ch 3, dc in each of next 9 sc, ch 1, sk next 17 sc (armhole opening), dc in each of next 20 sc, ch 1, sk next 17 sc (armhole opening), dc in each of next 10 sc, turn.

Row 7: Ch 1, sc in each dc and each ch across, turn. (42 sc)

Row 8: Ch 1, sc in each sc across, turn.

Row 9: Ch 3, dc in same st as beg ch-3, ch 1, 2 dc in next sc, [sk next sc, shell in next sc] rep across, turn. (21 shells)

Rows 10 & 11: Sl st into ch-1 sp of shell, beg shell in same ch-1 sp, shell in each ch-1 sp across, ending with dc in last dc of last shell, turn.

Rnd 12: Sl st into ch-1 sp of shell, beg shell in same ch-1 sp, shell in each ch-1

sp around, dc in last dc, join in 3rd ch of beg ch-3.

Rnd 13: Sl st into ch-1 sp of shell, beg shell in same ch-1 sp, ch 1, [shell in next ch-1 sp of next shell, ch 1] rep around, ending with shell in last dc, ch 1, join in 3rd ch of beg ch-3.

Rnd 14: Sl st into ch-1 sp of shell, beg shell in same ch-1 sp, ch 1, [shell in next ch-1 sp of shell, ch 1] rep around, join in 3rd ch of beg ch-1.

Rnd 15: Sl st into next ch-1 sp of shell, ch 1, *[sc, ch 2, 2 dc] in same ch-1 sp of shell, [sc, ch 2, 2 dc] in next ch-1 sp between shells, rep from * around, join in beg sc, fasten off.

Yoke trim

With size 6 hook, attach white in rem lp of Row 4 of dress, ch 1, [sc, ch 3, sc] in same st as beg ch-1, [sc, ch 3, sc] in each rem free lp across, fasten off.

SLEEVE

Make 2

Rnd 1: With size D hook, attach aqua at bottom of armhole, ch 1, work 24 sc around armhole opening, join in beg sc. (24 sc)

Rnd 2: Ch 1, sc in each of next 10 sc, 2 sc in each of next 4 sc, sc in each of next 10 sc, join in beg sc. (28 sc)

Rnd 3: Ch 1, sc in each of next 8 sts, hdc in each of next 2 sts, dc in each of next 8 sts, hdc in each of next 2 sts, sc in each of next 8 sts, join in beg sc.

Rnd 4: Ch 3, dc in each st around, join in 3rd ch of beg ch-3.

Rnd 5: Ch 1, [sc dec over next 2 dc] rep around, join in beg sc. (14 sc)

Rnds 6 & 7: Ch 1, sc in each sc around, join in beg sc.

Rnd 8: Ch 1, working in back lps only, sc in same st as beg ch-1, ch 3, [sc in next st, ch 3] rep around, join in beg sc, fasten off.

Sleeve trim

Rnd 9: With size 6 hook, attach white in rem free lp of Rnd 8, ch 1, [sc, ch 3, sc] in same st as beg ch-1, [sc, ch 3, sc] in each rem st around, join in beg sc, fasten off. Cut a 5-inch length of white ribbon. Fold ribbon into a bow and sew to front neckline. Sew 2 snap fasteners evenly sp down back opening.

ROMPER

Yoke

Row 1: With size D hook and pink pompadour, ch 11, sc in 2nd ch from hook, sc in each rem ch across, turn. (10 sc)

Rows 2–60: Ch 1, working in back lps only, sc in each st across, turn.

Row 61: Ch 1, working in ends of rows, work 92 sc across, fasten off, turn.

Row 62: Attach print yarn in front lp of first sc, working in front lps only, sc in each st across, turn.

Row 63: Ch 3, dc in each of next 9 sts, ch 1, sk next 24 sts (armhole opening), dc in each of next 24 sts, ch 1, sk next 24 sts (armhole opening), dc in each of next 10 sts, turn.

Row 64: Ch 3, dc in next 9 sts, 2 dc in next ch-1 sp, dc in each of next 24 sts, 2 dc in next ch-1 sp, dc in each of next 10 sts, turn. (48 dc)

Rows 65 & 66: Ch 3, dc in each dc across, turn.

Rnd 67: Ch 3, dc in each of next 23 dc, 2 dc in next dc, dc in each rem dc around, join in 3rd ch of beg ch-3. (49 dc)

Rnds 68 & 69: Ch 3, dc in each dc around, join in 3rd ch of beg ch-3, turn.

First leg

Rnd 70: Ch 3 (for crotch), sk next 23 dc, sl st in next dc, ch 3, dc in each rem dc, dc in each of the 3 chs for crotch, join in 3rd ch of beg ch-3, turn.

Rnd 71: Ch 1, sc in each of next 2 sts, [sc dec over next 2 sts, sc in each of next 2 sts] rep around, join in beg sc, turn.

Rnd 72: Ch 1, sc in each st around, join in beg sc.

Rnd 73: Ch 1, working in back lps only, sc in first st, ch 3, [sc in next st, ch 3] rep around, join in beg sc, fasten off.

Second leg

Rnd 70: Attach print in next st of Rnd 69, ch 3, dc in each rem st around, dc in opposite side of ch-3 of crotch foundation ch, join in 3rd ch of beg ch-3, turn.

Rows 71–73: Rep Rows 71–73 of first leg.

Leg trim

With size 6 hook, attach white in rem free lp of Rnd 72, ch 1, [sc, ch 3, sc] in same st, [sc, ch 3, sc] in each rem st around, join in beg sc, fasten off.

Top yoke trim

Row 1: With WS facing, attach print yarn in top of yoke, working in ends of rows, ch 1, sc in same st, work 29 sc evenly sp across neckline, turn. (30 sc)

Row 2: Ch 1, working in back lps only, sc in each st across, fasten off.

Row 3: With size 6 hook, attach white in rem free lp of Row 1, ch 1, [sc, ch 3, sc] in same st, [sc, ch 3, sc] in each rem st across, fasten off.

Bottom yoke trim

With size 6 hook, attach white in rem free lp of Row 61, ch 1, [sc, ch 3, sc] in same st, [sc, ch 3, sc] in each rem st across, fasten off.

Neckline trim & ties

With size 6 hook and white, ch 42, sc in first sc on neck edge, [ch 1, sc in next sc] rep across, ch 42, fasten off.

With rem 5-inch piece of ribbon, tie into a bow and sew to front of romper at neckline. Sew a snap fastener at back waistline.

SHOE

Make 2

Row 1: Starting at sole with size 6 hook and white, ch 5, sc in 2nd ch from hook, sc in each rem ch across, turn. (4 sc)

Rows 2–4: Ch 1, 2 sc in first sc, sc in each sc across to last sc, 2 sc in last sc, turn. (10 sc)

Row 5: Ch 1, sc in each sc across, turn.

Row 6: Rep Row 2. (12 sc)

Rows 7–14: Rep Row 5.

Row 15: Ch 1, sc dec over next 2 sc, sc in each sc across to last 2 sc, sc dec over next 2 sc, turn. (10 sc)

Rows 16 & 17: Rep Row 5.

Rows 18 & 19: Rep Row 15. (6 sc)

Row 20: Ch 1, sc in each sc across, do not turn.

Rnd 21: Working around outer edge of sole, ch 1, work 54 sc around, join in beg sc.

Rnd 22: Working in back lps only, ch 3, dc in each st around, join in 3rd ch of beg ch-3.

Rnd 23: Ch 3, dc in each dc around, join in 3rd ch of beg ch-3.

Rnd 24: Ch 3, dc in each of next 13 dc, [dc dec over next 2 dc] 10 times, dc in each rem dc around, join in 3rd ch of beg ch-3.

Rnd 25: Ch 1, sc in same st as beg ch-1, sc in each of next 11 sts, [sc dec over next 2 sts] 7 times, sc in each rem st around, join in beg sc.

Rnd 26: Ch 3, [fpdc around next st, bpdc around next st] rep around, join in 3rd ch of beg ch-3, fasten off.

Place shoes on doll. ■

DESIGN BY
BENDY CARTER

BABY BELINDA

Patterned after a life-size doll used in hospitals, Baby Belinda's realistic size and features will make her seem like a real "baby sister" for any little girl. She comes complete with a matching outfit, cuddly blanket, diaper and pacifier.

GAUGE

With hook size C, 5 sc = 1 inch; 6 sc rows = 1 inch
Check gauge to save time.

PATTERN NOTES

Weave in loose ends as work progresses.
Use hook size C unless otherwise stated.

To make a seamless doll, mark beg of each rnds with st marker, do not join.
Join rnds with a sl st unless otherwise stated.

Dress, pacifier holder, hat, booties and blanket can be used for 17–18-inch preemie baby. Diaper and crocheted pacifier are for doll only.

Use care while crocheting to changes within from rnds and rows and back to rnds.

DOLL

FOOT & LEG
Make 2

Rnd 1: With skin color, ch 10, 3 sc in 2nd ch from hook, sc in each of next 7 chs, 3 sc in last ch, working on opposite side of foundation ch, sc in each of next 7 chs. (20 sc)

INTERMEDIATE ●●●

SIZE 18-inch baby doll
Blanket: 27 inches square

MATERIALS
- J. & P. Coats Luster Sheen sport weight acrylic yarn (1/34 oz per ball): 5 balls each spa blue #821 (A) and white #001 (B), small amount natural #805 (C)
- Sport weight yarn: 8 oz skin color of choice
- Anchor embroidery floss: 4 skeins coffee medium #359, small amounts black #406, denim medium #921, white #2 and salmon very light #6
- Size E/4 crochet hook
- Size C/2 crochet hook or size needed to obtain gauge
- 8 (5/8-inch) buttons with 2 holes for sewing
- 4 (9mm) heart-shape buttons
- 2 size 1 snap fasteners
- 2 blue party favor plastic mini safety pins
- 10 ribbon accents
- 2 (2-inch) steel rings
- Powder blusher
- Fiberfill
- Stitch markers
- Sewing needle and thread
- Yarn needle

Rnd 2: [2 sc in each of next 3 sc, sc in each of next 7 sc] twice. (26 sc)

Rnd 3: [{Sc in next sc, 2 sc in next sc} 3 times, sc in each of next 7 sc] twice. (32 sc)

Rnd 4: [{Sc in each of next 2 sc, 2 sc in next sc} 3 times, sc in each of next 7 sc] twice. (38 sc)

Rnd 5: Sc in each sc around.

Rnd 6: Rep Rnd 5.

Row 7: [Sc in next sc, sc dec over next 2 sc] 4 times, sc in next sc, sl st in next sc, turn.

Rnd 8: Ch 1, sc in each sc around. (34 sc)

Row 9: Sc dec over next 2 sc, sc in each of next 4 sc, sc dec over next 2 sc, sl st in next sc, turn.

Rows 10–16: Ch 1, sc in each of next 6 sc, sl st in next unused sc, turn.

Rnd 17: Ch 1, sc in each sc around. (24 sc)

Rnds 18–32: Rep Rnd 5.

Rnd 33: Sc around, working 4 sc inc at front knee. (28 sc)

Rnd 34: Rep Rnd 5.

Rnd 35: Sc around, working 4 sc dec at front knee and 4 sc inc at back knee. (28 sc)

Rnd 36: Rep Rnd 5.

Rnd 37: Sc around, working 3 sc dec at front knee and 4 sc inc at back knee. (29 sc)

Rnd 38: Rep Rnd 5.

Rnd 39: Sc around, working 2 sc dec at front knee and 4 sc inc at back knee. (31 sc)

Rnds 40–44: Rep Rnd 5.

Rnd 45: Sc around, working 3 sc dec at inner leg. (28 sc)

Rnd 46: Rep Rnd 5.

Rnd 47: Sc around, working 2 sc dec at inner leg. (26 sc)

Rnd 48: Rep Rnd 5.

Rnd 49: Sc around, working 1 sc dec at inner leg. (25 sc)

Rnd 50: Rep Rnd 5.

Rnd 51: Sc in next st, [sc dec over next 2 sc, sc in next sc] 8 times. (17 sc)

Rnd 52: Rep Rnd 5.

Rnd 53: Sc in next sc, [sc dec over next 2 sc, sc in next sc] 5 times, sc in next sc, leaving a 6-inch length of yarn, fasten off. Stuff foot and leg, weave yarn through each sc of Rnd 53, pull tightly to close.

HAND
Make 4

Row 1: With skin color, ch 8, sc in 2nd ch from hook, sc in each rem ch across, turn. (7 sc)

Row 2: Ch 4, sc in 2nd ch from hook, sc in each of next 2 chs (thumb), sc in each of next 7 sc, turn. (10 sc)

Row 3: Ch 1, sc in each of next 7 sc, leaving rem 3 thumb sts unworked, turn. (7 sc)

Row 4: Ch 1, sc in each sc across, turn.

Row 5: Ch 4, sc in 2nd ch from hook, sc in each of next 2 chs, sl st in same sc at base of ch (little finger), sl st in each of next 2 sc, [ch 5, sc in 2nd ch from hook, sc in each of next 3 chs, sl st in same sc as last sl st on hand, sl st in next 2 sc] twice (ring finger and middle finger), ch 5, sc in 2nd ch from hook, sc in each of next 3 chs, sl st in same st as last sl st, leaving a long length of yarn, fasten off.

Holding 2 hand sections on top of each other, sew fingers and side of hand tog, leaving wrist open (opposite side of foundation ch).

ARM
Make 2

Rnd 1: Attach skin color in opposite side of foundation ch at wrist opening, ch 1, sc in each ch around. (14 sc)

Rnd 2: Sc around, working 3 sc inc evenly sp around. (17 sc)

Rnd 3: Sc in each sc around.

Rnds 4–11: Rep Rnd 3.

Rnd 12: Sc around, working 3 sc inc at back elbow. (20 sc)

Rnd 13: Rep Rnd 3.

Rnd 14: Sc around, working 3 sc dec at back elbow and 3 sc inc at front elbow. (20 sc)

Rnd 15: Rep Rnd 3.

Rnd 16: Sc around, working 2 sc dec at back elbow and 3 sc inc at front elbow. (21 sc)

Rnd 17: Rep Rnd 3.

Rnd 18: Sc around, working 1 sc dec at back elbow and 3 sc at front elbow. (23 sc)

Rnds 19–24: Rep Rnd 3.

Rnd 25: Sc in next sc, [sc in next sc, sc dec over next 2 sc] 7 times, sc in next sc. (16 sc)

Rnd 26: Rep Rnd 3.

Rnd 27: [Sc in next sc, sc dec over next 2 sc] 5 times, sc in next sc, leaving a 6-inch length of yarn, fasten off. Stuff hand and arm, weave rem length through sc sts of Rnd 27, pull tight to close opening, secure.

BODY

Rnds 1–6: Rep Rnds 1–6 of foot and leg. (38 sc)

Rnds 7–9: Rep Rnds 4–6 of foot and leg. (44 sc)

Rnd 10: Sc around, working 2 sc inc at both ends. (48 sc)

Rnd 11: Sc in each sc around.

Rnd 12: Rep Rnd 11.

Rnd 13: Sc around, working 5 sc inc at front. (53 sc)

Rnds 14 & 15: Rep Rnd 11.

Rnd 16: Sc in each st to center front, 4 sc in next st, draw up a lp, remove hook, insert hook in first sc of 4-sc group, pick up dropped lp and draw through st on hook, ch 1 to close (belly button), sc in each rem st around.

Rnds 17–46: Rep Rnd 11.

Rnd 47: Sc in each of next 3 sc, [sc dec over next 2 sc, sc in each of next 3 sc] 10 times. (43 sc)

Rnd 48: Rep Rnd 11.

Rnd 49: Sc around, working 3 sc dec on each side. (37 sc)

Rnd 50: Rep Rnd 11.

Rnd 51: Sc around, working 2 sc dec on each side. (33 sc)

Rnd 52: Rep Rnd 11, draw up a slight lp, remove hook, do not fasten off.

ATTACHING LEGS & ARMS
Note: *Use the ⅝-inch buttons to attach legs and arms to body.*

Run thread through 1 hole in button, through body from inside body to outside, through leg, through 1 hole of 2nd button, then back through other hole of 2nd button, back through same place on leg, back through same place on body, through other hole on first button, tie securely. It's important to go back through same place on body so that leg will be movable. Fasten arms to Rnd 46 of body in same manner as legs.

Slide first steel ring over neck of body (this ring will be used for head).

Rnd 53: Using 2nd steel ring, sc in each st of Rnd 52, working sc sts over 2nd ring, fasten off.

Stuff body with fiberfill.

EAR
Make 2

Row 1: With skin color, ch 17, starting in 2nd ch from hook, [sc dec over next 2 chs] 8 times, turn.

Rows 2 & 3: Ch 1, [sc dec over next 2 sts] rep across, turn. At the end of Row 3, leaving a length of yarn, fasten off.

HEAD

Rnd 1: Attach skin color to first ring, ch 1, 60 sc around ring, sl st to join in rep sc. (60 sc)

Rnd 2: Sc in each st around.

Rnd 3: Rep Rnd 2.

Rnd 4: [Sc in next sc, sc dec over next 2 sc] 3 times, sc in each of next 14 sc, [2 sc in next sc, sc in each of next 2 sc] 6 times, sc in each of next 10 sc, [sc in next sc, sc dec over next 2 sc] 3 times. (60 sc)

Rnds 5–8: Rep Rnd 2.

Rnd 9: Sc in each of next 28 sc, ch 4, sk next 4 sc (mouth opening), sc in each of next 28 sc.

Rnd 10: Sc in each of next 28 sc, sc in each of next 4 chs, sc in each of next 28 sc.

Rnd 11: Sc in each of next 24 sc, 2 sc in each of next 2 sc, [sc dec over next 2 sc] 4 times, 2 sc in each of next 2 sc, sc in each of next 24 sc. (60 sc)

Rnd 12: Rep Rnd 2.

Rnd 13: Sc in each of next 24 sc, 2 sc in each of next 2 sc, sc dec over next 2 sc, working in back lps only, sc in each of next 2 sts, working in both lps, sc dec over next 2 sc, 2 sc in each of next 2 sc, sc in each of next 24 sc.

Rnd 14: Sc in each of next 30 sc, *[yo, insert hook in unused lp 1 rnd below, yo, draw up a lp, yo, draw through 2 lps on hook] 3 times in same st, yo, draw, draw through all 4 lps on hook, rep from * once, sk the 2 sc sts directly behind, sc in each of next 30 sc.

Rnd 15: 2 sc in first sc, sc in each of next 5 sc, 2 sc in next sc, sc in each of next 16 sc, [sc dec over next 2 sc, sc in next sc] 6 times, sc in each of next 15 sc, 2 sc in next sc, sc in each of next 5 sc. (59 sc)

Rnds 16 & 17: Rep Rnd 2.

Rnd 18: Sc around, working 3 sc inc across forehead. (62 sc)

Rnds 19–27: Rep Rnd 2. At the end of Rnd 27, fasten off.

MOUTH

Rnd 1: With WS of head facing, attach skin color to mouth opening, work 12 sc around mouth opening, join in beg sc. (12 sc)

Rnds 2 & 3: Sc in each sc around.

Rnd 4: [Sc dec over next 2 sc] 6 times, leaving a length of yarn, fasten off. (6 sc)

Weave rem length through sts of Rnd 4, pull to close opening, secure.

FACIAL FEATURES

Sew ears to side of head. Using photo as a guide, outline eyes with skin color, working with embroidery thread, embroider eyes using white for eye, black for pupil and denim medium for iris. Embroider mouth with salmon very light. With coffee medium, embroider eyelashes and upper eyelids.

Enhance mouth with small amount of powder blusher.

TOP OF HEAD

Rnd 1: Attach skin color to last st of Rnd 27, ch 1, [sc in next sc, sc dec over next 2 sc] 20 times, sc in each of next 2 sc. (42 sc)

Rnd 2: Sc in each st around.

Rnd 3: [Sc in next sc, sc dec over next 2 sc] 14 times. (28 sc)

Rnd 4: Rep Rnd 2.

Rnd 5: [Sc in next sc, sc dec over next 2 sc] 9 times, sc in next sc. (19 sc)

Rnd 6: Rep Rnd 2.

Rnd 7: [Sc in next sc, sc dec over next 2 sc] 6 times, sc in next sc. (13 sc)

Rnd 8: Rep Rnd 2, leaving a length of yarn, fasten off.

Stuff head so that stuffing goes into head only and not down into body, otherwise head will not turn. Weave rem length through sts of Rnd 8, pull to close opening, secure.

HAIR

Using photo as a guide, and working outward from crown with long sts, with coffee medium thread, embroider hair around top of head.

ENSEMBLE

DRESS BODICE

Foundation row (RS): With hook size C and A, ch 54, sc in 2nd ch from hook, sc in each rem ch across, turn. (53 sc)

Note: Mark foundation row on RS with a scrap of CC yarn and use care when attaching yarn for each section to be

working in the proper direction.

Right back

Row 1: Ch 1, sc in each of next 11 sc, turn.

Row 2: Ch 1, sc in each sc across, turn.

Row 3: Ch 1, sc in each of next 10 sc, turn.

Row 4: Rep Row 2.

Row 5: Ch 1, sc in each of next 9 sc, turn.

Rows 6–13: Rep Row 2.

Row 14: Ch 1, sc in each of next 5 sc, turn. (5 sc)

Rows 15 & 16: Rep Row 2, fasten off.

Front

Row 1: Sk next 3 sts of foundation row, attach A, ch 1, sc in same st as beg ch-1, sc in each of next 24 sc, turn. (25 sc)

Rows 2–5: Ch 1, sc across to last st, leaving last st unworked, turn. (21 sc)

Rows 6–10: Ch 1, sc in each sc across, turn.

Right shoulder shaping

Row 11: Ch 1, sc in each of next 9 sc, turn.

Row 12: Ch 1, sc in each sc across, turn.

Row 13: Ch 1, sc in each of next 7 sc, turn

Row 14: Rep Row 12.

Row 15: Ch 1, sc in each of next 5 sc, turn

Row 16: Rep Row 12, fasten off.

Left shoulder shaping

With RS facing, attach A in first st of Row

10 on front, rep right shoulder shaping.

Left back

With RS facing, attach A in first st on bodice foundation row, rep right back. Sew shoulder seams.

Right button band

Row 1 (RS): Attach A at right back opening, ch 1, work 14 sc evenly sp across opening, turn. (14 sc)

Rows 2–4: Ch 1, sc in each sc across, turn. At the end of Row 4, fasten off.

Left buttonhole band

Row 1: Attach A at left back opening, ch 1, work 14 sc evenly sp across opening, turn.

Row 2: Ch 1, sc in each st across, turn.

Row 3: Ch 1, sc in same st as beg ch-1, [ch 2, sk 2 sts, sc in each of next 3 sts] twice, ch 2, sk next 2 sts, sc in next st, turn.

Row 4: Rep Row 2, fasten off.
Sew heart buttons opposite buttonholes.

Armhole trim

Make 2

Rnd 1: With WS facing, attach A at armhole opening, ch 1, work 36 sc evenly sp around opening, join in beg sc, fasten off.

Neckline trim

Row 1: With RS facing, attach A at neck opening, ch 1, work 42 sc evenly sp around opening, fasten off.

Left collar

Row 1: Attach B at left neck opening, ch 1, sc in same st as beg ch-1, sc in each of next 20 sc, turn. (21 sc)

Row 2: Ch 1, sc in same sc as beg ch-1, [ch 3, sk next sc, sc in next sc] 9 times, turn.

Rows 3–5: Sl st into ch-3 sp, ch 1, sc in same ch-3 sp, [ch 3, sc in next ch-3 sp] rep across, turn. At the end of Row 5, fasten off. (6 ch-3 sps)

Right collar

Rows 1–5: Attach B at right neck opening, rep Rows 1–5 of left collar.

SKIRT

Note: *Button bodice for ease in beg skirt.*

Rnd 1: Holding bodice upside down and working in opposite side of foundation ch of foundation row and in ends of buttonhole rows, working through both layers, with hook size E, attach A at back of bodice, ch 1, sc in same st as beg ch-1, [ch 3, sc in next st] rep around, ending with ch 3, sc in beg ch-3 sp.

Rnd 2: [Ch 3, sc in next ch-3 sp] rep around until skirt measures 6½ inches, ending with ch 3, sl st in 2nd ch of next ch-3 sp, fasten off.

SLEEVE

Sleeve cuff

Make 2

Rnd 1: With B, ch 22, join to form a ring, ch 1, sc in each ch around, join in beg sc. (22 sc)

Rnds 2 & 3: Ch 1, sc in each sc around, join in beg sc.

Sleeve

Rnd 1: Change to hook size E, ch 1, sc in same sc as beg ch-1, [ch 3, sk next sc, sc in next sc] 10 times, ch 3, sk next st, join in beg sc. (11 ch-3 sps)

Rnds 2–12: Sl st in next ch-3 sp, ch 1, sc in same ch-3 sp, [ch 3, sc in next ch-3 sp] rep around, ch 3, join in beg sc.

Sleeve cap

Row 1: Sl st in next ch-3 sp, ch 1, sc in same ch-3 sp, [ch 3, sc in next ch-3 sp] 9 times, turn.

Rows 2–6: Sl st in first ch-3 sp, ch 1, sc in same ch-3 sp, [ch 3, sc in next ch-3 sp] rep across, turn. At the end of Row 6, fasten off. (4 ch-3 sps)
Working in front lps only of armhole trim, sew sleeve into armhole opening easing in fullness. Sew 4 ribbon accents evenly sp across front of bodice.

BOOTIE

Make 2

Rnd 1: With B, ch 12, 3 sc in 2nd ch from hook, sc in each of next 9 chs, 3 sc in last ch, working on opposite side of foundation ch, sc in each of next 9 chs. (24 sc)

Rnd 2: [2 sc in each of next 3 sc, sc in each of next 9 sc] twice. (30 sc)

Rnd 3: [{Sc in next sc, 2 sc in next sc} 3 times, sc in each of next 9 sc] twice. (36 sc)

Rnd 4: [{Sc in each of next 2 sc, 2 sc in next sc} 3 times, sc in each of next 9 sc] twice. (42 sc)

Rnd 5: Ch 1, working in front lps for this rnd only, sc in each st around.

Rnd 6: Sc in each sc around.

Rnds 7 & 8: Rep Rnd 6.

Row 9: [Sc in next sc, sc dec over next 2 sc] 4 times, sc in next st, sl st in next st, turn. (34 sc)

Rnd 10: Ch 1, sc in each sc around.

Row 11: Sc dec over next 2 sts, sc in each of next 4 sts, sc dec over next 2 sts, sl st in next st, turn.

Rows 12–18: Ch 1, sc in each of next 6 sc, sl st in next unused sc, turn.

Rnd 19: Ch 1, sc in each sc around, join in beg sc. (28 sc)

Rnd 20: Ch 1, sc in same sc as beg ch-1, [ch 1, sk next sc, sc in next sc] 13 times, ch 1, join in beg sc.

Rnd 21: Change to hook size E, ch 1, sc in same sc as beg ch-1, [ch 3, sk next ch-1 sp, sc in next sc] 13 times, ch 3, sk next ch-1 sp, sc in next ch-3 sp, [ch 3, sc in next ch-3 sp] rep until cuff measures 1 inch from beg, ending with ch 3, sl st in 2nd ch of next ch-3 sp, fasten off.

TIE

Make 2

With A, ch 76, sc in 2nd ch from hook, sc in each rem ch across, fasten off. (75 sc)
Starting at center front, weave through ch-1 sps of Rnd 20, tie ends in a bow.

PACIFIER

Ring

With A, ch 6, join to form a ring, 6 sc in ring. Continue to work on the 6 sc only, sc around until a total of 144 sc are completed. Piece will look like a long tube, fasten off. Sew 1 sc on each end of 6-sc tube tog to form a ring.

Nipple

Rnd 1: Working in 5 rem sts on each end of ring, attach C in any sc, ch 1, sc in each sc around, join in beg sc. (10 sc)

Rnd 2: Ch 1, [sc dec over next 2 sc] 5 times, join in beg sc. (5 sc)

Rnds 3 & 4: Ch 1, sc in each sc around, join in beg sc. At the end of Rnd 4, leaving a length of yarn, fasten off.

Weave rem length through sts, pull to close opening, secure.

Disk

Rnd 1: With B, ch 8, join to form a ring, ch 1, 2 sc in each ch around, join in beg sc. (16 sc)

Rnd 2: Ch 1, sc in each sc around, join in beg sc.

Rnd 3: Ch 1, sc in same sc as beg ch-1, [ch 3, sk next st, sc in next st] 7 times, ch 3, sk next st, join in beg sc, fasten off.

Slip the disk over nipple and sew disk in place to ring.

Pacifier holder

Make 2

With A, ch 50, sc in 2nd ch from hook, sc in each rem ch across, fasten off.

Tie one pacifier holder into a bow.

Strap

Attach B in first sc of 2nd pacifier holder, ch 1, sc in same sc as beg ch-1, [ch 3, sk 1 st, sc in next st] rep across, ch 3, working in rem free lps on opposite side of foundation ch, sc in next st, [ch 3, sk 1 ch, sc in next ch] rep across, ch 3, join in beg sc, fasten off.

Sew end of strap to bow, then sew bow to front collar of dress. Sew heart button 4½ inches from end of opposite end of strap. Slip strap through ring of pacifier using ch-3 sp at end of strap for buttonhole.

DIAPER

Row 1: With hook size E and B, starting at front of diaper, ch 31, sc in 2nd ch from hook, sc in each rem ch across, turn. (30 sc)

Row 2: Ch 1, sc in each sc across, turn.

Rows 3–15: Rep Row 2.

Rows 16–21: Ch 1, sc in first sc, sc dec over next 2 sc, sc in each rem sc across, turn. (24 sc)

Rows 22–27: Rep Row 2.

Rows 28–37: Ch 1, sc in first sc, 2 sc in next sc, sc in each rem sc across, turn. (34 sc)

Rows 38–50: Rep Row 2.

Rnd 51: Change to hook size C, ch 1, sc evenly sp around outer edge of diaper, working 2 sc in each corner, join in beg sc, fasten off.

Place diaper around baby, tucking diaper in around legs. Mark position for snap placement and sew snaps on diaper. Sew play safety pins onto diaper.

HAT

Rnd 1: With A, ch 4, join to form a ring, ch 1, [sc in ring, ch 3] 5 times, join in beg sc. (5 ch-3 lps)

Rnd 2: Sl st into next ch-3 sp, ch 1, [sc, ch 3, sc] in same ch-3 sp as beg ch-1, ch 3, [{sc, ch 3, sc} in next ch-3 sp, ch 3] rep around, join in beg sc. (10 ch-3 sps)

Rnd 3: Rep Rnd 2. (20 ch-3 sps)

Rnd 4: Ch 3, sc in first ch-3 sp, [ch 3, sc in next ch-3 sp] 19 times.

Rnds 5–11: [Ch 3, sc in next ch-3 sp] 20 times.

Rnd 12: [Ch 3, sc in next ch-3 sp] 19 times, ch 3.

Rnd 13: Work 2 sc in next ch-3 sp, work 3 sc in each rem ch-3 sp around, do not join.

Rnds 14–17: Sc in each sc around.

Rnd 18: Change to hook size E, sl st in next sc, ch 1, sc in same sc as beg ch-1, [ch 3, sk 1 sc, sc in next sc] rep around, ch 3, join in beg sc, fasten off.

Sew 6 ribbon accents evenly sp over Rnds 14–17. Place hat on head.

BLANKET

Note: Work 5 rnds with A, [10 rnds with B, 10 rnds with A] twice.

Rnd 1: With hook size E and A, ch 4, join to form a ring, ch 1, [sc in ring, ch 3] 8 times, join in beg sc, turn.

Rnd 2: Sl st into ch-3 sp, ch 1, sc in same ch-3 sp, ch 3, [sc in next ch-3 sp, ch 3] rep around, join in beg sc, turn.

Rnd 3: Sl st into ch-3 sp, ch 1, [sc, ch 3, sc] in same ch-3 sp, *[ch 3, sc in next ch-3 sp] twice, [ch 3, sc in same ch-3 sp as last sc] twice, rep from * twice, [ch 3, sc in next ch-3 sp] twice, ch 3, join in beg sc, turn. (2 ch-3 sps each of 4 corners; 2 ch-3 sps on each side; total 16 ch-3 sps)

Rnd 4: Rep Rnd 2. (16 ch-3 lps)

Rnd 5: Sl st into ch-3 sp, ch 1, [sc, ch 3, sc] in same ch-3 sp, *[ch 3, sc in next ch-3 sp] 4 times across side edge of blanket, [ch 3, sc in same ch-3 sp as last sc] twice, rep from * twice, [ch 3, sc in next ch-3 sp] 4 times across side edge of blanket, ch 3, join in beg sc, turn. (2 ch-3 lps in each of 4 corners, 4 ch-3 lps on each side edge; total 24 ch-3 lps)

Rnd 6: Rep Rnd 2. (24 ch-3 lps)

Rnd 7: Sl st into ch-3 sp, ch 1, [sc, ch 3, sc] in same ch-3 sp, *[ch 3, sc in next ch-3 sp] 6 times across side edge of blanket, [ch 3, sc in same ch-3 sp as last sc] twice, rep from * twice, [ch 3, sc in next ch-3 sp] 6 times across side edge of blanket, ch 3, join in beg sc, turn. (2 ch-3 lps in each of 4 corners, 6 ch-3 lps on each side edge; total 32 ch-3 lps)

Rnds 8–45: Rep Rnds 6 and 7, adding 2 ch-3 sps in each side edge of blanket on each Rnd 7 rep. Each rep of Rnd 7 will add 8 ch-3 lps to the total. At the end of Rnd 45, fasten off. ■

Part of the charm that makes a house a home  are personal, handmade items that add a unique touch that cannot be replicated with store-bought accessories. They reflect the time and care we put into decorating our homes to make them distinctively our own. The beautiful accents presented in this chapter are sure

HOME ACCESSORIES SHOWCASE

 to showcase any decor in sophisticated style and gracious elegance and complement a variety of decorating tastes. Celebrate the place where you spend happy times with family and quiet time by yourself with distinctive handcrafted accessories that make your home uniquely personal.

ROSE SPLENDOR COVERLET

With an ornate beauty that defies its simplicity, this stunning throw evokes the feel of formal elegance, yet can perfectly accent any room with easy-living style. It works up beautifully in double-strand size 10 thread for a look that's extraordinary.

GAUGE

Motif across center from point to opposing point = 10 inches; 6 dc = 1 inch; 2 dc rnds = 1 inch
Check gauge to save time.

PATTERN NOTES

Weave in loose ends as work progresses.
Join rnds with a sl st unless otherwise stated.
Work 2 strands of same color cotton held tog throughout.

PATTERN STITCHES

Puff st: [Insert hook in st, yo, draw up a lp in indicated st, yo] 4 times, yo, draw through all 8 lps on hook.
Shell: 5 dc in indicated st.
Corner shell: 7 dc in indicated st.
Beg corner shell: [Ch 3, 6 dc] in indicated st.

MOTIF

Make 59
Rose front
Rnd 1 (RS): Beg at center front with 2 strands of mid rose, ch 4, join to form a

INTERMEDIATE ●●●
SIZE 58 x 70 inches, excluding tassels

MATERIALS

- J. & P. Coats Knit-Cro-Sheen crochet cotton size 10 (150 yds per ball): 32 balls mid rose #46A, 10 balls forest green #49
- J. & P. Coats Knit-Cro-Sheen crochet cotton size 10 (275 yds per ball): 26 balls white #1
- Size G/6 crochet hook or size needed to obtain gauge
- 59 (6mm) pearl beads
- Sewing thread to match mid rose
- Sewing needle
- Tapestry needle

ring, ch 1, [sc, ch 3] 6 times in ring, join in beg sc. (6 sc; 6 ch-3 sps)
Rnd 2: [{Hdc, 3 dc, hdc} in next ch-3 sp, sl st in next sc] 6 times. (6 petals)
Rnd 3: Holding petals forward, ch 1, sc in same sl st as beg ch-1, ch 3, [sc in next sl st, ch 3] 5 times, join in beg sc. (6 sc; 6 ch-3 sps)
Rnd 4: [{Hdc, 5 dc, hdc} in next ch-3

sp, sl st in next sc] 6 times. (6 petals)
Rnd 5: Holding petals forward, ch 1, sc in same sl st as beg ch-1, ch 4, [sc in next sl st, ch 4] 5 times, join in beg sc. (6 sc; 6 ch-4 sps)
Rnd 6: [{Hdc, 7 dc, hdc} in next ch-4 sp, sl st in next sc] 6 times. (6 petals)
Rnd 7: Holding petals forward, ch 1, sc in same sl st as beg ch-1, ch 5, [sc in next sl st, ch 5] 5 times, join in beg sc. (6 sc; 6 ch-5 sps)

Leaf
Make 6
Attach 2 strands of forest green in any sc of Rnd 7, ch 6, 3 sc in 2nd ch from hook, hdc in next ch, dc in each of next 3 chs, sl st in next ch-5 sp, ch 2, sl st in sc at base of beg ch-6, ch 2, sl st in next ch-5 sp on opposite side, working in opposite side of foundation ch of ch-6, dc in each of next 3 chs, hdc in next ch, join in beg sc, fasten off.

Rose back
Rnd 1: With WS of rose facing, attach 2 strands of mid rose around post of any sc of Rnd 1 of rose front, ch 1, sc around base of same sc, ch 3, [sc

around base of next sc of Rnd 1, ch 3] 5 times, join in beg sc. (6 sc; 6 ch-3 sps)

Rnd 2: Sl st into next ch-3 sp, holding leaves to back of work, ch 3, 4 dc in same sp, sl st in next ch-5 sp of Rnd 7 of rose front, [5 dc in next ch-3 sp, sl st in next ch-5 sp of Rnd 7 of rose front] 5 times, join in 3rd ch of beg ch-3, fasten off.

Background

Rnd 8: With RS of rose front facing, attach 2 strands of white through both rose front and rose back in sp between any 2 leaves to beg first corner, holding leaves forward, [ch 3, tr, ch 2, tr, dc] in same sp, ch 3, sc in center dc of next 5-dc group of Rnd 2 of rose back, ch 3, [{dc, tr, ch 2, tr, dc} in next sp, ch 3, sc in center dc of next 5-dc group on Rnd 2 of rose back, ch 3] 5 times, join in 3rd ch of beg ch-3.

Rnd 9: Sl st into next ch-2 sp, [ch 3, dc, ch 2, 2 dc] in same sp, [ch 3, sc in next ch-3 sp] twice, ch 3, *[2 dc, ch 2, 2 dc] in next ch-2 sp, [ch 3, sc in next ch-3 sp] twice, ch 3, rep from * around, join in 3rd ch of beg ch-3. (24 dc; 18 ch-3 sps)

Rnd 10: Sl st into corner ch-2 sp, [ch 3, dc, ch 2, 2 dc] in same sp, dc in each of next 2 dc, 2 dc in next sp, catching back lp of center sc at point of leaf to secure,

tr in next sp, 2 dc in next sp, dc in each of next 2 dc, [{2 dc, ch 2, 2 dc} in next corner ch-2 sp, dc in each of next 2 dc, 2 dc in next sp, catching back lp of center sc at point of leaf to secure, tr in next sp, 2 dc in next sp, dc in each of next 2 dc] times, join in 3rd ch of beg ch-3. (78 sts)

Rnd 11: Sl st into corner ch-2 sp, [ch 3, dc, ch 2, 2 dc] in same sp, dc in each of next 13 sts, [{2 dc, ch 2, 2 dc} in next corner ch-2 sp, dc in each of next 13 sts] 5 times, join in 3rd ch of beg ch-3. (102 dc)

Rnd 12: Sl st into corner ch-2 sp, [ch 3, dc, ch 2, 2 dc] in same sp, dc in each of next 17 sts, [{2 dc, ch 2, 2 dc} in next corner ch-2 sp, dc in each of next 17 sts] 5 times, join in 3rd ch of beg ch-3, draw up a lp, remove hook, do not fasten off. (126 dc)

Rnd 13: Attach 2 strands of mid rose in any corner ch-2 sp, ch 1, [sc, ch 5, sc] in same corner ch-2 sp, ch 7, puff st around post of first dc following ch-2 sp at corner on Rnd 10, ch 6, sc around post of 8th dc after ch-2 sp on corner of Rnd 12, ch 6, puff st around post of tr in Rnd 10, ch 6, sc around post of 14th dc after ch-2 sp on corner of Rnd 12, ch 6, puff st around post of last dc before corner on Rnd 10, ch 7, [{sc, ch 5, sc} in next corner ch-2

sp on Rnd 12, ch 7, puff st around post of first dc following ch-2 sp at corner on Rnd 10, ch 6, sc around post of 8th dc after ch-2 sp on corner of Rnd 12, ch 6, puff st around post of tr in Rnd 10, ch 6, sc around post of 14th dc after ch-2 sp on corner of Rnd 12, ch 6, puff st around post of last dc before corner on Rnd 10, ch 7] 5 times, join in beg sc, fasten off.

Rnd 14: Pick up dropped lp of white, sl st into next sc and ch-2 sp, [ch 3, dc, ch 1, sl st in back of 3rd ch of ch-5 sp of Rnd 13, ch 1, sk sc, ch 5, sc of Rnd 13, 2 dc] in same sp of Rnd 12, dc in each of next 7 dc, dc in next sc of Rnd 13 and next dc of Rnd 12 at the same time, dc in each of next 5 dc, dc in next sc of Rnd 13 and next dc of Rnd 12 at the same time, dc in next 7 dc, *in next corner ch-2 sp work 2 dc, ch 1, sl st in back of 3rd ch of ch-5 sp of Rnd 13, ch 1, sk sc, ch 5, sc of Rnd 13, 2 dc in same sp of Rnd 12, dc in each of next 7 dc, dc in next sc on Rnd 13 and next dc of Rnd 12 at the same time, dc in each of next 5 dc, dc in next sc of Rnd 13 and next dc of Rnd 12 at the same time, dc in next 7 dc, rep from * around, join in 3rd ch of beg ch-3, fasten off. (150 dc)

FILL-IN MOTIF
Make 8

Row 1: Beg at inner edge and working outward, with 2 strands of white, ch 26, dc in 4th ch from hook, dc in each rem ch across, turn. (24 dc)

Rows 2–10: Ch 3, dc in same st as beg ch-3, dc in each dc across to last dc, 2 dc in last dc, turn. At the end of Row 10, fasten off. (43 dc)

ASSEMBLY
Sew motifs tog with 2 strands white cotton according to assembly diagram. With sewing needle and thread, sew a pearl bead to the center of each motif.

EDGING
Rnd 1 (RS): Attach 2 strands of white cotton at first point at top of coverlet as indicated on diagram, ch 1, sc in each st around, inc and dec at inner and outer

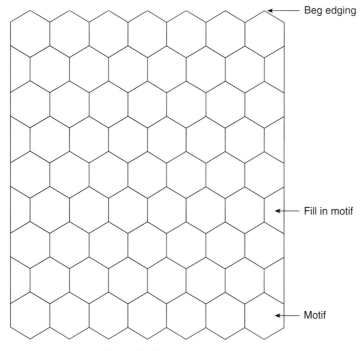

← Beg edging

← Fill in motif

← Motif

Assembly Diagram

▶ CONTINUED ON PAGE 157

PEARLS & LACE PHOTO FRAME

Adorn a simple purchased frame with this beautiful crocheted edging, and then add accents of lace, pearls and flowers to create an elegant display for a cherished photo. It's quick and easy to make, and perfect for a last-minute gift.

BEGINNER ● ●

SIZE Fits a 5 x 7-inch photo frame

MATERIALS

- J. & P. Coats Knit-Cro-Sheen crochet cotton size 10: 1 ball natural #62
- Size 7 steel crochet hook or size needed to obtain gauge
- 5 x 7-inch wooden frame with beveled edge
- 1 yd ½-inch-wide ecru flat beaded trim
- 1 yd ¾-inch-wide blue gathered lace
- 8 blue silk roses
- Hot-glue gun
- Starch
- Pinning board
- Plastic wrap
- Straight pins
- Tapestry needle

GAUGE

[1 shell, 1 fpdc] 3 times = 2 inches; 3 rows = 1 inch
Check gauge to save time.

▶ CONTINUED ON PAGE 171

DESIGN BY
MAGGIE PETSCH

OPPOSITES ATTRACT TABLE SET

Dainty hearts peeking through a lacy lattice overlay creates the romantic and reversible design in this stunning table set. Worked in double strands of size 10 thread, it's as durable as it is dazzling!

GAUGE

5 shells = 3 inches
Check gauge to save time.

PATTERN NOTES

Weave in loose ends as work progresses.
Join rnds with a sl st unless otherwise stated.
Work with 2 strands of cotton held tog throughout.
Materials listed will make 1 each of projects.

PATTERN STITCHES

Shell: 4 dc in indicated st or sp.
Beg shell: [Ch 3, 3 dc] in indicated st or sp.

PLACE MAT

Row 1: With 2 strands of red, ch 108, shell in 6th ch from hook, [sk next 3 chs, shell in next ch] rep across to last 2 chs, sk next ch, dc in next ch, turn. (26 shells)
Row 2: Ch 1, sc in first dc, [ch 5, sc between next 2 shells] rep across, ending with ch 5, sc in next ch, draw up

INTERMEDIATE ● ● ●
SIZE **Place mat:** 12 x 16½ inches
Coaster: 4½ inches square
Hot mat: 6¼ inches square
Napkin ring: 2¼ inches wide x 2 inches in diameter

MATERIALS

- DMC Cebelia crochet cotton size 10 (284 yds per ball): 3 balls each red #666 and white #1
- Size 1 steel crochet hook or size needed to obtain gauge
- 2 safety pins
- Straight pins
- Starch
- Tapestry needle

a lp, remove hook, insert safety pin in dropped lp, do not turn. (26 ch-5 sps)
Row 3: Attach 2 strands of white with a sl st in first sc, ch 3 (counts as first dc throughout), working in front of ch-5 sp of previous row, shell between 2nd and 3rd dc of first shell in row before last, shell between 2nd and 3rd dc of each shell across, dc in last sc, turn. (26 shells)

Row 4: Ch 1, sc in first dc, [ch 5, sc between next 2 shells] rep across, ending with ch 5, sc in 3rd ch of ch-3, draw up a lp, remove hook, insert safety pin in dropped lp, do not turn.
Row 5: Pick up dropped lp of red, remove safety pin, ch 3, working in front of ch-5 sps of previous row and under ch-5 sp directly below, shell between 2nd and 3rd dc of first shell, [working under next ch-5 sp directly below, shell between 2nd and 3rd dc of next shell] rep across, ending with dc in last red sc, turn. (26 shells)
Row 6: Rep Row 4.
Row 7: Pick up dropped lp of white, ch 3, working in front of ch-5 sps of last row and under ch-5 sps directly below, sell between 2nd and 3rd dc of first shell, [working under next ch-5 sp directly below, shell between 2nd and 3rd dc of next shell] rep across, dc in last white sc, turn. (26 shells)
Rows 8–79: Rep Rows 4–7, at the end of Row 79, fasten off white, turn.
Row 80: Pick up dropped lp of red, remove safety pin, ch 3, working under

ch-5 sp directly below, shell between 2nd and 3rd dc of first shell, [working under next ch-5 sp directly below, shell between 2nd and 3rd dc of next shell] rep across, ending with dc in last red sc, do not turn. (26 shells)

FIRST SIDE EDGING

Working along side of place mat from top to bottom, 5 dc in same st as last dc made, working through both thicknesses at once, [shell over side of end sc of next red ch-5 sp row and white st directly behind] 18 times, 6 dc over side of end sc of last red ch-5 sp row, join in first rem lp of foundation ch, fasten off, do not turn.

SECOND SIDE EDGING

With same side facing, attach 2 strands

of red with a sl st in last rem lp of foundation ch on opposite end of place mat, working along side of place mat from bottom to top, 6 dc over side of end sc of next red, ch-5 sp row and white st directly behind, [shell over side of end sc of next red ch-5 sp and white st directly behind] 18 times, 5 dc in same st as beg ch-3 of Row 80, join with a sl st in 3rd ch of beg ch-3, fasten off, do not turn.

BORDER

Rnd 1: With same side facing, attach 2 strands of white with a sl st between 2nd and 3rd dc of first shell, beg shell in same sp, *shell between 2nd and 3rd dc of each shell across to next 6-dc corner group, [shell between 2nd and 3rd dc of corner group, shell between 3rd and 4th dc of same corner group, shell

between 4th and 5th dc of same corner group], rep from * around working in rem lps across opposite side of foundation ch, shell in rem lp at base of each shell across to 6-dc corner group, rep between [ ] for corner group, join in 3rd ch of beg ch-3, turn.

Rnd 2: Sl st between first shell of last rnd and last shell made, ch 2, sl st between 2nd and 3rd dc of next shell, *ch 2, sl st between same shell and next 2-dc group, ch 2, sl st between same 2-dc group and next shell, [ch 2, sl st between 2nd and 3rd dc of next shell, ch 2, sl st between same shell and next shell] rep across to last shell before next 2-dc group, ch 2, sl st between 2nd and 3rd dc of last shell before 2-dc group, rep from * around, ending with ch 2, join in beg sl st, fasten off.

FINISHING

Starch lightly, pin out to size and let dry.

COASTER

Row 1: With 2 strands of red, ch 24, shell in 6th ch from hook, [sk next 3 chs, shell in next ch] rep across to last 2 chs, sk next ch, dc in last ch, turn. (5 shells)
Rows 2–7: Rep Rows 2–7 of place mat.
Rows 8–23: Rep Rows 4–7, at the end of Row 23, fasten off white, turn.
Row 24: Rep Row 80 of place mat.

FIRST SIDE EDGING

Working along side of coaster from top to bottom, 5 dc in same st as last dc made, working through both thicknesses at once, [shell over side of end sc of next red ch-5 sp row and white st directly behind] 4 times, 6 dc over side of end sc of last red ch-5 sp row, join in first rem lp of foundation ch, fasten off, do not turn.

SECOND SIDE EDGING

With same side facing, attach 2 strands of red with a sl st in last rem lp of foundation ch on opposite end of coaster, working along side of coaster from bottom to top, 6 dc over side of end sc of next red ch-5 sp row and white st directly behind, [shell over side of end sc of next red ch-5 sp row and white st directly behind] 4 times, 5 dc in same st as beg ch-3 of Row 24, join in 3rd ch of beg ch-3, fasten off, do not turn.

BORDER

Rnds 1 & 2: Rep Rnds 1 and 2 of place mat border.

FINISHING

Finish the same as place mat.

HOT MAT

Row 1: With 2 strands of red, ch 36, shell in 6th ch from hook, [sk next 3 chs, shell in next ch] rep across to last 2 chs, sk next ch, dc in last ch, turn. (8 shells)
Rows 2–7: Rep Rows 2–7 of place mat.
Rows 8–39: Rep Rows 4–7 of place mat, at the end of Row 39, fasten off white, turn.
Row 40: Rep Row 80 of place mat.

FIRST SIDE EDGING

Working along side of hot mat from top to bottom, 5 dc in same st as last dc made, working through both thicknesses, [shell over side of end sc of next red ch-5 sp

row and white st directly behind] 8 times, 6 dc over side of end sc of last red ch-5 sp row, join in first rem lp of foundation ch, fasten off, do not turn.

SECOND SIDE EDGING

With same side facing, attach 2 strands of red with a sl st in last rem lp of foundation ch on opposite end of hot mat, working along side of hot mat from bottom to top, 6 dc over side of end sc of next red ch-5 sp row and white st directly behind, [shell over side of end sc of next red ch-5 sp row and white st directly behind] 6 times, 5 dc in same st as beg ch-3 of Row 40, join in 3rd ch of beg ch-3, fasten off, do not turn.

BORDER

Rnds 1 & 2: Rep Rnds 1 and 2 of place mat border.

FINISHING

Finish the same as for place mat.

NAPKIN RING

FIRST HALF

Rnd 1: With 2 strands of red, ch 40, join to form a ring, beg shell in same st as joining, sk next 3 chs, [shell in next ch, sk next 3 chs] rep around, join in 3rd ch of beg ch-3, turn. (10 shells)

Rnd 2: Ch 1, sc between first 2 shells, ch 5, [sc between next 2 shells, ch 5] rep around, join in beg sc, draw up a lp, remove hook, insert safety pin in dropped lp, do not turn.

Rnd 3: Working in front of ch-5 sp of last rnd, attach 2 strands of white with a sl st between 2nd and 3rd dc of first shell, beg shell in same sp, shell between 2nd and 3rd dc of each shell around, join in 3rd ch of beg ch-3, turn. (10 shells)

Rnd 4: Rep Rnd 2.

Rnd 5: Pick up dropped lp of red, remove safety pin, working in front of ch-5 sps of last rnd, insert hook under ch-5 sp directly below and between 2nd and 3rd dc of first shell, yo, compete sl st, working under ch-5 sp, beg shell in same sp as sl st, [working under next ch-5 sp directly below, shell between 2nd and 3rd dc of next shell] rep around, join in 3rd ch of beg ch-3, fasten off, turn. (10 shells)

Rnd 6: Pick up dropped lp of white, remove safety pin, insert hook under ch-5 sp directly below and between 2nd and 3rd dc of first shell, yo, complete sl st, working under ch-5 sp, beg shell in same sp as sl st, [working under ch-5 sp directly below, shell between 2nd and 3rd dc of next shell] rep around, join in 3rd ch of beg ch-3, turn.

Rnd 7: Sl st between first shell of last rnd and last shell made, *ch 2, sl st between 2nd and 3rd dc of next shell, ch 2 **, sl st between same shell and next shell, rep from * around, ending last rep at **, join in beg sl st, fasten off, do not turn.

SECOND HALF

Rnd 1: With same side of napkin ring facing, attach 2 strands of red with a sl st in rem lp of foundation ch at base of any shell of Rnd 1 of first half, beg shell in same st, working in rem lps around, shell in st at base of each shell around, join in 3rd ch of beg ch-3, turn.

Rows 2–7: Rep Rows 2–7 of first half.

FINISHING

Starch lightly, shape and let dry. ■

ROSE SPLENDOR COVERLET ▶ CONTINUED FROM PAGE 152

point as necessary to maintain shape, join in beg sc, fasten off.

Note: *On Rnd 2, adjust the placement of sts to allow for the corner shells to fall at outer points and for sc dec sts to fall at inner points on short ends of coverlet.*

Rnd 2: Attach 2 strands mid rose at same point as Rnd 1, beg corner shell in same st, sk 2 sc, sl st in next sc, sk next 2 sc, [shell in next sc, sk next 2 sc, sl st in next sc, sk 2 sc] 4 times, sc dec at inner point, [shell in next sc, sk next 2 sc, sl st in next sc, sk next 2 sc] 4 times, sk next 2 sc, *corner shell in next st, sk next 2 sc, sl st in next sc, sk next 2 sc, [shell in next sc, sk next 2 sc, sl st in next sc, sk next 2 sc] 4 times, sc dec at inner point, [shell in next sc, sk next 2 sc, sl st in next sc, sk next 2 sc] 4 times, sk next 2 sc *, rep from * to * across top edge of coverlet, corner shell in last point, sk next 2 sc, sl st in next sc, sk next 2 sc, **shell in next sc, sk next 2 sc, sl st in next sc, sk next 2 sc **, rep from ** to ** across straight edge of coverlet, rep from * to * across bottom of coverlet, rep from ** to ** across last straight edge of coverlet, join in 3rd ch of beg ch-3, fasten off.

TASSEL

Make 14

With mid rose, cut 48 strands of crochet cotton each 10 inches in length. Holding all strands even tog, tie a separate length of crochet cotton tightly around strands at center. Fold strands in half at tied point and tie a 10-inch length tightly around folded strands 1¼ inches below top. Blend ends of tying strand in with tassel strands. Using tying length at top of each tassel. Attach tassel to center dc of shell at point. Attach a tassel to each point on each short end of coverlet. Trim ends even. ■

DESIGN BY
KATHERINE ENG

STARFLOWERS RUNNER & PILLOW TOPPER

A garden of flowers in a rainbow of pretty spring colors will brighten your home year-round with this fresh floral set that makes a great project for using up partial balls of colorful size 10 thread.

GAUGE

Rnds 1 and 2 = ⅞ inch; square = 4½ inches

Check gauge to save time.

PATTERN NOTES

Weave in loose ends as work progresses.

Join rnds with a sl st unless otherwise stated.

PATTERN STITCHES

Medium shell (for flower): [Hdc, dc, tr, ch 3, tr, dc, hdc] in indicated st.

Small shell: [2 dc, ch 2, 2 dc] in indicated st.

Large shell: [3 tr, ch 3, 3 tr] in indicated st.

RUNNER

SQUARE

Rnd 1 (RS): With mid rose (maize), ch 4, join to form a ring, ch 1, 12 sc in ring, join in beg sc. (12 sc)

Rnd 2 (RS): Ch 1, sc in first sc, ch 1, [sc in next sc, ch 1] rep around, join in

INTERMEDIATE ●●●

SIZE **Runner:** 14 x 23½ inches
Pillow topper: 14 inches square

MATERIALS

- Coats Knit-Cro-Sheen crochet cotton size 10: 450 yds new ecru #61, 120 yds each spruce #179 and mid rose #46A, 100 yds maize #123, 64 yds crystal blue #25, 21 yds lilac #36, 12 yds almond pink #35
- Size B/1 crochet hook or size needed to obtain gauge
- 12–13-inch ruffled lilac pillow
- Tapestry needle

beg sc, fasten off. (12 ch-1 sps)

Rnd 3 (RS): Draw up a lp of maize (crystal blue) in any ch-1 sp, ch 1, sc in same ch sp, ch 2, [sc in next ch-1 sp, ch 2] rep around, join in beg sc, sl st into ch-2 sp.

Rnd 4 (RS): Ch 1, sc in same ch sp, medium shell in next ch-2 sp, [sc in next ch-2 sp, medium shell in next ch-2 sp] rep around, join in beg sc.

Rnd 5 (RS): Ch 1, sc in same sc as joining, ch 1, sk next st, sc in next st, *ch 1, sk next st, [{sc, ch 2} 3 times and sc] in next ch-3 sp, [ch 1, sk 1 st, sc in next st] 3 times, rep from * around, ending with ch 1, sk last st, join in beg sc, fasten off, turn.

Rnd 6 (WS): Draw up a lp of spruce (mid rose) in ch-2 sp at point of any petal, ch 1, sc in same sp, *ch 1, sk next sc, hdc in next ch-2 sp, ch 1, sk next sc, dc in next ch-1 sp, [ch 1, sk next sc, tr in next sp] twice, ch 1, sk next sc, dc in next ch-1 sp, ch 1, sk next sc, hdc in next ch-2 sp, ch 1, sk next sc **, sc in next ch-2 sp, rep from * around, ending last rep at **, join in beg sc, turn.

Rnd 7 (RS): Ch 1, sk over sts, work 2 sc in each ch-1 sp around, join in beg sc, fasten off, turn. (84 sc)

Rnd 8 (WS): Draw up a lp of crystal blue (spruce) in first sc of previous rnd, ch 1, [sc, ch 2, sc] in same sc, [ch 1, sk next 2 sc, {sc, ch 2, sc} in next sc] twice, *ch 2, sk 3 sts, [sc, ch 3, sc] in next sc, ch 3, sk next 4 sc, [{sc, ch 2,

sc} in next sc, ch 1, sk next 2 sc] 4 times, [sc, ch 2, sc] in next sc, ch 3, sk next 4 sc, [sc, ch 3, sc] in next sc, ch 2, sk next 3 sc **, [{sc, ch 2, sc} in next sc, ch 1, sk next 2 sc] 4 times, [sc, ch 2, sc] in next sc, rep from *, ending last rep at **, [{sc, ch 2, sc} in next sc, ch 1, sk next 2 sc] twice, join in beg sc, fasten off, turn.

Note: *On Rnd 9, use care to work in specified sts only, skipping over other sts and sps.*

Rnd 9 (RS): Draw up a lp of new ecru in first ch-2 sp of previous rnd, ch 1, sc in same ch-2 sp, small shell in next ch-2 sp, sc in next ch-2 sp, *ch 2, large shell in next ch-3 sp, ch 2, sc in next ch-2 sp **, [small shell in next ch-2 sp, sc in next ch-2 sp] twice, rep from * around, ending last rep at **, small shell in last ch-2 sp, join in beg sc. (4 large shells; 8 small shells; 12 sc)

Rnd 10 (RS): Ch 1, sc in same sc, ch 3, [sc, ch 2, sc] in ch-2 sp of small shell, ch 3, sc in next sc, *[sc, ch 3, sc] in next ch-2 sp, sc in next tr, ch 3, [sc, ch 4, sc, ch 6, sc, ch 4, sc] in corner ch-3 sp of large

shell, ch 3, sk next 2 tr, sc in next tr, [sc, ch 3, sc] in next ch-2 sp, sc in next sc **, [ch 3, {sc, ch 2, sc} in next ch-2 sp of small shell, ch 3, sc in next sc] twice, rep from * around, ending last rep at **, ch 3, [sc, ch 2, sc] in next ch-2 sp of small shell, ch 3, join in beg sc, fasten off. Arrange squares 3 x 5 in alternate colors beg with pattern color 1 and making sure that points of stars are all facing in the same direction.

Work Rnd 10 around first square, then join others as follows, continuing in pattern st, connect ch-2 sps at side small shell points and corner ch-4 and ch-6 sps. To connect ch-2 sps, ch 1, drop lp, draw lp under to over through opposite ch-2 sp, ch 1 and continue. To connect ch-4 sps, ch 2, drop lp, draw lp under to over through opposite ch-4 sp, ch 2 and continue. To connect ch-6 sps, ch 3, drop lp, draw lp under to over through opposite ch-6 sps, ch 3 and continue. Continue to rep until all 15 squares are joined.

BORDER

Note: *Shell for border rnd is [3 dc, ch 2, 3 dc] in indicated st. Work in specified sts and sps, skipping over other sts and sps.*

Rnd 1 (RS): Draw up a lp of new ecru in first ch-4 sp to left of any corner ch-6 sp, ch 1, sc in same sp, *ch 1, shell in next ch-3 sp (at center between corner shell and next shell), ch 1, sc in next ch-2 sp, ch 1, shell in next sc, ch 1, sc in next ch-2 sp, ch 1, shell in next ch-3 sp (at center between last shell and corner shell), ch 1, sc in next ch-4 sp **, ch 1, 3 dc in next ch-6 sp, ch 2, 3 dc in next ch-6 sp, ch 1, sc in next ch-4 sp, rep from * around working at each corner, rep pattern from * to **, ch 1, 7 dc in corner ch-6 sp, ch 1, sc in next ch-4 sp, join in beg sc, sl st into next ch-1 sp.

Rnd 2 (RS): Ch 1, sc in same sp, *ch 1, sk 1 dc, sc in next dc, ch 1, sk next dc, [sc, ch 3, sc] in next ch-2 sp, ch 1, sk 1 dc, sc in next dc, ch 1, sk next dc, sc in next ch-1 sp, ch 2, sk next sc, sc in next

▶ CONTINUED ON PAGE 173

DESIGN BY
BRENDA STRATTON

PASSIONFLOWER BEADED DOILY

A large, beautiful beaded flower takes center stage in this exquisite doily blooming with delightful texture and radiant color. The beadwork is artfully carried through to the dainty picot-like edging for a perfect finishing touch.

GAUGE

Rnds 1–9 of doily = 4¼ inches; 3 tr rnds = 1½ inches

Check gauge to save time.

PATTERN NOTES

Weave in loose ends as work progresses.

Join rnds with a sl st unless otherwise stated.

PATTERN STITCHES

Bead dc (bdc): Yo, insert hook in indicated st, yo, draw up a lp, slide a bead up to hook, [yo, draw through 2 lps on hook] twice, push bead through to front.

Dc dec: Yo, insert hook in indicated st, yo, draw up a lp, yo, draw through 2 lps on hook, yo, insert hook in next st, yo, draw up a lp, yo, draw through 2 lps on hook, yo, draw through all 3 lps on hook.

Beg dc dec: Ch 2, yo, insert hook in next st, yo, draw up a lp, [yo, draw through 2 lps on hook] twice.

Cluster (cl): [Yo, insert hook in next st, yo, draw up a lp, draw through 2 lps on hook] 3 times, yo, draw through all 4 lps on hook.

INTERMEDIATE ●●●

SIZE 14½ inches in diameter

MATERIALS
- Crochet cotton size 10: 350 yds white, 150 yds each dark lavender and dark green
- Size 5 steel crochet hook or size needed to obtain gauge
- 642 (4mm) clear dark lavender faceted beads
- White thread
- Sewing needle

Beg cl: Ch 2, [yo, insert hook in next st, yo, draw up a lp, yo, draw through 2 lps on hook] twice, yo, draw through all 3 lps on hook.

Split dc: Yo, draw up a lp in indicated sp, yo, draw through 2 lps on hook, yo, draw up a lp in next sp, yo, draw through 2 lps, yo, draw through rem 3 lps on hook.

Sc dec: Draw up a lp around post of same dc, draw up a lp in next free sc of Rnd 1, draw up a lp around post of next dc, yo, draw through all 4 lps on hook.

2-sc dec: Draw up a lp in each of next 3 sts, yo, draw through all 4 lps on hook.

Beaded picot (bp): [Sc, push up 3 beads, ch 1, sc] in same sp.

Beaded puff st dec (bps dec): Ch 2, [yo, draw up a 1/4-inch lp] twice in each of next 3 ch-2 sps at dip between scallops, yo, draw through all lps on hook, ch 1, push up 3 beads, ch 1, sl st in top of bps dec, ch 2.

DOILY CENTER

Rnd 1 (RS): Thread 138 beads onto white crochet cotton, ch 6, join to form a ring, ch 1, 12 sc in ring, join in beg sc. (12 sc)

Rnd 2: [Ch 3, bdc, dc] in same sc, ch 2, sk 1 sc, [{dc, bdc, dc} in next sc, ch 2, sk 1 sc] rep around, join in 3rd ch of beg ch-3. (12 dc; 6 bdc)

Rnd 3: [Ch 3, bdc] in same st, bdc in next bdc, [bdc, dc] in next dc, ch 2, sk next sp, [{dc, bdc} in next dc, bdc in next bdc, {bdc, dc} in next dc, ch 2, sk next sp] rep around, join in 3rd ch of beg ch-3. (12 dc; 19 bdc)

Rnd 4: [Ch 3, bdc] in same st, bdc in each of next 3 bdc, [bdc, dc] in next dc,

ch 2, sk next sp, [{dc, bdc} in next dc, bdc in each of next 3 bdc, {bdc, dc} in next dc, ch 2, sk next sp] rep around, join in 3rd ch of beg ch-3. (12 dc; 30 bdc)

Rnd 5: Ch 3, bdc in each of next 5 bdc, dc in next dc, ch 2, dc in next ch sp, ch 2, [dc in next dc, bdc in each of next 5 bdc, dc in next dc, ch 2, dc in next ch sp, ch 2] rep around, join in 3rd ch of beg ch-3. (18 dc; 30 bdc)

Rnd 6: Ch 3, bdc in each of next 5 bdc, dc in next dc, ch 2, [dc, ch 3, dc] in next dc, ch 2, [dc in next dc, bdc in each of next 5 bdc, dc in next dc, ch 2, {dc, ch 3, dc} in next dc, ch 2] rep around, join in 3rd ch of beg ch-3.

Rnd 7: Beg dc dec over first 2 sts, bdc in each of next 3 bdc, dc dec in next 2 sts, ch 2, dc in next dc, ch 2, [dc, ch 3, dc] in next ch-3 sp, ch 2, dc in next dc, ch 2, [dc dec in next 2 sts, bdc in each of next

3 bdc, dc dec over next 2 sts, ch 2, dc in next dc, ch 2, {dc, ch 3, dc} in next ch-3 sp, ch 2, dc in next dc, ch 2] rep around, join in 2nd ch of beg ch-2.

Rnd 8: Beg dc dec over next 2 sts, bdc in next bdc, dc dec over next 2 sts, ch 2, [dc in next dc, ch 2] twice, [dc, ch 3, dc] in next ch-3 sp, ch 2, [dc in next dc, ch 2] twice, [dc dec over next 2 sts, bdc in next bdc, dc dec over next 2 sts, ch 2, {dc in next dc, ch 2} twice, {dc, ch 3, dc} in next ch-3 sp, ch 2, {dc in next dc, ch 2} twice] rep around, join in 2nd ch of beg ch-2.

Rnd 9: Beg cl, ch 2, [dc in next dc, ch 2] 3 times, [dc, ch 3, dc] in next ch-3 sp, ch 2, [dc in next dc, ch 2] 3 times, [cl over next 3 dc, ch 2, {dc in next dc, ch 2} 3 times, {dc, ch 3, dc} in next ch-3 sp, ch 2, {dc in next dc, ch 2} 3 times] rep around, join in top of beg cl, fasten off. (48 dc; 6 cl)

Petal outline

Note: The petal outline trim is worked on surface of doily around outer edge of the flower petals inserting hook around the post of the outer dc of petals.

Rnd 1: Attach dark lavender around post of beg ch-3 of Rnd 1, ch 1, *sc in same st, [2 sc around post of outermost dc of next rnd] 7 times, 3 sc in top of cl at point of petal, now working down opposite side of same petal, [2 sc around post of outermost dc of next row] 7 times, sc dec, rep from * around, join in beg sc, fasten off.

Leaf

Make 6

Row 1: Attach dark green with a sl st in top of dc between any 2 petals of Rnd 5, ch 3, 4 dc in same st as beg ch-3, turn. (5 dc)

Row 2: Ch 3, dc in next dc, 2 dc in next

► CONTINUED ON PAGE 172

DESIGN BY
DONNA NICKELL

CIRCLE OF ROSES DOILY

The heirloom beauty of Irish crochet is creatively displayed in this large and lovely antique-style doily. Roses in a soft, neutral shade present an unusual colorway that will beautifully blend with any decor.

GAUGE

Rose = 2¾ inches in diameter; 3 cl rnds = 1¾ inches
Check gauge to save time.

PATTERN NOTES

Weave in loose ends as work progresses.
Join rnds with a sl st unless otherwise stated.

PATTERN STITCHES

4-tr cl: Yo hook twice, insert hook in indicated st, yo, draw up a lp, [yo, draw through 2 lps on hook] twice, rep from * 3 times, yo, draw through all 5 lps on hook.

Beg 4-tr cl: Ch 3 (counts as first tr), *yo hook twice, insert hook in indicated st, yo, draw up a lp, [yo, draw through 2 lps on hook] twice, rep from * twice, yo, draw through all 4 lps on hook.

DOILY

Rnd 1 (RS): With white, ch 10, join to form a ring, ch 3, 24 dc in ring, join in 3rd ch of beg ch-3. (25 dc)

Rnd 2: Ch 1, sc in same st as beg ch-1,

INTERMEDIATE ●○○

SIZE 24 inches in diameter
MATERIALS
- South Maid crochet cotton size 10: 1 ball each white #1, spruce #179 and new ecru #429
- Size 5 steel crochet hook or size needed to obtain gauge
- 11 (6mm) pearl beads
- Toothpicks
- Fabric glue
- Tapestry needle

ch 25, [sc in next dc, ch 25] rep around, join in beg sc. (25 ch lps)

Rnd 3: Sl st in first 13 chs of next lp, ch 3 (counts as first dc throughout), 2 dc in same ch lp, [ch 7, 3 dc in next ch lp] rep around, ending with ch 4, tr in 3rd ch of beg ch-3 to position hook in center of last ch lp.

Rnd 4: Ch 3, 2 dc in same ch sp as beg ch-3, [ch 7, 3 dc in next ch-7 sp] rep around, ending with ch 4, tr in 3rd ch of beg ch-3.

Rnd 5: Ch 3, 2 dc in same ch sp as beg ch-3, [ch 9, 3 dc in next ch-7 sp]

rep around, ending with ch 4, dtr in 3rd ch of beg ch-3.

Rnd 6: Ch 3, 2 dc in same ch sp as beg ch-3, [ch 11, 3 dc in next ch-9 lp] rep around, ending with ch 6, dtr in 3rd ch of beg ch-3.

Rnd 7: Beg 4-tr cl in same ch sp, ch 14, [4-tr cl in next ch-9 lp, ch 14] rep around, join in 3rd ch of beg ch-3. (25 cls)

Rnd 8: Sl st into next ch lp, [beg 4-tr cl, ch 10, 4-tr cl] in same ch-14 lp, ch 3, [{4-tr cl, ch 10, 4-tr cl} in next ch-14 lp, ch 3] rep around, join in 3rd ch of beg ch-3. (50 cls)

Rnd 9: Sl st into next ch lp, [beg 4-tr cl, ch 6, 4-tr cl] in same ch lp, ch 3, 4-tr cl in next ch-3 sp, ch 3, [{4-tr cl, ch 6, 4-tr cl} in next ch-10 lp, ch 3, 4-tr cl in next ch-3 sp, ch 3] rep around, join in 3rd ch of beg ch-3. (75 cls)

Rnd 10: Sl st into next ch lp, [beg 4-tr cl, ch 4, 4-tr cl] in same ch lp, *[ch 3, 4-tr cl in next ch lp] twice, ch 3 **, [4-tr cl, ch 4, 4-tr cl] in next ch lp, rep from * around, ending last rep at **, join in 3rd ch of beg ch-3. (100 cls)

Rnd 11: Sl st into center of next ch lp, ch 7 (counts as first dc, ch 4 throughout), *4-tr cl in next ch lp, [ch 3, 4-tr cl in next ch lp] twice, ch 4 **, dc in next ch lp, ch 4, rep from * around, ending last rep at **, join in 3rd ch of beg ch-7. (75 cls)

Rnd 12: Sl st into center of next ch lp, ch 7, *4-tr cl in next ch lp, ch 3, 4-tr cl in next ch lp, ch 4 **, [dc in next ch lp, ch 4] twice, rep from * around, ending last rep at **, dc in next ch lp, ch 4, join in 3rd ch of beg ch-7. (50 cls)

Rnd 13: Sl st into center of next ch lp, ch 7, *4-tr cl in next ch lp **, [ch 4, dc in next ch lp] 3 times, ch 4, rep from * around, ending last rep at **, [ch 4, dc in next ch lp] twice, ch 4, join in 3rd ch of beg ch-7. (25 cls)

Rnd 14: Sl st into center of next ch lp, ch 7, [dc in next ch lp, ch 4] rep around, join in 3rd ch of beg ch-4, fasten off. (100 dc)

Rnd 15: Attach spruce with a sl st in any dc of Rnd 14, 4-tr cl in same dc, sl st in next dc, [4-tr cl in same dc, sl st in next dc] rep around, fasten off.

ROSE
Make 11

Rnd 1: With new ecru, ch 6, join to form a ring, ch 5 (counts as first dc, ch 2), [dc in ring, ch 2] 7 times, join in 3rd ch of beg ch-5. (8 dc; 8 ch-2 sps)

Rnd 2: [Sc, hdc, 3 dc, hdc, sc] in each ch-2 sp around, join in beg sc. (8 petals)

Rnd 3: [Ch 4, sc in sp between 2 sc sts of petals] rep around. (8 ch-4 sps)

Rnd 4: [Sc, hdc, 5 dc, hdc, sc] in each ch-4 sp around, join in beg sc.

Rnd 5: [Ch 5, sc in sp between 2 sc sts of petals] rep around. (8 ch-5 sps)

Rnd 6: [Sc, hdc, 7 dc, hdc, sc] in each ch-5 sp around, join in beg sc.

Rnd 7: [Ch 6, sc in sp between 2 sc sts of petals] rep around.

Rnd 8: [Sc, hdc, dc, 7 tr, dc, hdc, sc] in each ch-6 sp around, join in beg sc, fasten off.

Sew a pearl bead to center of rose.

LEAF
Make 12

Rnd 1: With spruce, ch 23, sc in 2nd ch from hook, ch 3, sk next 2 chs, dc in next ch, ch 3, sk next 2 chs, tr in next ch, [ch 3, sk next 2 chs, dtr in next ch] twice, ch 3, sk next 2 chs, tr in next ch, ch 3, sk next 2 chs, dc in next ch, ch 3, sk next 2 chs, [dc, ch 4, dc] in last ch, working on opposite side of foundation ch, ch 3, sk next 2 chs, dc in next ch, ch 3, sk next 2 chs, tr in next ch, [ch 3, sk next 2 chs, dtr in next ch] twice, ch 3, sk next 2 chs, dc in next ch, ch 3, sl st to join in beg sc.

Rnd 2: Ch 3, 3 dc in next ch-3 sp, [dc in next st, ch 4, sl st in top of last st, 3 dc in next ch-3 sp] 6 times, dc in next dc, ch 4, sl st in top of last dc, [3 dc, ch 4, sl st in top of last dc, 3 dc] in next ch-4 sp, [dc in next st, ch 4, sl st in top of last st, 3 dc in next ch-3 sp] 7 times, join in 3rd ch of beg ch-3, to form stem, ch 11, sc in 2nd ch from hook, sc in each of next 9 chs, sl st in next st of leaf, fasten off.

FINISHING

Place doily on a flat surface. Using photo as a guide, positioning as desired, place 2 leaves and a rose at center of doily. Place rem leaves and roses around outer edge of doily as desired. Using a toothpick, place a small dot of fabric glue to hold in place. Then tack leaves and roses securely in place with needle and thread. ∎

DESIGN BY
GLENDA WINKLEMAN

NAVY HOUNDSTOOTH RUG

A unique stitch pattern creates a distinctive and reversible houndstooth design in this handsomely styled rug that's predominantly navy on one side and white on the other. Double-strand bulky weight yarn makes it both cozy and durable.

GAUGE

7 sts = 3 inches; 7 rows = 3 inches
Check gauge to save time.

PATTERN NOTES

Weave in loose ends as work progresses.
Join rnds with a sl st unless otherwise
stated.
Work with 2 strands of yarn held tog
throughout.

RUG

Row 1 (RS): With navy, ch 58, sc in 2nd
ch from hook, dc in next ch, [sl st in next
ch, dc in next ch] 27 times, sc in last ch,
turn. (28 dc; 27 sl sts, 2 sc)

Row 2: Ch 1, sc in first sc, sl st in next
dc, [dc in next sl st, sl st in next dc] 27
times, sc in last sc, fasten off, turn.

Row 3: Attach white in first sc, ch 1, sc
in same sc as beg ch-1, dc in next sl st,
[sl st in next dc, dc in next sl st] 27 times,
sc in last sc, fasten off, turn.

BEGINNER ●●●

SIZE 28½ x 35 inches

MATERIALS

- Coats & Clark Red Heart Grande Craft
  bulky yarn (6 oz per skein): 3 skeins each
  white #2101 and navy #2885
- Size M/13 crochet hook or size
  needed to obtain gauge
- Yarn needle

Row 4: Attach navy in first sc, ch 1, sc in
same sc as beg ch-1, sl st in next dc, [dc
in next sl st, sl st in next dc] 27 times, sc
in last sc, fasten off, turn.

Rows 5–82: Rep Rows 3 and 4. At
the end of Row 82, do not fasten off
navy, turn.

Row 83: With navy, rep Row 3,
fasten off.

BORDER

Rnd 1 (RS): Attach navy in first sc at
beg of Row 83, ch 1, *sc in each st
across to next corner, ch 1, sc in end st
of each of next 2 rows, [sk next row, sc in
end st of next row] rep down side edge of
rug, ending with sc in last row, ch 1, rep
from * around, join in beg sc, fasten off.

SIDE BORDER

Note: *Work side border on each long
side of rug.*

Row 1: Working across long edge of rug
only, attach navy with sl st in last sc on
width of rug, ch 1, sc in corner ch-1 sp,
sc in each of next 4 sc, [2 sc in next sc,
sc in each of next 5 sc] rep across to 3
sc from next corner ch-1 sp, 2 sc in next
sc, sc in each of next 2 sc, sc in corner
ch-1 sp, sl st in next sc across width of
rug, turn.

Row 2: Ch 1, sk sl st, sc in each sc
across, sl st in sl st, fasten off. ■

DESIGN BY
ROSE PIRRONE

WILD IRISH ROSE PILLOW

An heirloom-style motif and dainty edgings are the simple, yet elegant, crochet embellishments that turn a ready-made pillow into a sophisticated home accent. Sport weight acrylic yarn in a variety of colors can create a rainbow of different decorating looks!

GAUGE

Irish rose = 3⅞ inches in diameter
Check gauge to save time.

PATTERN NOTES

Weave in loose ends as work progresses. Join rnds with a sl st unless otherwise stated.

FLAT PETAL FLOWER

First petal

Row 1: Starting at center with vanilla, leaving a 4-inch length at beg, ch 2, sc in 2nd ch from hook, ch 7, dc in first ch of ch-7, turn.

Note: *All petals will start in the same ch as first petal.*

Row 2: Ch 6, dc in first dc, ch 2, sk next 2 chs, dc in next ch, turn.

Row 3: Ch 6, dc in first dc, ch 2, sk 2 chs, dc in next dc, ch 2, sk next 2 chs, dc in next ch, turn.

Row 4: Ch 6, dc in first dc, [ch 2, sk next 2 chs, dc in next dc] twice, ch 2, sk next 2 chs, dc in next ch, turn.

Row 5: Ch 6, dc in first dc, [ch 2, sk

INTERMEDIATE ●●○

SIZE 16 inches square

MATERIALS

- J. & P. Coats Luster Sheen 3-ply sport weight acrylic yarn (150 yds per ball): 1 ball vanilla #7
- Size F/5 crochet hook or size needed to obtain gauge
- Zweigart's 16-inch prefinished pillow cover: Stockholm #1318 eggshell
- 16-inch pillow form
- ⅝-inch flat pearl shank button
- Ruler
- Scissors
- Straight pins
- Disappearing ink fabric marking pen
- Sewing needle and thread

next 2 chs, dc in next dc] 3 times, ch 2, sk next 2 chs, dc in next dc, fasten off.

Second petal

Row 1: Attach vanilla in opposite side of foundation ch of first petal, ch 1, sc in same st, ch 7, dc in first ch of ch-7, turn.

Rows 2–5: Rep Rows 2–5 of first petal.

Third–fifth petals

Rep Rows 1–5 of second petal.

After all 5 petals are completed, pull on rem beg length of first petal at center to close opening and secure rem length.

Edging

Rnd 1: Attach vanilla to first sc at bottom of any petal, working along the sides and top of petal, 4 sc in each side sp, 9 sc in each corner sp around outer edge of flat petal flower, join in beg sc.

Rnd 2: Sk the first and last sc of each petal, sc in each sc around, join in beg sc, fasten off.

IRISH ROSE

Rnd 1: Leaving a 2-inch length of vanilla at beg, ch 2, 18 sc in 2nd ch from hook, join in beg sc, pull rem beg length to close opening, secure. (18 sc)

Rnd 2: Ch 1, sc in same st as beg ch-1, ch 5, sk next 2 sc, [sc in next sc, ch 5, sk next 2 sc] rep around, join in beg sc. (6 ch-5 sps)

Rnd 3: Ch 1, [sc, 7 dc, sc] in each ch-

► CONTINUED ON PAGE 173

TWILIGHT LAGOON AFGHAN

Softly blended colors and a creative arrangement transform small, simple granny squares into a dazzling work of art in this magnificent design. A floral centerpiece on Tunisian crochet completes the striking effect.

GAUGE

Square = 4 x 4 inches; afghan st center, 17 sts = 4 inches; 16 rows = 4 inches
Check gauge to save time.

PATTERN NOTES

Weave in loose ends as work progresses. Join rnds with a sl st unless otherwise stated.

ROSE & WHITE SQUARE

Make 60

Rnd 1: With hook size H and light old rose, ch 4, join to form a ring, ch 4 (counts as first hdc, ch 2 throughout), [3 hdc in ring, ch 2] 3 times, 2 hdc in ring, join in 2nd ch of beg ch-4. (12 hdc; 4 ch sps)

Rnd 2: Sl st into next ch, ch 4, *2 hdc in same ch sp, hdc in each hdc across to next corner ch sp **, 2 hdc in next ch sp, ch 2, rep from * 3 times, ending last rep at **, hdc in same ch sp as beg ch-4, join in 2nd ch of beg ch-4, fasten off. (28 hdc; 4 ch sps)

Rnd 3: Attach white in first ch-2 sp of previous rnd, rep Rnd 2, fasten off. (44

INTERMEDIATE ●●○

SIZE 52 x 52 inches
MATERIALS
- Bernat worsted weight yarn: 16 oz light old rose #3024, 12 oz each medium willow #00431 and medium old rose #00436
- Phentex Merit worsted weight yarn (50 grams per ball): 8 balls white #00101, 3 balls olive #11526
- Coats & Clark Red Heart TLC Essentials worsted weight yarn: 12 oz medium thyme #2673
- Small amounts of pearl cotton or fingering weight yarn in light and dark rose shades and 1 shade of green
- Size H/8 crochet hook or size needed to obtain gauge
- Size G/6 afghan crochet hook or size needed to obtain gauge
- Size C/2 crochet hook
- Tapestry needle

hdc; 4 ch sps)

Rnd 4: Attach medium old rose in first ch sp of previous rnd, ch 1, 2 sc in same ch sp, *sc in each hdc across side

of square **, 4 sc in next ch sp, rep from * 3 times, ending last rep at **, 2 sc in same ch sp as beg 2-sc, join in beg sc, fasten off. (60 sc)

GREEN SQUARE

Note: Make a total of 60 squares, working 10 squares in each of the 6 color sequences as indicated, repeating rose and white square pattern.

Rnds 1 & 2: With olive (olive, willow, willow, thyme, thyme), rep Rnds 1 and 2.

Rnd 3: With willow (thyme, olive, thyme, olive, willow), rep Rnd 3.

Rnd 4: With thyme (willow, thyme, olive, willow, olive), rep Rnd 4.

DIAGONAL SQUARE

Make 8

Note: While working the 8 diagonal squares, when pattern indicates green, do not work all the squares the same, use the 3 greens on varying sequence of colors as in green square.

Rnd 1: With light old rose, ch 4, with green, join to form a ring, ch 3, with light old rose, ch 1, 3 hdc, ch 2, 3 hdc in ring,

with green, ch 2, 3 hdc, ch 2, 2 hdc in ring, join in 2nd ch of green beg ch-3.

Rnd 2: With green sl st in next ch, ch 3, with light old rose, ch 1, 2 hdc in same ch sp, hdc in each hdc across side of square, 2 hdc, ch 2, 2 hdc in next ch sp, hdc in each hdc across side edge, 2 hdc in next ch sp, with green, ch 2, 2 hdc in same ch sp, hdc in each hdc across side edge, 2 hdc, ch 2, 2 hdc in next ch sp, hdc in each hdc across side edge, 1 hdc in same ch sp as beg ch, join in 2nd ch of beg ch-3 of green.

Rnd 3: Rep Rnd 2 using white and a 2nd shade of green.

Rnd 4: With medium old rose and a 3rd shade of green, rep same color sequence as in Rnd 2, working 4 sc in each corner ch sp and 1 sc in each hdc across each side edge, join in beg sc, fasten off.

AFGHAN CENTER SQUARE

Row 1: With afghan hook size G and white, ch 66, insert hook in 2nd ch from hook, yo, draw up a lp, retaining all lps on hook, [insert hook in next ch, yo, draw up a lp] rep across (66 lps on hook), yo, draw through first lp on hook, [yo, draw through 2 lps on hook] rep across until 1 lp rem on hook.

Rows 2–62: Sk first vertical bar, [insert hook under next vertical bar, yo, draw up a lp] rep across retaining all lps on hook (66 lps on hook), yo, draw through first lp on hook, [yo, draw through 2 lps on hook] rep across until 1 lp rem on hook.

At the end of last rep, do not fasten off.

Border

Rnd 1: With white, ch 1, sc evenly sp around outer edge of afghan square, working 3 sc in each corner, join in beg sc, fasten off.

Rnd 2: Attach medium old rose in top right edge in center sc of corner st of square, ch 1, sc in same center corner st, sc in each sc across top, 3 sc in center corner sc, sc in each sc to bottom left edge, 2 sc in center corner sc, attach willow, sc in same corner st, sc in each sc across bottom edge, 3 sc in center corner sc, sc in each sc to top right corner, work 2 sc in same center corner sc as beg st, join in beg sc, fasten off.

JOINING

Using afghan diagram as a guide, whip-stitch squares tog on the WS, randomly scattering the 6 green color sequence squares in the green section of diagram. The st count of the afghan square is greater than the st count of the surrounding squares. To ensure the piece will join properly, simply sk over a few sts along the afghan square edges as needed. With RS facing, place afghan square as center of joined squares, matching yarn color of afghan squares and changing as color changes, sc center square to afghan.

AFGHAN BORDER

Rnd 1: Attach medium old rose with sl st in top right corner, working in back lps only, ch 1, sc in same sc, [ch 1, sk 1 sc, sc in next sc] rep around outer edge working [sc, ch 1, sc] in each corner st and changing to thyme while working over green section of afghan, join in beg sc, fasten off.

Rnd 2: Attach white in any sc of previous rnd, ch 1, sc in same sc, ch 1, sk next ch-1 sp, [sc in next sc, ch 1, sk next ch-1 sp] rep around, join in beg sc.

Rnd 3: Sl st into next ch-1 sp, [ch 3, dc, ch 2, 2 dc] in same ch sp, sk next ch-1 sp, [{2 dc, ch 2, 2 dc} in next ch-1 sp, sk next ch-1 sp] rep around, join in 3rd ch of beg ch-3.

Rnd 4: Sl st into ch-2 sp, ch 3, 6 dc in same ch-2 sp, sc in next ch-2 sp, [7 dc in next ch-2 sp, sc in next ch-2 sp] rep around, join in 3rd ch of beg ch-3, fasten off.

APPLIQUÉ

Notes: *Use pearl cotton or fingering yarn for applique.*

Work all appliques with size C hook.

First light rose flower

Row 1: With green, ch 66, sl st in 2nd ch from hook, sl st in each of next 5 chs, sc in each of next 15 chs, hdc in each of next 44 chs, fasten off.

Row 2: Working in opposite side of foundation ch of Row 1, attach light rose in 26th st from the sl st end, ch 1, sc in same st as beg ch-1, ch 3, sc in next st, [sc in next st, ch 3, sc in next st] rep to point (sl st end of flower), [sc, ch 3, sc] in point, working down opposite edge along sts, [sc in next st, ch 3, sc in next st] rep down edge working in sl sts, sc sts and first 5 hdc sts, fasten off.

Second light rose flower

Row 1: With green, ch 50, sl st in 2nd ch from hook, sl st in each of next 5 chs, sc in each of next 15 chs, hdc in each of next 28 chs, fasten off.

Row 2: Rep Row 2 of first light rose flower.

Dark rose flower

Row 1: With green, ch 45, sc in 2nd ch from hook, sc in each rem ch across, fasten off.

Row 2: Working in opposite side of foundation ch, attach dark rose in 8th st from the end, ch 1, sc in same st as beg ch-1, sc in each of next 7 sts, 3 sc in point, working in back lps only on opposite edge, sc in each of next 8 sts, turn. (19 sc)

Row 3: Ch 1, working in back lps only, sc in each of next 8 sts, 2 sc in next st, sc in next st, 2 sc in next st, sc in each of next 8 sts, turn. (21 sc)

Row 4: Ch 1, working in back lps only, sc in each of next 9 sts, 2 sc in next st, sc in

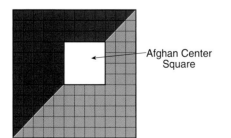

Afghan Diagram

Afghan Center Square

SQUARE KEY
■ Rose & white square
▨ Green square
▧ Diagonal squares

next st, 2 sc in next st, sc in each of next 9 sts, fasten off. (23 sts)

Make 2 more dark rose flowers, working Row 1 with green, ch 30 for first and ch 27 for 2nd. Rep Rows 2–4 with dark rose the same as first dark rose flower.

Long leaf
Row 1: With green, ch 36, sc in 2nd ch from hook, sc in next ch, hdc in each of

next 2 chs, 2 dc in next ch, [dc in each of next 4 chs, 2 dc in next ch] 5 times, dc in next ch, hdc in each of next 2 chs, sc in each of next 2 chs, fasten off.

Short leaf
Row 1: With green, ch 31, sc in 2nd ch from hook, sc in next ch, hdc in each of next 2 chs, 2 dc in next ch, [dc in each of next 4 chs, 2 dc in next ch] 4 times, dc in

next ch, hdc in each of next 2 chs, sc in each of next 2 chs, fasten off.

FINISHING
Using photo as a guide, sew appliqués to afghan center square. ■

PEARLS & LACE PHOTO FRAME ▶ CONTINUED FROM PAGE 153

PATTERN NOTES
Weave in loose ends as work progresses. Join rnds with a sl st unless otherwise stated.

PATTERN STITCHES
Shell: [2 dc, ch 2, 2 dc] in indicated sp.
Beg shell: [Ch 3, dc, ch 2, 2 dc] in indicated sp.
3-dc shell: [3 dc, ch 2, 3 dc] in indicated sp.
4-dc shell: [4 dc, ch 2, 4 dc] in indicated sp.

FRAME
Foundation: Ch 4, dc in 4th ch from hook, ch 3, dc in sp between ch-4 and last dc, [ch 3, dc in sp between ch-3 and last dc] rep until there are 80 sps, taking care not to twist foundation, join.
Rnd 1: Sl st into next sp, ch 1, sc in same sp, shell in next sp, sc in next sp, [shell in next sp, sc in next sp] 10 times, 3-dc shell in next sp for corner, sc in next sp, [shell in next sp, sc in next sp] 7 times, 3-dc shell in next sp for corner, sc in next sp, [shell in next sp, sc in next sp] 11 times, 3-dc shell in next sp, sc in next sp, [shell in next sp, sc in next sp] 7 times, 3-dc shell in next sp for corner, join in beg sc. (36 shells; 4 corner 3-dc shells)
Rnd 2: Sl st into ch-2 sp of next shell, beg shell in same sp, fpdc around next sc, [shell in next shell, fpdc around next sc] 10 times, *4-dc shell in next corner ch-2 sp, fpdc around next sc, [shell in next shell, fpdc around next

sc] 7 times *, 4-dc shell in next corner ch-2 sp, fpdc around next sc, [shell in next shell, fpdc around next sc] 11 times, rep * to *, 4-dc shell in next corner ch-2 sp, fpdc around next sc, join in 3rd ch of beg ch-3.
Rnd 3: Sl st into ch-2 sp of shell, beg shell in same sp, fpdc around fpdc, [shell in next shell, fpdc around fpdc] 10 times, *dc in each of next 4 dc, shell in corner ch-2 sp, dc in each of next 4 dc, fpdc around fpdc, [shell in next shell, fpdc around fpdc] 7 times *, dc in each of next 4 dc, shell in corner ch-2 sp, dc in each of next 4 dc, fpdc around fpdc, [shell in next shell, fpdc around fpdc] 11 times, rep from * to *, dc in each of next 4 dc, shell in corner ch-2 sp, dc in each of next 4 dc, fpdc around fpdc, join in 3rd ch of beg ch-3.
Rnd 4: Sl st into ch-2 sp of shell, beg shell in same sp, fpdc around fpdc, [shell in next shell, fpdc around fpdc] 10 times, *dc in each of next 6 dc, shell in corner ch-2 sp, dc in each of next 6 dc, fpdc around fpdc, [shell in next shell, fpdc around fpdc] 7 times *, dc in next 6 dc, shell in corner ch-2 sp, dc in each of next 6 dc, fpdc around fpdc, [shell in next shell, fpdc around fpdc] 11 times, rep from * to *, dc in each of next 6 dc, shell in corner ch-2 sp, dc in each of next 6 dc, fpdc around fpdc, join in 3rd ch of beg ch-3.
Rnd 5: Sl st into ch-2 sp of shell, ch 1, [sc, ch 3] twice in same sp, sc between next 2 dc, ch 3, fpsc around next fpdc, [ch 3, sc between next 2 dc, ch 3, {sc,

ch 3} twice in next ch-2 sp, sc between next 2 dc, ch 3, fpsc around next fpdc] 9 times, ch 3, *[sc in sp between next 2 dc, ch 3] 7 times, [sc, ch 3] twice in next corner ch-2 sp, [sc between next 2 dc, ch 3] 7 times, ch 3, fpsc around fpdc *, [ch 3, sc between next 2 dc, ch 3, {sc, ch 3} twice in next ch-2 sp, sc between next 2 dc, ch 3, fpsc around fpdc] 7 times, ch 3, rep * to *, [ch 3, sc between next 2 dc, ch 3, {sc, ch 3} twice in next ch-2 sp, sc between next 2 dc, ch 3, fpsc around next fpdc] 11 times, ch 3, rep from * to *, [ch 3, sc between next 2 dc, ch 3, {sc, ch 3} twice in next ch-2 sp, sc between next 2 dc, ch 3, fpsc around next fpdc] 7 times, ch 3, rep from * to *, ch 3, sc in sp between next 2 dc, ch 3, join in beg sc, fasten off.

FINISHING
Starch frame, pin to plastic wrap covered pinning board to dry.

Glue crocheted frame to front of wooden frame, mitering crocheted lace at corners.

Glue blue lace over edge of crocheted frame taking care to keep beading straight.

Note: *Because of the beading the ecru lace cannot be mitered. Instead, cut 4 individual pieces of lace to fit respective sides of the inner bevel of the picture frame.*

Glue ecru flat beaded trim over edge of blue lace. Glue the silk roses in clusters of 2 over the raw edges of the lace at each corner. ■

dc, dc in each of next 2 dc, turn. (6 dc)

Row 3: Ch 3, [dc dec over next 2 sts] twice, dc in last dc, turn. (4 dc)

Row 4: Ch 2, [yo, draw up a lp in next st, yo, draw through 2 lps on hook] 3 times, yo, draw through all 4 lps on hook, fasten off.

OUTER DOILY PORTION

Rnd 1: Attach white in ch-3 sp at any corner of Rnd 9 of doily center, ch 1, *catching tip of leaf, sc in same sp, [ch 3, sc in next sp] 3 times, sk next sp, 7 tr in back lp of center dark lavender sc at tip of flower petal (picking up white lp of same dc for added strength), sk next sp, [sc in next sp, ch 3] 3 times, rep from * around, join in beg sc. (36 ch-3 lps; 42 tr)

Rnd 2: Sl st into next sp, ch 1, sc in same sp, ch 3, sc in next sp, sk next sp, [2 tr in next tr, ch 1] 6 times, 2 tr in next tr, sk next sp, *[sc in next sp, ch 3] 3 times, sc in next sp, sk next sp, [2 tr in next tr, ch 1] 6 times, 2 tr in next tr, sk next sp, rep from * around, ending with sc in next sp, ch 3, sc in next sp, ch 1, hdc in beg sc. (84 tr; 18 ch-3 sps)

Rnd 3: Ch 1, sc in same sp, *[2 tr in each of next 2 tr, ch 1] 6 times, 2 tr in each of next 2 tr, sk next sp **, sc in next sp, rep from * around, ending last rep at **, join in beg sc, fasten off. (168 tr; 36 ch-1 sps)

Rnd 4: Sk next 12 tr, attach white in next ch-1 sp, ch 1, sc in same sp, [ch 5, sc in next sp] 3 times, ch 7, sk next 8 tr, sc in next ch-1 sp, *[ch 5, sc in next ch-1 sp] 5 times, ch 7, sk next 8 tr, sc in next ch-1 sp, rep from * around, ending with ch 5, sc in next ch-1 sp, ch 5, join in beg sc.

Rnd 5: Sl st into center of next sp, ch 1, sc in same sp, ch 5, [sc in next sp, ch 5] twice, [tr, ch 5] twice in next sp, *[sc in next sp, ch 5] 5 times, [tr, ch 5] twice in next sp, rep from * around, ending with [sc in next sp, ch 5] twice, join in beg sc, fasten off. (42 ch-5 sps)

Rnd 6: Attach white in ch-5 sp between

any 2 tr, [ch 4 (counts as first tr throughout), 8 tr] in same sp, [sc in next sp, ch 5] 5 times, sc in next sp, *9 tr in next sp, [sc in next sp, ch 5] 5 times, sc in next sp, rep from * around, join in 4th ch of beg ch-4. (54 tr; 30 ch-5 sps)

Rnd 7: [Ch 4, tr] in same tr, ch 1, [2 tr in next tr, ch 1] 7 times, 2 tr in next tr, [sc in next sp, ch 5] 4 times, sc in next sp, *[2 tr in next tr, ch 1] 8 times, 2 tr in next tr, [sc in next sp, ch 5] 4 times, sc in next sp, rep from * around, join in 4th ch of beg ch-4. (108 tr; 24 ch-5 sps)

Rnd 8: [Ch 4, tr] in same tr, 2 tr in next tr, [ch 1, 2 tr in each of next 2 tr] 8 times, [sc in next sp, ch 5] 3 times, sc in next sp, *[2 tr in each of next 2 tr, ch 1] 8 times, 2 tr in each of next 2 tr, [sc in next sp, ch 5] 3 times, sc in next sp, rep from * around, join in 4th ch of beg ch-4. (216 tr; 18 ch-5 sps)

Rnd 9: Ch 4, tr in each of next 3 tr, [ch 1, tr in each of next 4 tr] 8 times, [sc in next sp, ch 5] twice, sc in next sp, *[tr in each of next 4 tr, ch 1] 8 times, tr in each of next 4 tr, [sc in next sp, ch 5] twice, sc in next sp, rep from * around, join in 4th ch of beg ch-4. (216 tr; 12 ch-5 sps)

Rnd 10: Ch 4, tr in each of next 3 tr, [ch 2, tr in each of next 4 tr] 8 times, sc in next sp, ch 5, sc in next sp, *[tr in each of next 4 tr, ch 2] 8 times, tr in each of next 4 tr, sc in next sp, ch 5, sc in next sp, rep from * around, join in 4th ch of beg ch-4, fasten off. (216 tr; 6 ch-5 sps)

Rnd 11: Attach dark green in last ch-5 sp worked, ch 1, [sc, ch 2, sc] in same sp, sc in next sc, [sc in each of next 4 tr, 3 sc in next ch-2 sp] 8 times, sc in each of next 4 tr, sc in next sc, *[sc, ch 2, sc] in next ch-5 sp, sc in next sc, [sc in each of next 4 tr, 3 sc in next ch-2 sp] 8 times, sc in each of next 4 tr, sc in next sc, rep from * around, join in beg sc, fasten off. (384 sc; 6 ch-2 sps)

Rnd 12: String 216 beads onto white cotton, working across scallop (tr section of doily), attach white in 2nd sc of 2nd

3-sc group to the left of any ch-2 sp, ch 1, sc in same sc, sc in each of next 47 sc, *sk next 2 sc, ch 2, sc in next ch-2 sp, ch 2, sk next 2 sc **, sc in each of next 60 sc, rep from * around, ending last rep at **, sc in each of next 12 sc, join in beg sc. (366 sc)

Rnd 13: Ch 1, sc in same st, ch 3, sk 1 sc, bdc in each of next 4 sc, [ch 3, sk 1 sc, sc in next sc, ch 3, sk 1 sc, bdc in each of next 4 sc] 6 times, work split dc over next 2 ch-2 sps, ch 1, *bdc in each of next 4 sc, [ch 3, sk 1 sc, sc in next sc, ch 3, sk 1 sc, bdc in each of next 4 sc] 8 times, ch 1, work split dc over next 2 ch-2 sps, ch 1, rep from * 4 times, bdc in each of next 4 sc, ch 3, sk 1 sc, sc in next sc, ch 3, sk 1 sc, bdc in each of next 4 sc, ch 3, sl st in top of beg sc. (216 bdc)

Rnd 14: Sl st into next ch-3 sp, ch 1, sc in same sp, *sc in each of next 2 sc, ch 2, sc in each of next 2 sc, 2 sc in next sp, ch 2 **, 2 sc in next sp, rep from * around, ending last rep at **, join in beg sc, fasten off.

Rnd 15: String 288 beads on dark lavender cotton, attach in first sc of Rnd 14, ch 1, sc in same sc, sc in each of next 3 sc, [bp in next ch-2 sp, sc in each of next 4 sc] 12 times, bps dec over next 3 ch-2 sps, *sc in each of next 4 sc, [bp in next ch-2 sp, sc in each of next 4 sc] 15 times, bps dec over next 3 ch-2 sps, rep from * around, ending with [sc in next 4 sc, bp in next ch-2 sp] 3 times, join in beg sc, fasten off.

Center Trim

Rnd 1: With dark lavender, ch 5, join to form a ring, ch 1, 8 sc in ring, join in beg sc. (8 sc)

Rnd 2: Ch 1, sc in same sc, ch 3, [sc in next sc, ch 3] rep around, join in beg sc, fasten off.

With white thread, invisibly sew center trim to center of passionflower. Sew 8mm pink bead to center of center trim. ■

WILD IRISH ROSE PILLOW ▶ CONTINUED FROM PAGE 167

BRAID

Note: To measure braid, place on a flat surface to measure, do not stretch.

Inner braid

With vanilla, [ch 3, 2 dc in 3rd ch from hook] rep until braid measures 46 inches, fasten off.

Outer braid

With vanilla, [ch 3, 2 dc in 3rd ch from hook] rep until braid measures 66 inches to fit around outer edges of pillow.

FINISHING

Pin flat petal flower to center of pillow cover and stitch in place. Sew Irish rose centered over flat petal flower. Sew pearl button to center of Irish rose. Measure and mark an 11-inch square for frame around flower. Pin inner braid around 11-inch frame, using care when turning corners that the braid remains consistent as on sides. Sew inner braid to cover.

Insert pillow form into cover. Pin outer braid around outer edge of pillow, using care when turning corners that the braid remains consistent as on sides. Sew outer braid to pillow. ■

5 sp around, join in beg sc. (6 petals)

Rnd 4: Ch 1, sc in same st as joining, ch 7, [sc in first sc of next petal, ch 7] rep around, join in beg sc.

Rnd 5: Ch 1, [sc, 9 dc, sc] in each ch-7 sp around, join in beg sc.

Rnd 6: Ch 1, sc in same st as beg ch-1, ch 8, [sc in first sc of next petal, ch 8] rep around, join in beg sc.

Rnd 7: Ch 1, [sc 11 dc, sc] in each ch-8 sp around, join in beg sc.

Rnd 8: Ch 1, sc in same st as beg ch-1, ch 9, [sc in first sc of next petal, ch 9] rep around, join in beg sc.

Rnd 9: Ch 1, [sc, 13 dc, sc] in each ch-9 sp around, join in beg sc, fasten off.

STARFLOWERS RUNNER & PILLOW TOPPER ▶ CONTINUED FROM PAGE 159

ch-1 sp, rep from * around, working at each corner ch 1, sk 1 dc, sc in next dc, ch 1, sk next dc, [sc, ch 3, sc, ch 4, sc, ch 3, sc] in next dc, ch 1, sk 1 dc, sc in next dc, ch 1, sk next dc, sc in next ch-1 sp, ch 2, sk next sc, sc in next ch-1 sp, join last ch 2 in beg sc, fasten off.

PILLOW TOPPER

Notes: Make 5 of pattern 1 and 4 of pattern 2 in parentheses. Join squares 3 x

3. Then sew onto pillow top with matching thread through sts of Rnd 10 of squares.

Work Rnds 1 and 2 with maize (lilac), Rnds 3–5 with mid rose (maize), Rnds 6 and 7 in spruce (mid rose), Rnd 8 with lilac (almond pink) and Rnds 9 and 10 and border with new ecru. ■

GENERAL INSTRUCTIONS

Please review the following information before working the projects in this book. Important details about the abbreviations and symbols used are included.

HOOKS

Crochet hooks are sized for different weights of yarn and thread. For thread crochet, you will usually use a steel crochet hook. Steel crochet-hook sizes range from size 00 to 14. The higher the number of the hook, the smaller your stitches will be. For example, a size 1 steel crochet hook will give you much larger stitches than a size 9 steel crochet hook. Keep in mind that the sizes given with the pattern instructions were obtained by working with the size thread or yarn and hook given in the materials list. If you work with a smaller hook, depending on your gauge, your project size will be smaller; if you work with a larger hook, your finished project's size will be larger.

GAUGE

Gauge is determined by the tightness or looseness of your stitches, and affects the finished size of your project. If you are concerned about the finished size of the project matching the size given, take time to crochet a small section of the pattern and then check your gauge. For example, if the gauge called for is 10 dc = 1 inch, and your gauge is 12 dc to the inch, you should switch to a larger hook. On the other hand, if your gauge is only 8 dc to the inch, you should switch to a smaller hook.

If the gauge given in the pattern is for an entire motif, work one motif and then check your gauge.

UNDERSTANDING SYMBOLS

As you work through a pattern, you'll quickly notice several symbols in the instructions. These symbols are used to clarify the pattern for you: brackets [], curlicue brackets {}, asterisks *.

Brackets [] are used to set off a group of instructions worked a number of times. For example, "[ch 3, sc in ch-3 sp] 7 times" means to work the instructions inside the [] seven times. Brackets [] also set off a group of stitches to be worked in one stitch, space or loop. For example, the brackets [] in this set of instructions, "Sk 3 sc, [3 dc, ch 1, 3 dc] in next st" indicate that after skipping 3 sc, you will work 3 dc, ch 1 and 3 more dc all in the next stitch.

Occasionally, a set of instructions inside a set of brackets needs to be repeated, too. In this case, the text within the brackets to be repeated will be set off with curlicue brackets {}. For example, "[Ch 9, yo twice, insert hook in 7th ch from hook and pull up a loop, sk next dc, yo, insert hook in next dc and pull up a loop, {yo and draw through 2 lps on hook} 5 times, ch 3] 8 times." In this case, in each of the eight times you work the instructions included in brackets, you will work the section included in curlicue brackets five times.

Asterisks * are also used when a group of instructions is repeated. They may either be used alone or with brackets. For example, "*Sc in each of the next 5 sc, 2 sc in next sc, rep from * around, join with a sl st in beg sc" simply means you will work the instructions from the first * around the entire round.

"*Sk 3 sc, [3 dc, ch 1, 3 dc] in next st, rep from * around" is an example of asterisks working with brackets. In this set of instructions, you will repeat the instructions from the asterisk around, working the instructions inside the brackets together.

STITCH GUIDE

Front Loop (a) Back Loop (b)

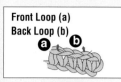

Chain (ch)

Yo, draw lp through hook.

Slip Stitch Joining

Insert hook in beg ch, yo, draw lp through.

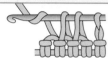

Front Post/Back Post Dc

Fpdc (a): Yo, insert hook from front to back and to front again around the vertical post (upright part) of next st, yo and draw yarn through, yo and complete dc.

Bpdc (b): Yo, reaching over top of piece and working on opposite side (back) of work, insert hook from back to front to back again around vertical post of next st, yo and draw yarn through, yo and complete dc.

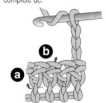

Single Crochet (sc)

Insert hook in st (a), yo, draw lp through (b), yo, draw through both lps on hook (c).

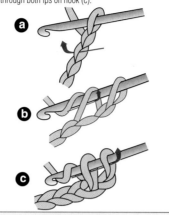

Half-Double Crochet (hdc)

Yo, insert hook in st (a), yo, draw lp through (b), yo, draw through all 3 lps on hook (c).

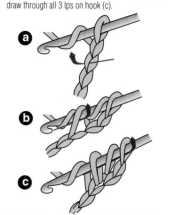

DECREASING

Single Crochet Decrease

Dec 1 sc over next 2 sts as follows: Draw up a lp in each of next 2 sts, yo, draw through all 3 lps on hook.

Double Crochet Decrease

Dec 1 dc over next 2 sts as follows: [Yo, insert hook in next st, yo, draw up lp on hook, yo, draw through 2 lps] twice, yo, draw through all 3 lps on hook.

Double Crochet (dc)

Yo, insert hook in st (a), yo, draw lp through (b), [yo, draw through 2 lps] twice (c, d).

Treble Crochet (tr)

Yo hook twice, insert hook in st (a), yo, draw lp through (b), [yo, draw through 2 lps on hook] 3 times (c, d, e).

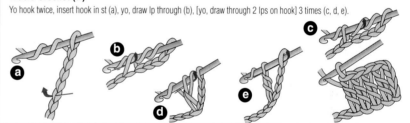

SPECIAL STITCHES

Chain Color Change (ch color change)

Yo with new color, draw through last lp on hook.

Double Crochet Color Change (dc color change)

Drop first color, yo with new color, draw through last 2 lps of st.

Reverse Single Crochet (reverse sc)

Working from left to right, insert hook in next st to the right (a), yo, draw up lp on hook, complete as for sc (b).

Stitch Abbreviations

The following stitch abbreviations are used throughout this publication.

beg	begin(ning)
bl(s)	block(s)
bpdc	back post dc
ch(s)	chain(s)
cl(s)	cluster(s)
CC	contrasting color
dc	double crochet
dec	decrease
dtr	double treble crochet
fpdc	front post dc
hdc	half-double crochet
inc	increase
lp(s)	loop(s)
MC	main color
p	picot
rem	remain(ing)
rep	repeat
rnd(s)	round(s)
RS	right side facing you
sc	single crochet
sk	skip
sl st	slip stitch
sp(s)	space(s)
st(s)	stitch(es)
tog	together
tr	treble crochet
trtr	triple treble crochet
WS	wrong side facing you
yo	yarn over

Crochet Hooks

METRIC	US
.60mm	14 steel
.75mm	12 steel
1.00mm	10 steel
1.25mm	8 steel
1.50mm	7 steel
1.75mm	5 steel
2.00mm	B/1
2.50mm	C/2
3.00mm	D/3
3.50mm	E/4
4.00mm	F/5
4.50mm	G/6
5.00mm	H/8
5.50mm	I/9
6.00mm	J/10

Yarn Conversion

OUNCES TO GRAMS

1	28.4
2	56.7
3	85.0
4	113.4

GRAMS TO OUNCES

25	⅞
40	1⅖
50	1¾
100	3½

Crochet Abbreviations

US	INTL
sc—single crochet	dc—double crochet
dc—double crochet	tr—treble crochet
hdc—half-double crochet	htr—half treble crochet
tr—treble crochet	dtr—double treble crochet
dtr—double treble crochet	trip—triple treble crochet
sk—skip	miss

YARNS

Bedspread weight	No. 10 cotton or Virtuoso
Sport weight	3-ply or thin DK
Worsted weight	thick DK or Aran

Check tension or gauge to save time.

SPECIAL THANKS

Carol Alexander
French Provincial, Lady Iris

Amy Brewer
Silver Moon Purse

Kazimiera Budak
Wagon Wheels Table Runner

Jo Ann Burrington
Baby Snowsuit & Patchwork Blanket

Bendy Carter
Baby Belinda, Cotton Candy Capelet
Set, Goose-Chase Puzzle Book, Post
Stitch Review

Paula Clark
Elegant Edgings

Donna Collinsworth
Black Ice Purse

Deborah Davidson
Scarlet Ribbons Shawl

Dot Drake
Island in the Sky Doily, Majestic Braids,
Renaissance Beauty Doily, Sweet
Victorian Table Topper

Katherine Eng
Starflowers Runner & Pillow Topper

Norma Gale
Earring Elegance

Kathleen Garen
Persian Tiles

Hartmut Hass
Butterflies in Flight Valance

Sharon Hatfield
Fast & Fun Hooded Sweaters

Kathleen Power Johnson
Hyacinth's Party Dress, Tunisian
Tapestry Jacket & Hat

Roseanne Kropp
Sunday-Best Bib

Jennifer Moir
Pineapple Sunshine Doily

Donna Nickell
Circle of Roses Doily

Maggie Petsch
Limpet Shell Purse, Opposites Attract
Table Set

Rose Pirrone
Wild Irish Rose Pillow

Angel Rhett
Charleston Rose

Sandy Rideout
Desert Oasis

Karen Rigsby
His & Her Gingham Afghans, Twilight
Lagoon Afghan, Underwater Adventures

Ann Smith
Lemon Drops Sweater, Zebra Stripes
Purse

Brenda Stratton
Heritage Lace Coverlet & Doily,
Passionflower Beaded Doily, Pearls
& Lace Photo Frame, Pretty Posies
Layette, Rose Splendor Coverlet,
Victorian Princess Purse, Vintage Floral
Lace Doily

Margret Willson
American Mosaic, Diamond Rio Jacket,
Fuchsia Fantasy Ripple Pullover, Jazzy
Jewels Vest, Woodland Jacket

Angela Winger
Leopold

Glenda Winkleman
Navy Houndstooth Rug, Tapestry Floral

Lori Zeller
Pretty Patti, Sweet Summer Shoes